The Contemporáneos Group

The Contemporáneos Group
Rewriting Mexico
in the Thirties and Forties

SALVADOR A. OROPESA

 University of Texas Press, Austin

Copyright © 2003 by the University of Texas Press

All rights reserved
Printed in the United States of America

First edition, 2003

Requests for permission to reproduce material from this work should
be sent to Permissions, University of Texas Press, Box 7819, Austin,
TX 78713-7819.

♾ The paper used in this book meets the minimum requirements of
ANSI/NISO Z39.48-1992 (R1997) (Permanence of Paper).

Library of Congress Cataloging-in-Publication Data

Oropesa, Salvador A., 1961–
    The Contemporáneos Group : rewriting Mexico in the thirties and
forties / Salvador A. Oropesa. — 1st ed.
        p.   cm.
    Includes bibliographical references and index.
    ISBN 0-292-76057-4 (hardcover : alk. paper)
    1. Contemporáneos (Literary group)   2. Mexican literature—20th
century—History and criticism.   I. Title.
    PQ7153.O76 2003
    863'.609972—dc21
                                                                2002011188

To Leah and Cristina

Contents

Acknowledgments

The process from manuscript to book is long and needs the help of many people. I want to start with the same critics noted in the Introduction, maestros like Frank Dauster, Merlin H. Forster, Seymour Menton, and John S. Brushwood. If they had not written what they did, we would have to be doing so now. They studied Mexican literature because they loved and respected the country, its people, and its art. I have humbly tried to learn from them.

I also have to thank my wife, Leonides Covarrubias Comadurán, who taught me almost everything I know about her birth country, Mexico, and immersed me in her unending *norteña* family. The father of this project is David William Foster, the best literary coach on this side of the Río Bravo. Many people read parts of the manuscript and gave me invaluable insight: Mel Arrington, Douglas Benson, Bob Clark, Rose Costantino, Melissa Fitch, Laura Kanost, Darrell Lockhart, Mary K. Long, Bradley Nelson, Bradley Shaw, Chuck Thorpe, Chris Weimer, and Kim Wiggans. They are my friends. When translations of texts existed, I used them (references can be found in the Bibliography); but Bradley Shaw and I modified most of them to suit our common taste. The rest of the translations are our own. I also want to thank the anonymous reader for the University of Texas Press and Miguel González-Gerth of the University of Texas, second reader of the manuscript. Their suggestions were crucial. In 1995 I attended a National Endowment for the Humanities (NEH) Summer Seminar under the direction of Elias Rivers and Georgina Sabat-Rivers at the State University of New York at Stony Brook. I thank them very much for their generosity in inviting me and for the opportunity to enjoy their wisdom and erudition. The Office of the Dean of the College of Arts and Sciences at Kansas State University granted me a sabbatical in the fall of 1998 during which I was able to write an important part of the manuscript. I also want to thank my colleagues at Kansas State University, including Maureen Ihrie, who is now pursuing other interests. Special thanks to the two department heads during recent years, Michael Ossar and Robert Corum. Finally I want to thank Theresa May, Rachel Jennings, Kathy Lewis, and the staff of the University of Texas Press for their help and impeccable professionalism.

Parts of this manuscript were published as articles in *Chasqui, Monographic Review/Revista Monográfica,* and *Romance Languages Annual* and as a chapter of the book *Echoes and Inscriptions: Comparative Approaches to Early Modern Spanish Literatures,* edited by Christopher B. Weimer and Barbara A. Simerka (Lewisburg, Pa.: Bucknell University Press, 2000).

Introduction

Frank Dauster and Merlin H. Forster in the United States and Octavio Paz and Guillermo Sheridan in Mexico, among several others, taught us about the importance of the writers of the Contemporáneos. Little by little these literary critics were able to rewrite the Mexican canon and give these authors the place they deserved in Mexican letters.

In spite of the significance of the Contemporáneos, the novel of the Revolution in literature, Diego Rivera's murals in painting, and the movies of the golden age ended up representing the essential and official Mexico. But the poems, short stories, and plays of the Contemporáneos remained impassive by the sanctioned texts, with their skewed look, giving modern readers not just a new perspective but a different gaze, a new way to view reality—like Marcel Proust—and a new approach to perceive the different Mexicos. Theirs was not the Mexico of the beautiful Aztecs of the murals and the stylized serapes of the movies; theirs was the Mexico of the enlightened bourgeoisie and the *alemanista* middle class. The Contemporáneos knew well the literature and art of the Western world and decided that Mexican letters had to play a significant role. They studied colonial and modern Mexican literature not from a nationalist perspective but as a process of legitimization of modern Mexico and its true leaders, businesspeople and civilian presidents. The Contemporáneos were not afraid to utter the names of countries like Spain and the United States; they recognized all Spanish literature as their own and integrated the literature of the United States as part of their canon, the new classics like Edgar Allan Poe and the avant-garde literature from the Imagists and black poets. They also enjoyed U.S.

popular culture like the movies and glossy magazines that came from the other side. The Contemporáneos realized that the new forms of capitalism could create a massive middle class that could spend money and time for their own enlightenment and to give meaning to their leisure. Although they did not succeed completely in their efforts to create a literature independent of the state, at least they tried to harmonize public and private art. Another goal was to bridge the different types of culture, to create a porous national literature in which different cultural forms could merge; their aim was not just to start literary journals for the elite, which they did, but to write magazines for the middle class and movie scripts for the masses.

In this book I want to bring to the reader's attention a few important developments in the wonderful literature of the Contemporáneos. The first is their fascination with baroque literature. They did a very good reading of the texts of the seventeenth century and learned from them that literature is a necessary instrument of power and legitimization; absolute and democratic governments need literature to reproduce their ideology. The writers of the Renaissance brought literature back to the court, to the privileged minority. The humanists did the first modern, Western reading of the classics: they pillaged them, they translated, and above all they chose what fit their artistic and ideological needs and tossed away what they did not want. Then the writers of the following century, the so-called baroque, took the literature away from the palaces and made an urban commodity out of it. These archaic middle-class writers were bureaucrats from the lower steps of nobility, libertine clerics, protofeminist nuns, theater people, and academics of literary salons and literary taverns—writers who could do filigree literature, twist mythology, hide obscene references, and merge Latin and the slang of the slaves. They even wrote the first queer—and homophobic—modern literature.

The Contemporáneos writers had read romantic literature and the sentimental versions of symbolism that recycled romanticism at the end of the nineteenth century. But they were not interested in their *añoranza*, the Porfiriato's nostalgia about itself when it still was a young regime full of possibilities. They were interested in the urban vision of Leopoldo Lugones. They added Buenos Aires and Argentina on their map of the literary world. After Lugones came the Mexican Ramón López Velarde, a poet who could make poems of the conversations in the streets and create characters in his poems to analyze himself.

In this study I center my interest on baroque literature because it was a literature of crisis, of unending social, economic, and ideological crises where the extremes of individualism and an oppressive absolutist state were always in conflict. New Spain also gave Mexico its first important writers in Spanish, the patriarchs of Mexican letters; and in an unbelievable act of transvestism, the father of Mexican literature was a woman.

I also pay special attention to satiric literature because there is a tradition, especially when studying colonial satire, of reading it as liberal and subversive literature. After the seminal study published by Dustin Griffin in 1994 by the University of Kentucky Press, we can perform a better, more moderate and accurate reading of satire. I also pay attention to figures of speech. Contemporary critics neglected them, but they stressed the joy of literature as a game of erudition and witticism.

The two main writers I have chosen to study are Salvador Novo and Xavier Villaurrutia, the generation of two. The reasons for my choice are easy to understand: they wrote first-class literature, enjoyed their social standing, had similar literary taste, and embarked on a renovation of Mexican literature. The novel of the Revolution and Rivera's murals gave the impression that they were the only voice of Mexico. They were outstanding but dogmatic art. Novo and Villaurrutia aimed instead to be important voices of a polyphonic Mexico. When Novo discovered indigenous literature, he learned Nahuatl; he did not intend to represent it or to engage in *indigenismo*. Novo and Villaurrutia were also gay writers, like many others of the avant-garde all over the Western world. This is important because it brought new topics to their literature, including a new way to represent desire. It also made them more aware of the need for individual rights and for a liberal-conservative capitalism to rule Mexico's economy, a political system that could develop niches for difference and otherness. In this kind of political environment dissident groups could survive better and move from the margin to the center.

The second part of the book is dedicated to two little-known writers who have been associated with the Contemporáneos. The first is the painter Agustín Lazo, Xavier Villaurrutia's partner. I analyze two of Lazo's fine plays and a third text that he may have written in collaboration with Villaurrutia. What Lazo brings to Mexican theater is craft, the taste for very well constructed plays which are part of a complex machinery that is dismantled in front of the spectator and reconstructed again to teach the viewer new topics. Two of these are the representation of the closet and Mexico's history from the point of view of the new middle classes of the *alemanismo* so that they could learn how they were related to the Second Empire and the *porfirista* era of the haciendas.

The second writer is Guadalupe Marín, wife of Diego Rivera and Jorge Cuesta. She wrote two novels that I would label literary documents. They are not first-class literature, although they read better than Jaime Torres Bodet's avant-garde novels, which are part of the canon. The very few people who read the novels considered them mere personal revenge, and they soon disappeared from shelves and literary discussions. But these texts are very important because they represent women's struggle to have a voice, to move from being the object of the masculine and heterosexual gaze (Lupe was the *encuerada nacional* of Rivera's frescoes) to a desperate attempt to have a view of their own. After marrying Cuesta, Lupe was involved in the identity gender crisis of some of the Contemporáneos writers, who had to struggle to give a voice to their homosexuality and gayness in their literature in the context of Mexican machismo and compulsory heterosexuality. Lupe explores illness and madness, normalcy and aberration, the construction of gender and how it is related to the construction of national identity. She may not be the most skilled writer, but with her energy and originality she adds an important element to the history of the Contemporáneos that justifies her inclusion in this study.

The last chapter is another variation on the meaning of the writer as a public figure in modern society. It analyzes Novo's journey from the status of intellectual to that of celebrity. He abandoned what he called his grandiose *obra* and immersed himself in the world of popular culture: op-ed articles, gossip, radio, and television. Novo started a new type of novel or soap opera in which he was the protagonist and a number of invited guests and celebrities formed his supporting cast. This café society with an intellectual patina was a huge success. For the first time in history the new mass media could create a kind of national backyard, and Novo intended to be at its center.

The Contemporáneos Group

1)≣ Neo-Baroque

Introduction to the Concept of Neo-Baroque

The subtitle of José Antonio Maravall's book *Culture of the Baroque* (1980) is *Analysis of a Historical Structure*. Maravall's definition of historical structure is "the figure — or mental construction — in which we are shown a complex of facts endowed with an internal articulation wherein the intricate network of relations taking place between such facts is systematized and acquires meaning" (1986: xxxvi). In the development of the concept of the baroque, Maravall states that it is impossible to use this terminology outside the context of seventeenth-century Europe, although it is always possible to use the term when substructures of the content or mental constructions found in various historical contexts are isolated for study.

Raymond Williams, in *Marxism and Literature* (1985 [1977]), describes the dynamic concept of culture in the chapter "Dominant, Residual, and Emergent," where he defines the functioning of the residual: "any culture includes available elements of its past . . . The residual, by definition, has been effectively formed in the past, but it is still active in the cultural process, not only and often not at all as an element of the past, but as an effective element of the present" (122). Therefore it is possible to have a neo-baroque in the twentieth century if these residuals end up forming a "structure of feeling" (Williams 1985 [1977]: 128–135), whose definition is very similar to Maravall's definition of "mental construction." The advantage of Williams's structure over Maravall's *construcción* is that it can be applied to any study in the humanities, while Maravall's is only concerned with history.

Of course, Williams's structure is not the only epistemological possibility to go from history to culture. Fredric Jameson's "ideologeme" as he defines it in *The Political Unconscious* (1986 [1981]) is also very useful: "A historically determinate conceptual or semic complex which can project itself variously in the form of a 'value system' or 'philosophical concept,' or in the form of a protonarrative, a private or collective narrative fantasy" (115). It is in this context that the ideologeme "baroque" can escape the historical rigidity of the historical structure "baroque," and the term can then be applied to the neo-baroque semic complexes of the avant-garde in Mexico in the twentieth century.

The Spanish poetic Generación de 1927 has always been associated with the baroque since its inception, because 1927 was the tricentennial observance of the death of Luis de Góngora. Dámaso Alonso and Gerardo Diego brought to the attention of the other writers of Spain and Hispanic America the importance of Góngora (born 1561) and the richness, the challenges, and the novelty of his literature. The parallel in Mexico to the Generación de 1927 is the Contemporáneos group. Various critics have documented the influence of the baroque period on the Mexican avant-garde, but it has not been analyzed; they have only stated that it exists. In Mexico the neo-baroque arrived by way of Góngora and Francisco de Quevedo, of course, and Sor Juana Inés de la Cruz (1651–1695), through her rediscovery thanks to writers like Amado Nervo, Ermilo Abreu Gómez (future target of Novo's satire), and Alfonso Reyes. Roberto González Echevarría clarifies this point:

> While it is a commonplace of Spanish literary history to say that the Generation of '27 in Spain looked to Góngora for inspiration, the fact is that the revision that brought about Góngora's rediscovery began in Spanish America with the *modernistas* — José Martí and Rubén Darío in particular — and continued in the writings of the Mexican Alfonso Reyes during the teens. (1993: 195)

Víctor García de la Concha offers a wonderful quotation from Miguel de Unamuno that summarizes the whole situation: "Rubén didn't come from Paris, but from Góngora" (González Echevarría 1993: 69). Mervyn R. Coke-Enguídanos has examined the relationship between Rubén Darío and Quevedo, studying in Darío's sonnet "La poesía castellana" how the Nicaraguan assimilates, interprets, and imitates the sonnet form using Quevedo's technique (1988: 47–48). Alberto Forcadas (1972) has effectively ended the controversy about the influence of Góngora on Darío (which Dámaso Alonso and Emilio Carilla thought was very weak), following Ricardo Senabre Sempere, who demonstrated that Darío knew Góngora's poetry well. Forcadas offers more examples to illustrate Darío's knowledge of Góngora's poetry and how he was influenced by him. Rex Hauser (1993) has also studied the presence of similar metaphors in Góngora and in Darío.

According to Octavio Paz, mannerist periods correspond to epochs of crisis. He perceives an obvious, if not clearly understood, relation between the emergence of subjectivism and the several expressions of mannerism: baroque, romantic, symbolist, and avant-garde (1982/1988: 52). It is interesting to notice how Paz connects the baroque and the avant-garde: he sees them as parallel movements or phenomena. Paz calls for the study of this relationship, and others have followed his advice.

In *The Baroque Narrative of Carlos de Sigüenza y Góngora: A New World Paradise* (1993), Kathleen Ross notes that the so-called Barroco de Indias has been analyzed as two different ideologemes. Octavio Paz and José Lezama Lima understand this baroque as oxymoronic, therefore symbolic, thus forming a true baroque of the Americas. For instance, Carlos de Sigüenza y Góngora uses the baroque framework to put together all his ideological and artistic contradictions: his loyalty to the Creole community, his rewriting of the *crónicas* of the previous century, his allegiance to the cause of Hernán Cortés, and his revision of historical sources while paying lip service to the necessity of respecting them. The wide array of baroque devices allows him to combine all these theoretical and poetic challenges. In contrast, John Beverley (1980) sees this phenomenon as an imperial baroque of Spanish origin and analyzes it using a materialist approach. The problem of putting all the emphasis on the imperial dimension of the artistic movement is that it does not give enough importance to the liberating dimension of the baroque and its flexibility to give voice to the new realities of the Americas. Ross proposes the following: "My own investigation is indebted to these materialist and symbolic critiques, but I wish to go beyond the dichotomy that considers them mutually exclusive paradigms. A literary analysis that takes into account findings from history is a path out of this critical dead end" (1993: 5). Her analysis is very successful because she achieves true New Historicism, drawing upon history and poststructuralism, including gender studies.

Ross's epistemological model is at the core of this book. The main problem of New Historicism has been that literary critics have embarked on historical studies without having a sufficient knowledge of the history of the period they are analyzing; the solution for this gap in erudition has been to apply false universals that only concern specific contexts and historical periods—for example, the use of gender models of the middle-upper class Victorian family (the so-called *normal* nuclear family) to work with Hispanic colonial literature.

Octavio Paz in *Children of the Mire* (1974) gives the historical reason for the importance of the baroque poets in modern Spanish poetry. According to González Echevarría: "Paz underscores an unpleasant, yet unavoidable fact: that there are no first-rate romantic poets in Spanish . . . Without a recent tradition on which to base their search for a poetic language, modern Hispanic poets had to look back to the Baroque" (1993: 115). It must be noticed that several characteristics of baroque literature would later form part of the Spanish avant-garde, the most important one being the dissolution of mimetic language. Salvador Novo, Xavier Villaurrutia, Jorge Cuesta, and the rest of the Contemporáneos group could identify themselves with this position. They were working at the margins of Mexican culture, attacked by those who read their literature as outside of the Mexican mainstream and against the *true* concept of nationality. It cannot be forgotten that the new orthodoxy created by the Mexican Revolution was firmly established in the mimetic language of realism, the novel of the Revolution, and did not wish to explore new possibilities to explain (and possibly denounce) the chaos produced by the Revolution. González Echevarría continues: "Góngora's poetry is inclusive rather than exclusive, willing to create and incorporate the new, literally in the forms of neologisms. He is anxious to overturn the tyranny of syntax, making the hyperbaton the most prominent feature of its poetry" (1993: 115).

What connects the baroque and the avant-garde writers of the Contemporáneos group is this idea of inclusiveness. The writers of the baroque exploited classical literature: they revisited the classics, chose the elements they wanted, and made new cultural artifacts out of them. Decorum did not apply here, because the classical texts could be decontextualized and recycled without showing respect for the original or, in any case, creating a new decorum to replace the old. These writers enjoyed the classics but were not overwhelmed by them. It was *imitatio*, but of a very particular form, for it included slang, the language of African slaves, popular songs like ballads and songs linked to dance, obscene tavern songs, and nursery rhymes. It also included the "epistemology" of popular culture, like the presence of the author in the puppet show and circus and fair artifacts like the anamorphosis (e.g., paintings where certain parts could only be seen from an angle). *Don Quijote* is a good example of these techniques. All these cultural artifacts could be used to make literature, putting together highbrow and lowbrow culture (or what we know today as popular culture).

The baroque was an attempt to reconcile the tension between the rationalism of the Renaissance (René Descartes) and the irrational forces of the seventeenth century (Gottfried Wilhelm Leibniz). Paolo Rossi (1995) has noticed that hundreds of books of the baroque period refer to the term *novus* (new). In addition, the New World was being explored, new stars were discovered, and the microscope opened up more new worlds to explore. As a result:

> The rejection of the exemplarity of classical culture (on which the humanists had insisted) took on strongly polemical overtones and in many cases (as in these lines of verse by Perrot de la Sale) took the forms of a rejection of classical culture itself: "De Grec et de Latin, mais point de connaissance. On nous munit la teste en notre adolescence." (In our adolescence they stuff our heads with Greek and Latin but not with knowledge). (Rossi 1995: 278)

It is the same with the Mexican avant-garde writers of the Contemporáneos, who were not satisfied with the scientific knowledge of the Porfiriato. The dynamism of the United States as an economic and cultural force could not compete in their eyes with the "official" French culture, which was being overwhelmed by the new cultural forms from the north (poetry, painting, cinema, architecture, music, vaudeville, etc.) in both high and pop culture. González Echevarría says:

> Góngora's style is not always "high," nor does he attempt to purge reality of base or heterogeneous elements. Reality did not enter his formula either to be accepted or rejected; its representation did. And here Góngora, like Cervantes and Velázquez, liked to juxtapose received forms of representation — "high" and "low" — critically. Everything can be part of beauty, even that which is not altogether comprehensible, and worse yet, even that which appears to be ugly, grotesque, or monstrous. (1993: 115)

For Novo and Villaurrutia, the discovery of the baroque model(s) gave them the opportunity to use literally everything: classical literature as understood by their models, the language of the streets of Mexico City with its *albures* (puns with sexual content); the language of lowclass *nacos*, *merolicos* (charlatans), and *carpas* (stand-up comedians like

Cantinflas and Roberto Soto); Nahuatl; obscenity; the lyrics of popular songs; the quick language of radio, newspaper, and wire news; Aztec culture; U.S. newsreels; trendy words in French and English (even *pachuco*) to create their own slang; the literary models of the United States or Spain—which had been taboo for political reasons—and the "traditional" French models as well. In addition, this discovery and recuperation of the baroque allowed them to recycle New Spanish colonial literature and the Spanish writers of the past or contemporary literature like the Generación de 1927, all of which were very well known to the young Mexican writers.

Above all, this gave them the opportunity to escape the temptation of converting the Revolution into a master narrative. They rejected the possibility of creating a lay religion out of the ideals of the Revolution, which they did not share. Novo as a child had been witness to the murder of his uncle by Villista troops and was not very fond of the revolutionary heroes. The baroque was the model to write free literature in a context of oppression. The last and most important quotation from González Echevarría on this topic states:

> This aesthetics of difference is another way of saying that the Baroque incorporates the Other; it plays at being the Other . . . The Baroque assumes the strangeness of the Other as an awareness of the strangeness of Being. Being is being as monster, at once one and the other, the same and different . . . An awareness of otherness within oneself, of newness. In this way the Baroque is a phenomenon parallel to Descartes's meditation on the self as thinking subject that questions all received knowledge. The feeling of being in the Baroque is more concrete than Descartes's *cogito;* it is more tangible. It is a sense of one's own rarity, of oddity, of distortion. Hence the plurality of New World Culture, its being-in-the-making as something not quite achieved, of something heterogeneous and incomplete, is expressed in the Baroque. (1993: 198–199)

Novo, Villaurrutia, and other writers of the group were gay in the modern sense of the term (cf. Smith 1986); the baroque was the perfect ideologeme to problematize their gender and their art. Writers like Salvador Novo, Federico García Lorca, and others detected early that there was a possibility of doing a queer reading of writers like Luis de Góngora, Francisco de Quevedo, Sor Juana Inés de la Cruz, or María de Zayas y Sotomayor. They realized that Góngora's mannerism (an effeminate Italian style) had been read by Góngora's foes as the opposite of masculine/Spanish (Díaz-Ortiz 1999b). They labeled this manner-ism affectation and declared that those who wrote in this style were sodomites, also insinuating that there was more than friendship be-tween the Count of Villamediana and Góngora. Góngora brought the beauty of the masculine body to his poetry (e.g., Canción 388, with its male desire for another man like the Sun; the pilgrim in the *Soledades;* and the male body of Acis and its genitalia, as seen through the eyes and the desire of a woman, Galatea).

Quevedo has a different perspective (Díaz-Ortiz 1999a). He dis-guises himself as homophobic and outs Góngora a number of times. He despises *bujarrones* (old faggots), *putos* (faggots), and *italï-anos* (Italï-anus). But at the same time Quevedo dedicates one book to the anus, "Gracias y desgracias del ojo del culo" (Fortunes and Misfortunes of the Asshole), and seven entries to the anus and its functions in *Diccionario privado de Francisco de Quevedo* (Private Dictionary by Francisco de Quevedo). Bringing the buttocks and the anus to the center of his po-etry, he challenges the phallocentrism of the dominant culture. He is also a model for writing poems in which the gender is disguised, where it is not easy for the reader to discern if the poetic voice and the object of desire are male or female, a technique that will be copied by the po-ets of the Generación de 1927 and the Contemporáneos group.

From María de Zayas they learned the performativity of gender (Charnon-Deutsch 1999). Her use of cross-dressing, masquerade, and androgyny deconstructs the expectations of being a man or a woman. Zayas also represents in a very detailed manner the dangers of patriar-chal heterosexuality, which brings inequality to the relationship be-tween men and women. Sor Juana (Altamiranda 1994) is a model for different reasons. The first one is obvious: she is Mexican and the most important representative of the Barroco de Indias. The cultural and ide-ological models could be European, but she taught future generations that one could adapt them to the American reality and make them one's own. She is the prodigy of the baroque, performing at court; she is the modern writer acting the role of a celebrity. Sor Juana also put gender at the center of her production and had to defend herself from the at-tacks she endured for being a woman working on exclusively male is-sues, like theology.

The baroque also served to question the fact of writing in what would come to be known as a third-world context. The baroque was the perfect connection to jump-start the modern Mexican culture of the twentieth century. The Revolution had ended the nineteenth century, but the young writers realized that the first cultural models created by the Revolution still belonged to that century. Modernity was a gap to be filled, and with their youth, erudition, and boasting they could (re)write modern Mexican culture. Octavio Paz, as González Echevarría says, was puzzled by the rejection of romantic models. This is not strange if we consider that the main function of romanticism was to provide an ideological base for nationalism.

Philip Silver's thesis about Spain's National Romanticism is that it is formed by the restitution of a modern Castilian-Andalusian tradition. Latin American *modernismo* and Castilian-Andalusian romanticism are parallel phenomena in that — instead of the latter causing the former — both were sparked by European high romanticism, as Octavio Paz indirectly suggests. The key word here is "high," which is why I have emphasized the importance given to popular forms in baroque literature. If Silver is right, we can infer that the main reason that romanticism and *modernismo* could not be the models for the avant-garde writers was because these literary traditions had given less importance to popular forms or had understood popular texts as a rural phenomenon through which it was possible to rescue the soul of the people. Novo and Villaurrutia were interested mainly in popular urban culture and in dismantling the nationalist ideological base of the Mexican state of romantic origin.

The Mexican Crisis of the Thirties: The Case of Novo

According to Maravall the most commonly used term in reference to the baroque is "crisis." And these crises form "a gesticulating culture, one of dramatic expression [that] was produced whenever a situation of conflict arose between the energies of the individual and the ambit containing it" (1986: 36). There are two key ideas in this paragraph (one lost in translation): "imposición represiva [repressive imposition]" (28), and "gesticulación [dramatic expression]." The first one has its origin in the absolutism inaugurated with the Catholic kings and spread in the following centuries. The second is the product of the conflict between the individual and the ambit. What is this ambit like? According to Maravall: "We are faced — not only in Spain, but in all of Europe — with an epoch that, in all spheres of collective life, saw itself dragged along by irrational forces, by appeals to violence, the multiplying of crimes, moral laxity, and hallucinating forms of devotion. All these aspects resulted from the situation of pathos wherein the underlying social crisis was exteriorized and expressed in manifestations of the epoch's general mentality" (1986: 53). Maravall assigns four characteristics to the culture of the baroque: "Guided" (57–78), "A Mass Culture" (79–103), "Urban" (104–125), and "Conservative" (126–148). We have already toned down the conservative aspect, giving emphasis, as Rossi demonstrates, to the continuation of the *novus* paradigm of the Renaissance.

According to the Mexican historians Héctor Aguilar Camín and Lorenzo Meyer, when General Lázaro Cárdenas (1934–1940) became president of Mexico, a new period of Mexican history began: the end of *caudillismo* and the beginning of the presidential regime (*presidencialismo*). The termination by Cárdenas of the political influence of Plutarco Elías Calles, and *callismo* in general, was the beginning of a new historical structure (and/or structure of feeling) that produced social anomies (Maravall 1986: 411–470) similar to those found in the European baroque of the seventeenth century.[1] The most important fact is the foundation of a central power similar to the absolutist king: the Mexican president. To perpetuate these political ideologemes and their modes of government, both systems underwent an enormous ideological depreciation to rationalize these absolute powers (e.g., the divine justification given by absolute kings at a time of Cartesian philosophy). In the Mexican case, presidents had to justify the lack of democracy by means of flamboyant electoral campaigns. Thus, the given definition of "baroque" can be applied to the Mexico of the postrevolutionary period.[2] The divorce between the ideological foundations of the Mexican Republic (liberalism and utopian socialism) and the course the presidents followed is reflected in the profound ironies of the Contemporáneos' writings and paintings.

The Mexican writer José Emilio Pacheco, Novo's personal secretary, collected most of the articles written by Novo between 1934 and 1940 in a single volume, *La vida en México en el período presidencial de Lázaro Cárdenas* (Life in Mexico during the Presidency of Lázaro Cárdenas, 1964). In the magazine *Hoy* (Today) Novo had a column called "La semana pasada" (Last Week) which he used to criticize the authoritarian leftist policies of President Cárdenas. This column became obligatory reading for the new urban, postrevolutionary middle classes. According to Pacheco, Novo was "the creator and importer of new, modern journalism among us" (14). He would end up being the best-paid writer of the moment and an integral part of other modern urban activities like cinema, publicity, and radio as well. Allowing for their obvious differences, Novo is Mexico's Walter Winchell.

A close reading of Novo's first articles evokes a very serious writer, extremely technical at times, who uses sophisticated statistics. But little by little the style of the author became more relaxed, and he let verbal pyrotechnics form part of the political/literary game he was developing, the so-called *novocablos*. Novo began to create neologisms based on those invented by Quevedo and Góngora during the baroque period: the Spanish exiles of the Civil War (1938) were "puñicerrados coñidicientes" (foul-mouthed closed fists; 1964: 456). Novo cultivated a "gesticulating dramatic expression," which made him a neo-baroque writer: the *arbitrista*, the satiric poet, reactionary at times — the urban writer who used the same verbal weapons already displayed by Góngora, Sor Juana, and Quevedo. Novo sharpened his claws and was ready to fight in the jungle of Mexican letters.

The aphorism *homo homini lupus*, resurrected by the baroque period, can also be used to define the Mexico of the thirties. Very different social and ideological movements tried to impose their political and economical interests as well as their definition of what revolutionary Mexico should be on others: liberalism, Marxism, communism, Stalinism, Trotskyism, socialism, fascism, agrarianism, indigenism, multiracism (*mestizaje*), *indigenismo*, unionism, Catholicism (the Cristero War), traditionalism, treason (*malinchismo*) — all made more complex by the followers of José Vasconcelos, Plutarco Elías Calles, Venustiano Carranza, Francisco Madero, Pancho Villa, Emiliano Zapata, and other political leaders. This is an unfinished list, but it is useful in explaining the agony created in Mexican intellectuals in their quest for enough signs of identity to square the circle of finding a new definition of fatherland/motherland. It also explains the complex and contradictory political pressures imposed upon artists.

Guillermo Sheridan, in his book *Los Contemporáneos ayer* (The Contemporáneos Yesterday, 1985), explains the first battle in the polemics over the true meaning of contemporary Mexican literature. Painting formed part of the controversy because the muralists also participated in the public debate, especially Diego Rivera (see Chapter 3 for discussion of the ways in which Rivera gave his own definition of Mexico). Sheridan's study "1922: Lamecazuelas contra vanguardistas" (1922: Pot-Suckers against Vanguardists, 1985: 120–146) can be summarized in this quotation from José Joaquín Blanco: "And what in the early twenties was an anticolonial movement later on became folklore for tourists and magic barbarousness; from a vital, tropical anticivilization of wild inspiration, it became nationalist demagoguery" (1983: 126).

Novo and the Contemporáneos group wanted a Mexican literature open to the beneficial influences of foreign ideas even if, on occasion, they attacked these ideas. They enjoyed the articles and poems of José Ortega y Gasset's magazine *Revista de Occidente*, the French novels of Marcel Proust and André Gide, the avant-garde poetry of the Imagists in the United States, and the poetry of the Harlem Renaissance.

This position drew a strong reaction from the nationalists of the Mexican Revolution. These nationalists belonged to the two extremes of the political spectrum: both fascists and Communists joined forces against the moral decadence of the avant-garde, including the Contemporáneos. The other important avant-garde group, the Estridentistas, defended the nationalistic positions. They in turn attacked the "exotics" (the others, the non-Mexicans) and requested the dismissal from public office of the poets open to foreign influence. The theory of otherness developed by González Echevarría (and Octavio Paz) provides an idea of the difference between the two poetic groups: the inclusiveness of the Contemporáneos and the exclusiveness of the Estridentistas. Some of the Contemporáneos who had minor positions in the state bureaucracy lost them because of the pressures of those who opposed them. The most common insult besides "exotic" was "effeminate"; later on the Estridentista writer Manuel Maples Arce, a parliament member during the Cárdenas administration, said in the House of Representatives: "[This is] the comedy of the fags and the cynicism of the pederasts shielded under the new publicity of Proust and Gide" (Sheridan 1985: 132).

According to Paz, the attacks against the Contemporáneos group came from two different sources. The first attack happened in 1932 and had its origin in the reactionary right of the newspaper *Excélsior* (1987: 96) in the form of a diatribe against the secretary of education, Narciso Bassols, who had protected the young poets. The second offensive came from the Cárdenas government, from the revolutionary left, where the Contemporáneos were denounced "as reactionary . . . exquisite, decadent, and cosmopolitan" (1987: 98). Víctor Díaz Arciniega (1989) has found six major polemics after the Revolution: in 1926 the central issue was effeminate literature versus revolutionary right and privilege; in 1932 the discussion focused on classicism and nationalism in the arts and Marxism and liberalism in teaching; in 1947 the question was whether the Revolution itself was in crisis and also if there was any way to identify Mexicanness; in 1961 at issue was Mexican socialism and its reality in comparison with the Cuban Revolution; in 1968 the topic was the end of the revolutionary system and the need for younger generations to participate in public life and politics; and as late as 1978 the question of Mexican cultural reality was again discussed. The recent crises of the Institutional Revolutionary Party (PRI), the assassinations of prominent Mexican political figures and television personalities, narcoterrorism, and the Zapatista movement are widely discussed nowadays by intellectuals and the mass media.

Nueva grandeza mexicana *(New Mexican Grandeur, 1946)*

More than fifty years after its first edition, the only possible word to describe Salvador Novo's *Nueva grandeza mexicana* today is "perfection." In 1946 the Federal District of Mexico City had a public contest for books eulogizing the metropolis, which Novo won. He donated the generous award of $2,000 to a literacy campaign patronized by his friend the Contemporáneos writer Jaime Torres Bodet (Paz 1994), who was secretary of public education at the time. This was an attempt by Novo to win the favor of the new administration. That year marked the transition between the presidencies of Manuel Avila Camacho (1940–1946) and Miguel Alemán Valdés (1946–1952), the first civilian to serve as president after the 1910 Revolution. Novo was named head of the Department of Theatrical Productions at the Instituto Nacional de Bellas Artes, where he served throughout the presidency of the rightist Alemán Valdés.

Now the question is how a conventional piece, a mixture of history book and tourist pamphlet, has become a classic of Mexican literature. The 1992 edition used for this study, with an introduction by Carlos Monsiváis, was published by Hermes but funded by the National Council for the Culture and Arts. The name of the collection is "Cien de México," a series of 100 masterpieces of Mexican literature, a literary compilation like those made famous by Vasconcelos to bring high culture to the Mexican people.

In his article "El barroco y el neobarroco" (Baroque and Neo-Baroque), Severo Sarduy disagrees with Robert Jammes, a French critic who considers a ballad by Góngora a minor text because it is based on another ballad by Lope de Vega. According to Jammes, Góngora's ballad is just a parody subordinated to a major text. Sarduy not only disputes this but goes on to say: "For a Latin American text to belong to a major genre, it has to be the deformation of a previous text; then this text will be read like a filigree [*en filigrana*], and this will be the only reading providing pleasure. And this will be more valid in the future, because the references and the knowledge of the reader will be more sophisticated, and more filigree texts will come, as well as the products of other deformations" (1972: 175). According to Sarduy, Jammes creates an unnecessary hierarchy of the texts. In my view Sarduy is right; examples by Bernardo de Balbuena and Ramón María del Valle-Inclán show how literary texts can be constructed using different cultural elements, including lowbrow culture. What Sarduy means to say in an ostentatious way is that Hispanic American culture is by nature a mestizo culture. Spanish is a transported language with an important tradition of being at a crossroads, always receiving foreign influences. Hispanic American culture is formed mainly of Western cultural texts that attempt to transcend imperialistic ideology. These texts are part of the Western canon and at the same time aim to transcend the Europeanness of this canon.

The text that Novo deformed according to the terminology of Sarduy is *Grandeza mexicana* (Mexican Grandeur) by Bernardo de Balbuena, written in 1603 and published in 1604. Balbuena was born in Valdepeñas, Ciudad Real, Spain, in 1562 and at the age of twenty-two moved to New Spain, where his father lived. He stayed in the Americas for the rest of his life except for four years that he spent in Spain (1606–1610) to receive an academic degree and advance his ecclesiastic career. He died in 1627 in San Juan, Puerto Rico, where he was bishop. Balbuena, as a member of the Barroco de Indias (or is it a Renacimiento de Indias?), is someone between two paradigms: Spain and Europe on one side and America as a new reality with its own personality and idiosyncrasy on the other. Novo, as the son of an immigrant from Spain, always saw himself as someone between two cultures and two countries. This does not mean that he considered himself a Spaniard, but at least he felt that he owed some kind of respect to his father's country and that Spain was part of his heritage. The Revolution and the postrevolutionary period were marked by a strong sentiment against the former metropolis, and there was a great deal of rhetoric against Spain, which started during independence, continued during the Reforma, and increased during the Porfiriato. This lasted until the first refugees of the Spanish Civil War came to Mexico during the presidency of Lázaro Cárdenas; at that time Novo felt obliged to criticize some of the new immigrants when they abused the generosity Mexico had shown them. It has to be said that Spain was an exception to Novo's iconoclasm.[3] He did not avoid criticizing Spain, but he spared it very harsh or unjustified criticism at a moment when Spain was fair game for the Revolution, its people, and its institutions. Other organizations and personalities were not so lucky.

Novo was always marked by the fact that his father was from Galicia, Spain. Michael Alderson, who has written the best biographical account of Novo, begins his work with a translation of a well-known poem by Novo, "La historia" (History; 1961: 340) from his book *Espejo* (Mirror, 1933):

¡Mueran los gachupines!
My father is a gachupín,
full of hate the teacher looks at me
and tells us of the War of Independence
and how the Spaniards were evil and cruel
with the Indians—he is Indian—
and all the children shout death to the gachupines.

But I object
and think that they are very stupid:
That's what history says
but how are we to know it?   (1994: XI)

A second poem, also from *Espejo*, should be included in this biographical account: "Retrato de familia" (Family Portrait):

My father, my mother, I
I can hardly recognize myself here.
They say that I have something of the two of them
but that I look more like him;
he already died,
people are always right.   (1994: 74)

Despite this, Novo's reaction to nationalism was mainly intellectual; he decided to fight the ultranationalism of the Revolution because a policy of isolation was not good for the country and was against the definition of Mexico as a Western nation within the context of the Americas as well (Sheridan 1984). His reaction was also literary, because nationalism is linked to romanticism. Modern nations in Europe and in America were constructed using literary myths developed during the romantic period (Juaristi). Bypassing romanticism when constructing new subjectivities, modern writers could avoid the nationalist master narrative and its irrational myths.

The intertextuality of *Grandeza* and *Nueva grandeza* emphasizes the question of the origin of Mexico. *Grandeza* is a seminal Creole text of the Barroco de Indias that describes Mexico City as a European city. According to Balbuena, the beginning of Mexico City occurs when the destruction of the old Aztec city is complete and a new, European city is erected in its place: "Of whose noble birth, second to none / this great city was born anew / ascending, prosperous and fecund" (1963: 15).[4] The idea is clear: Mexico City is a reborn city, second to none (*sin segundo*), but also with the possibility of denying the first Aztec city, Tenochtitlan —*sin segundo* meaning that the Spanish city he is describing is the first one. Balbuena calls the Indians *gentes extrañas* (strange people, 15) and uses the phrase *indio feo* (ugly Indian, 86). The indigenous population is excluded from his description of the city; they belong to the otherness.[5] Balbuena's explanation is devastating: "And let's admire the theater of fortune, / because less than one hundred years ago this looked like / humble huts, scum, and the lagoon; / and not even one old lump left standing, / from its first foundation renewed / this greatness and wonder has been erected."[6] Not even *un terrón* (a lump) of the old city has been saved; every single chunk has been replaced by a new European/American city. Balbuena compares Mexico City throughout the poem with the well-known European cities and mythical metropolises of the past: Troy, Rome, Venice, Thebes, Memphis. He does not make a single comparison with other cities of Old Spain; he does not want Mexico City competing with the sister cities there.

The parallel in Novo's *Nueva grandeza* is the American city, as it had been depicted during World War II in the newsreels and in the movies and in the model of society designed by Franklin Delano Roosevelt and his New Deal policies. The new Mexican City of 1946 is very different from the 1910 provincial city at the beginning of the Revolution. The phenomenon parallels Balbuena's comparison with the old Tenochtitlan. Mary Kendall Long in her dissertation has studied the textual construction of Mexico City in *El joven* and *Nueva grandeza*. The chapter "Writing the City" (1995: 165–219) "explores the implications of the fact that for Novo 'writing the city' is also reading what has been written and finding possibilities for his own place in the canon" (1995: iv). This is another dimension of the intertextuality between *Nueva grandeza* and the chronicles of the colonial past. The other key text of the colony mentioned by Novo is *México en 1554: Tres diálogos latinos* by Francisco Cervantes de Salazar, who had been named the first official chronicler of the city. Novo inserted himself into the lineage of official city historians.

Maravall (1980) says that baroque literature is by nature official, the public discourse of the new state.[7] In this context, Long quotes Margo Glantz:

> In Mexico a phenomenon that had started several decades ago has been exacerbated lately. It is the absolute institutionalization of culture. Everything goes through the system, and being a writer means being in some way mediated by power, and at the same time having the benefits of power. One can enjoy many privileges thanks to writing. In Mexico one can be in key places just for writing and writing with certain repercussion. A writer who says things in the newspaper that can be dread is immediately harnessed by the State and becomes part of it. His books are published in important editions, are distributed; the writer is on television, he is interviewed. On the other hand, there is a polarization between "gerontocracy" and "ephebocracy": old writers determine who the really important young writers are and castrate them. They make them essential, inflate them so much that the old writers destroy the new ones. (Long 1995: 108; cf. Mercado 1992)[8]

The discourse of dissidence is silenced by the state. The process is double: in one direction the state tries to integrate dissident discourses into the official form of the state; and in the other, the writer aims to be part of the official discourse, to become integrated into the dwindled polyphony of the country.

The key word repeated throughout *Grandeza* is *interés* (profit). *Grandeza* states that peace and commerce, when brought together, bring affluence to a nation. In the same way, *Nueva grandeza* declares that the *pax mexicana* of President Alemán Valdés and the stability all over the country will bring prosperity to the nation. The capitalist model should be the vehicle necessary to make Mexico a true Western nation. To Balbuena *el interés* is "[t]he sun that vivifies the world; / what preserves, rules, and makes it grow, / shields, defends, and fortifies it" (1963: 11). This surely must be one of the first examples of a passionate defense of capitalist modes for the Mexican economy. Balbuena tells us that people work for money: the farmer, soldier, merchant, actor, shepherd, officer, tailor, sailor, conqueror, clerk, lawyer, doctor, peddler, priest, abbot, sacristan. All of them work because they see in their professions a means to better themselves and their families. But Balbuena goes further in his economic theories; he dares to affirm: "if [people] help each other, and they obey, / and if in this network and human connection / men with their own world stay, / the appealing profit holds their hands, / reinforces pleasure and makes them grow strong, / and with itself makes the whole level even" (12). Mercantilism produces a perfect social equilibrium, with the balance based on all doing their jobs and the obedience of those who are in inferior positions: the hierarchy has to be respected. There is a utopian echo in this stanza: New Spain as a new country lacks the class defects of Old Spain, although caste should be respected.

Another ideological point that could be of interest to Novo is the inversion of the topos of *menosprecio de corte* (contempt for the court), which in Balbuena becomes *menosprecio de aldea* (contempt for the village, the rural area): "Small towns, small, everything is work, / gossip, murmur, small talk, invention, / a lie, envy, and everything that goes on [t]here" (1963: 35). Or, as it is said in contemporary Mexico, "pueblo chico, infierno grande" (a small town is a big inferno). An example by Novo of the transition from small city to large metropolis is discussed in the analysis of *Nueva grandeza* below. Both Balbuena and Novo follow the classical models of the *laudes Italiae* and *laudes Romae*, in which the panegyrist had to laud first the situation of the city and then the rest of its advantages, including the arts and sciences (Curtius 1955: 228).

For Mary Kendall Long, "the 'crónica de la ciudad' has much in common with the chronicles which address broader themes. In particular, the tendency to find national definitions in the ephemeral details of daily life and the tension caused by having the transitory newspaper chronicle serve also as a repository of issues with a potential for historical permanence. These tensions are made more intriguing by the existence of an 'official' position by the 'Cronista de la ciudad' " (1995: 179). It has to be said in this context that the most intriguing intertextuality between *Nueva grandeza* and newspapers is within Novo himself. *Nueva grandeza* is a stylization of his raw materials in everyday newspapers. It is the opportunity to give organicity to his own materials and to demonstrate that his writing on a daily basis for the newspapers and magazines serves a purpose of national interest.

Monsiváis (1992) says in his prologue that Novo wants to imprint on his articles and essays brief and different rhythms. These rhythms come not from poetry or "acoustic attainment" but from the accumulation of information, erudition, intelligence, high-quality prose, classical culture, and everyday life, with everything ruled by an extraordinary love of the present: Golden Age and Manhattan, Quevedo and the new poetry in English. The melting point is irony, the leery distance that asks for the reader's "bad faith" (1992: 10). According to Monsiváis's "love of the present," Novo is not a utopian writer. He belongs to the bourgeoisie and is very proud of his accomplishments as a self-made man. But he agrees with Balbuena that a harmonious society can be achieved if a social contract is put in place and the different sectors of society do their respective jobs. The man of the baroque was a *fieri*. And Novo wants to establish a parallelism between himself and the city of his success. An analysis of Monsiváis's words indicates the rigor of Novo's prose: information, erudition, intelligence, quality, classical and modern culture. There is no philosophical wandering or speculation as in utopian essayists, but rather the reality of the brand-new large city and Novo's erection of a textual reality parallel to the new Mexico City skyline.

According to Monsiváis, this way of representing urban life reveals the direct influence of André Gide (1992: 13). Marcel Proust is the other author who comes to mind; both Frenchmen wrote about the poetic content of the new urban life of the beginning of the twentieth century. In the *Avila Camacho* book Novo names Proust four times yet never mentions Gide; but in the *Alemán Valdés* book he mentions Gide eight times and Proust six. Both authors are very influential because Novo learned from them to recount urban life and the closet.

Monsiváis says that *Nueva grandeza* is an *alemanista* book, because it attempts to create a symbolic Mexico City where all social classes live in harmony. This may be true, but Novo is not that naïve; as Monsiváis himself says, he always appeals to the "bad faith" of the reader. Novo needs an accomplice reader to complete the text. What is more, Monsiváis's progressive interpretation of "reactionary" *alemanismo* is correct from a 1992 perspective, but it distorts *Nueva grandeza*—to Novo, Alemán's government meant an important advance toward a *normal* and civil society: at last, the end of military rule in Mexico and the beginning of a civilian society. The demonstration of this premise is in the fact that Secretary Torres Bodet became the de facto vice-president and ideologue of the administration, especially in his function as Alemán's ghostwriter and architect of the reform of article 3 of the constitution, which ended the socialist education implemented by President Cárdenas. It is not just that Torres Bodet had started his political career as Vasconcelos's personal secretary; as a Vasconcelista ideologue he was ruling the SEP (Secretariat of Public Education) and fulfilling the Vasconcelista creed as much as Mexican means permitted. Novo was a firm defender of the role of the state in promoting culture as a complement and aid to the private sector. The accomplishments during his term as head of the Department of Theatrical Productions, Instituto Nacional de Bellas Artes, are outstanding (see Novo 1967).

Following a pattern created by Balbuena, Novo's book is divided into seven parts, each one beginning with a line from a poem by Balbuena. Both *Grandeza mexicana* and *Nueva grandeza* are glosses. In her seminal book *A Poetics of Postmodernism* (1988), Linda Hutcheon quotes Vincent Leichs:

> Intertextuality posits both an uncentered historical enclosure and an abysmal decentered foundation for language and textuality; in so doing, it exposes all contextualizations as limited and limiting, arbitrary and confining, self-serving and authoritarian, theological and political. However paradoxically formulated, intertextuality offers a liberating determinism. (127)

Hutcheon continues this line of thought at a later juncture:

> In American postmodernism, the different comes to be defined in particularizing terms such as those of nationality, ethnicity, gender, race, and sexual orientation. Intertextual parody of canonical American and European classics is one mode of appropriating and reformulating — with significant change — the dominant white, male, middle-class, heterosexual, European culture. It does not reject it, for it cannot. Postmodernism signals its dependence by its *use* of the canon, but reveals its rebellion through its ironic *abuse* of it. (130)

Some readers will be surprised by the presence of the term "postmodernism" in the context of the analysis of a 1946 book by a Mexican author, but this is the term that can best explain the intertextual relationship between Novo's text and the cultural contexts with which he is working. The Spanish term *ámbito* defines Novo's textual construction: it includes "boundary," "scope," and "context" in the same word. *Nueva grandeza* is a new cultural *ámbito* to explain Mexico City. Novo's use of neo-baroque techniques to construct his text positions him in the Western tradition and at the same time, as Hutcheon explains, provides him with the tools to assemble a genuine Mexican product that is simultaneously unquestionably Western and something else.

Sarduy and Hutcheon coincide because postmodernism and the neo-baroque respond to the same phenomenon or cluster of phenomena. For instance, the concept of the neo-baroque as developed by Omar Calabrese (1992) is no more than the conventional definition of postmodernism as defined by Hutcheon, among others. Beverley (1994) is another critic who has joined the concepts of baroque and postmodernism.

Nueva grandeza does not have a prologue or an introduction by the author; the first chapter functions as a presentation of the whole book and its structure. The text is narrated in the first person by the author, and the narratee is a "provinciano" from Monterrey, a good friend who comes to Mexico City for the first time. The text also uses the real reader as implied reader. This technique enables the author to entertain the real reader and at times to demand participation in the text. The reader does not tire or get bored either, because once in a while he or she is challenged by the text and has to make a choice or a guess. Novo, as a publicist and radio, newspaper, and magazine writer, knows how to find a balance between erudition and entertainment. This is the Aristotelian and Horatian tradition of amusing and teaching with a modern twist, giving more importance to the entertainment factor in order to reach a wider audience. In *Nueva Grandeza* Novo storms the literary establishment; he aims to achieve both goals: to write a high-quality literary product that is at the same time a commodity. This is the postmodern dimension of Novo, which explains why a book written in 1946 reads like a contemporary text:

> I was going to impress with inside knowledge a provincial who was
> coming to town for the first time. At the same time, for my own part, I
> was going to savor the nostalgia of old memories of the city. (1992: 21)

The key word is *añoranza* (nostalgia). Theorists of postmodernity have hypothesized about the nostalgia of late capitalism, but we know little about these early manifestations of nostalgia. In Novo's case, it appears that he was aware that the presidency of Alemán was going to represent a big change in Mexico, possibly the true modernization of the country, and the certainty that Mexico City was on its way to becoming incomprehensible due to its magnitude. At the very beginning of the book Novo alludes to "mi pericia y mi conocimiento de todos sus secretos" (1992: 21), "inside knowledge," but he is conscious that from that moment on (1946) any writer would be unable to grasp the totality of the city. The metropolis was going to end up eluding and overwhelming its inhabitants. Andrew Ross has studied the influence of the intellectual to define modern, urban culture (1989: 135–170). He has noticed how, according to Susan Sontag (1966: 288), in an age of mass culture the dandy is in charge of defining nostalgia. The young urbanites like Novo were in charge of deciding which elements of the old Porfirian culture, or even the Imperial period, could be rescued as commodities to be consumed by the nouveaux riches of the postrevolutionary period and vicariously by the masses through magazines and movies (e.g., the nostalgia in the movies made by Indio Fernández).[9]

One of the techniques the narrator uses to show the city to his friend is modern, like the city: "Suddenly, like a 'dissolve' in a film, the reality of our bus was washed out on the screen of my memories" (1992: 22). The narrator in some cases tries to narrate not in prose but in images. This introductory chapter promises a whole vision of the city, perhaps the last possible one. Critics have read *Nueva grandeza* as a sanitized account of Mexico City (Monsiváis 1992: 16), but this is only half true. Let us remember that Monsiváis said that the "bad faith" of the reader was needed to fill in the blanks produced by the text. On page 23 we find a veiled reference to prostitution and an attack on the greed of the generals of the Revolution and on page 24 a reference to the body odors of taxi drivers (odors that Novo loved because he was very fond of making love to taxi drivers, as he explains in his memoirs, *La estatua de sal* [The Pillar of Salt]). And on page 25 he describes the origins of the term *mordida* (bribe). From the very beginning of the book Novo is telling the reader to take care, because he is always able to find a cunning way to present much more than the apparent eulogy of the city.

We now turn to analysis of Novo's literary strategies. One interesting example of intertextuality describes prostitutes: "provocativo maquillaje de albayalde y fuchina roja" (a bold and provocative makeup of white lead and red fuchsine; 23); this is the *modernista* and grotesque mode of description used by Ramón del Valle-Inclán. The narrator equates himself with the Spaniard, an acid descriptor of the harshness of the social realities of the Spain of the Restauración, Spain's Victorian period, and the first two decades of the twentieth century. Valle-Inclán was also a caustic portrayer of exotic Mexico in *Sonata de estío* (Summer Sonnet, 1903). In *Luces de bohemia* we can find two references to prostitutes and *albayalde:*

> La vieja sórdida, bajo la máscara de albayalde, descubre las encías sin dientes, y tienta capciosa a DON LATINO. (1993a: 128) [THE OLD HAG's white chalk mask cracks as she gives a toothless grin in a pathetic attempt to tempt DON LATINO. (1993b: 152)]

> El rostro albayalde de la otra vieja peripatética. (1993a: 135) [The chalk-like face of another prostitute. (1993b: 155)]

The neo-baroque intertextuality is active because the new literary texts are constructed with pieces of culture. In this case the first edition of Valle-Inclán's play is from 1920 and the second and final edition from 1924, a key moment in the avant-garde art. *Bohemian Lights* represents the most important major work of the avant-garde in Spanish in terms of creating literature with remnants of marginal texts; the *esperpento* is the creative process of deforming lowbrow and highbrow culture to create a new text where the positivist definition of culture is destroyed. By definition, the *esperpento* is bathetic.

The references to Walter Winchell as a U.S. paradigm comparable to Novo enter into this game of intertextualities. Valle-Inclán's model, according to editor Alonso Zamora Vicente, was Salvador María Granés, whose specialty was to write parodies of major works (1993a: 23–24). He wrote *La golfemia* based on Giacomo Puccini's *La bohème*. Valle-Inclán includes in his text writers like Alejandro Sawa and Rubén Darío, characters from his own books like El Marqués de Bradomín, and real people from the cafés of Madrid. Other cultural artifacts used by Valle are *Hamlet* and *Life Is a Dream* by Pedro Calderón de la Barca. He mentions famous people, including writers, singers, bullfighters, and politicians: Miguel de Unamuno, King Alfonso XIII, la Infanta Isabel de Borbón, Pastora Imperio, Antonio Maura, Joselito, El Marqués de Alhucemas (1993a: 25). The language is based on the urban slang of the lower classes of Madrid and the journalistic idiom of the newspapers.

Novo's reference to Valle-Inclán is not an exercise in the nostalgia of modernism but the recognition of a new way of making literature, the way to develop a new literary tradition able to narrate the urban city of the twentieth century. Everything has to be redone, because language is not being renovated by a group of intellectuals in their ivory towers but by the new reality of the city: cabaret, *carpas*, newspapers, the radio, songs, political speeches and their parodies, the mixture for the first time of people coming from all the regions of any given country (Novo himself was from Coahuila), the new celebrities. The new reality is also the collapse of the figure of the unchallenged intellectual like the scientist during the Porfiriato. In Valle's list Unamuno has to compete with a stunningly beautiful gypsy singer like Imperio or a draconian politician like Maura or a legendary bullfighter like Joselito. They all have in common the new culture of celebrity developed by the mass media. This example illustrates the previous quotation from Hutcheon and the use made by an American writer like Novo of Europe's cultural patrimony to construct New World reality.

In the chapter dedicated to restaurants, bars, theater, movies, and cabaret, "Gifts, Occasions for Contentment," as in the previous section, Novo delivers more than he promises for the attentive reader. The first example is when he tells about the Club de Banqueros, one of the most important private clubs in the city:

I might even have been indiscreet enough to tell my friend that below us, in the Alley of the Countess, beside which the building topped by the Banker's Club rises proudly and opulently, there was a hundred years ago a dirty tortilla shop, with an open drain running by it, swarming with dogs. Here, rescued by a charitable old woman, grew Payno's romantic hero. And I could have told him that the Sanborn's of the border, where we might have eaten or bought toothpaste, or a suit, or silver, or toys, or paintings, or candy, or laxatives, or admired a fresco by Orozco, is the Palace of Tiles. The Marquis of San Francisco wrote its complete history. Before becoming what it is, it housed the Jockey Club, rendezvous of the scientific "tight folk." (1992/1967: 30–31) [10]

This paragraph is paradigmatic of what we as readers can expect from Novo. Readers do not get a detailed description of what the Club de Banqueros is—and the privileges of its membership—but other information. The first circumstance the narrator shares with us is "si yo fuera miembro" (29): Novo distances himself from the *apretado* group, the financial elite of Mexico. And then he defines them:

I should have taken my friend to the Banker's Club, and we would have shared with these gentry the neurotic privilege of feeling ourselves, on the terrace overlooking the Alameda, the lords of Mexico and the authors of its development, after downing some highballs in front of Angel Zárraga's murals. (1992/1967: 31) [11]

Now that the narrator has distanced himself from the *apretados*, he can label them neurotics because they "feel" themselves to be the owners and authors of Mexico's development. But they are not, as Novo implies with this periphrasis. The neo-baroque technique is useful to be able to say more than what is expected in a conventional text. It is very important to use the anachronistic preposition *cabe* to introduce the club, because it suggests that this social institution is antiquated and passé. The gradation first moves downward and then goes upward. This technique harks back to the baroque text *Grandeza mexicana* by Balbuena that inspired Novo's document. The Club de Banqueros is according to Novo the "crown" of the building; but in the archaeological movement downward he brings to the surface the layers beneath the elitist club: (1) a dirty tortilla factory; (2) an open sewer; (3) stray dogs; (4) Payno. Novo uses the neo-baroque as the system to describe the city because it enables him to unmask the reality of the metropolis without removing that mask. He creates a modern emblem to describe the club. The simple truth is that the *banqueros* float upon the shit of the city. Even the reference to Miguel Payno is not innocent. Payno had been able to portray Mexican society as a whole with *Los bandidos de Río Frío* (1889–1891) without moralizing and by using mild satire, exactly what Novo is doing (Sefchovich 1987: 38).

The second place used to deconstruct the city is Sanborn's (29–30), a general store resembling those in the United States, a sign of the new times. The adjective to describe the store is *frontero* (of the border), an example of the transition between the United States and Mexico. The United States after World War II had consolidated its position as paradigm of modernity and triumph. Another neo-baroque technique is the enumeration to describe the store: toothpaste, a suit, silver, trinkets, pictures, candy, a purgative, as examples of the neocolonial situation; two of the terms are key: "trinkets" recalls the treats brought by Spaniards to deceive the Indians, and "purgative" brings the body and its orifices to the surface of text. Scatology had an important tradition in the baroque. Novo, like Quevedo, is challenging the aseptic client of Sanborn's, the follower of Manuel Antonio Carreño's norms of hygiene (cf. Oropesa 1992 on Laura Esquivel), and reminding the reader of the attempt of the new society created by the Victorian period (the Porfiriato in Mexican terms) to hide the body. On a linguistic level, the presence of words like *apretados, flaneo, lambiscón,* and *ruletear* brings slang to the text.

It was also the baroque that brought *germanía* (criminal slang) to literature. Neal Gabler, analyzing the function of slang in the newspaper columns of Walter Winchell, says:

> Language in the twenties was assuming a new and energizing role in the culture. Like so much else in the decade, slang was a form of cultural democracy; it was a way for the disenfranchised to reclaim their language from the genteel elites. Slang aerated English and in doing so created a new language, a kind of subversive tongue that was especially attractive to young, urban Americans. To know which words were in vogue, to know what "scram" meant and "palooka" and "belly laughs" and "lotta baloney" and "pushover," was like being part of a secret society—one from which the arbiters of good taste were obviously excluded. For these readers, then, language wasn't just a means of expression; it was a nosethumbing, a fashion, an entertainment, and a way of showing one was in the know when being in the know was an important differentiation. (1994: 71)

Of course, there are important differences between Novo and Winchell, but they shared the same kind of urban upbringing, the school of the streets, and their appreciation of the dynamic forces of the city. Novo's advantage over Winchell is that he had a classical education; but he always considered an integral part of his development to have come from the street—knowing its language, its mores and standards. At a very young age Novo had begun his gay life in the streets of Mexico City. He knew the language of the people because like Pier Paolo Pasolini he had made love to them. When they are at Ambassadeurs, Novo shows his friend the famous journalists:

> If at the moment they were noisily cheerful, if they began to stagger a little, none would guess it the next morning when their columns, models of austerity, thundered against governmental corruption and the poverty into which the ineptitude of the Revolutionary authorities has sunk the common people who do not eat because everything costs the nose on your face, because it has been necessary to import corn, and, on the other hand, because we are threatened with Communism. (1992/ 1967: 39) [12]

In this case Novo uses litotes and displacement of meaning. It appears that he is attacking journalists, but he is one of them—he is also writing adverse things about the government on a daily basis; at that time he had been an editorial writer for more than ten years. So instead of describing a luxurious bar, as he should be doing, he is attacking the government:

> The Revolution had just triumphed. It was a peasant revolution, and the reviews made fun of the bumpkin, the pot-bellied, foxy, or simply stupid farmer as portrayed on the stage by "buddy" Beristáin. This was an elementary punning humor at the expense of the coarse stupidity of the countryman considered to be the popular prototype of the times of Zapata, the direct descendant of the buffoon or fool of the early Spanish theater. At that time Beristáin was still "he who gets slapped," the one who gets it from his tormentors but usually repays them to the amusement of the public, which thus is able to feel a personal and evident superiority. Roberto Soto, who was later to concentrate in his potbelly a whole epoch of the Revolution and of the capital and of the humor proper to both . . . When Calles raised up Morones, as fat as Soto, Soto hit on the happy notion of offering to the politically repressed citizenry in his *Lírico* theater a hilarious safety valve by ridiculing fat labor leaders and pistol-packing congressmen. (1992/1967: 46–47) [13]

Novo uses several levels of analysis: (1) historical origin (the Revolution); (2) identification of the synecdochical theatrical character, the *payo;* (3) identification of the main rhetorical device used by the *payo,* the pun; (4) the literary origin in classical literature of this character; (5) identification of the Revolution with *zapatismo,* implying that this movement within the Revolution was defeated; (6) the intertextuality of the *revista* genre with American slapstick movies; (7) explanation of how this form of humor works on the public; (8) identification of Soto's belly as synechdochical of the new political situation; (9) reference to the centralist government where the capital and the country converge; and (10) Morones as paradigm of the new politician, the congressman with a pistol. These levels of analysis serve to demonstrate the degree of sophistication of Novo's way of writing *Nueva grandeza.* His synechdochical method of writing has to be noticed, because it is very risky — you can only choose one part to represent the whole, and if your example is flawed the entire system will collapse. But at the same time it gives the text an exhilarating rhythm, like the news on the radio or in newspapers. Walter Winchell could again be compared to Novo: "From his years in vaudeville he had learned a breezy patois and a brisk rhythm that allowed him to whittle a wisecrack to its essentials" (Gabler 1994: 36).

Many times the only purpose of this kind of language was to parody and deconstruct the oratory of the politicians. Novo says:

> There dawned a confused and oratorical period when the word reigned, promising everything but committing itself to nothing, which the intelligent newspapers labeled demagogic. The sensitive antenna that registered this new vibration and hit on the style of humor into which the new generation discharged its frustrations was called Cantinflas, another timely ripened growth of the city. If the verbal and logical chaos that our age projects through the lips of Cantinflas has achieved fame and recognition outside the city, and indeed almost everywhere thanks to the movies, it is because outside of Mexico, too, men stifle in a climate of verbal flux, mental confusion, promises that commit one to nothing, rhetoric, and unintelligible, vain juggling with words. Have we not had ringing speeches from Hitler, Churchill, Molotov, Eden, Goebbels, Roosevelt, Stalin, De Gaulle, Franco, Perón, Lombardo Toledano? (1992/1967: 47) [14]

Novo uses litotes again when he says that the newspapers labeled the epoch "demagogic," a paronomasia on the medical terminology of problems in speech to imitate Cantinflas's talk, and two enumerations — one in the semantic field of words, and the second an interesting gathering of politicians: dictators and elected officials in democratic regimes. The only Mexican is Lombardo Toledano, the secretary of labor during the Cárdenas presidency. A key word underlines this way of writing: the English word "high-ball," to create the sensation that the only true modernity can come from the United States and that the Mexican elite is dominated by other elites. Again, the text is a demythification of the Revolution.

These are just representative examples of what can be found throughout the book. Let us move to the final pages, where there is a summary of what modern Mexico is:

> From Chapultepec Heights, the city seemed to float in a light halo that threw its skyline into relief. It spilled over the valley, stretched between the centuries, alive and eternal. Like a huge, jealous mother, it watched for its tired children to come home. Under its roofs, in the cry of the new-born baby, in the young lover's kiss, in the man's dreams, in the mother's womb, in the tradesman's ambition, in the gratitude of the exile, in luxury and squalor, and in the pretentiousness of the banker and the worker's muscles, in the stones shaped by the Aztec and the churches built by the *conquistadores,* in the naïve palaces built in the times of Díaz, in the schools, the hospitals, the parks laid out by the Revolution, the Grandeur of Mexico now slept, drew into the future, stored up its strength — survived. (1992/1967: 131) [15]

The panorama of the city has to come from above, where the real power of the country is, where the residence of the president and the mansions of the Mexican "aristocracy" are. The city is a giant womb, a maternal woman taking care of her sons and daughters. The city is the fruit of all civilizations: Aztecs, Spaniards, Creoles, and the mestizos of the Revolution. All social classes are represented in this city, even the exiles, mainly from Spain. All times form part of the city: its past, the present, and the projection of the city toward its future. And, of course, following Góngora's advice, they are making love.

2 ⫘ *Gay and Baroque Literatures*

El joven *(The Young Man, 1925)*

Salvador Novo's *El joven* is usually explained as a new novel based on the figure of young men popularized by gay writers like Marcel Proust and André Gide. Besides this influence, the figure of the wandering young man already existed in classical literature, especially in the baroque period. In 1952 Antonio Vilanova published his seminal article "El peregrino de amor en las *Soledades* de Góngora" (The Love Pilgrim in Góngora's *Solitudes*). Vilanova starts by quoting Juan de Jáuregui, who wrote *Antídoto contra las "Soledades"* (Antidote against the *Solitudes*):

> You have a young man, the main character you present, and you do not give him a name. He went to the sea and came from the sea, without knowing how, or why; he is just an onlooker. He does not say either a good or a bad thing, does not open his mouth. He only does a very selfish discourtesy and an absurdity: he forgets his absent lady, the one that cost him so many quarrels when leaving the sea; and he falls in love with the farmer's daughter, the one that got married in her father's house, where he had been courteously lodged. And this does not serve any purpose for the plot of the story but to spoil it and to finish it without any art or contentment. (1952: 421) [1]

Jáuregui's satiric tone does not prevent him from doing an accurate analysis of the main character of the *Soledades:* an unknown, purposeless, erratic young man. The first to defend Góngora after Jáuregui's attack was D. Francisco de Córdoba, the abbot of Rute, who wrote *Examen del Antídoto* (Examination of the Antidote). He tried to provide organicity to the plot of the poem, but he did not succeed. In his attempt to explain the structure of the *Solitudes* he brought to the readers' attention the great epic poems of antiquity like Homer's *Odyssey* and Virgil's *Aeneid*; but he does not dare to label the *Soledades* an epic. This is Córdoba's "defense":

> But to follow this attempt, it is obligatory to notice first to which genre this Poem of the *Solitudes* belongs. The result will be to know if the Poem is capable of greatness, it will be known if it has it, and if there is a reason for the Poem to be great. Leaving aside several opinions, it is taken for granted that it is not dramatic; neither can it be Epic; neither the story nor the action is of a hero, or famous person, nor is the versification proper. Still less is it romance, even if it has mixed elements, because the versification does not help; besides there are not Princes as subjects of the Poem, nor Courts, wars, adventures, as in Ariosto, Tasso the Elder, and Alamani. It is not Bucolic although it has Shepherds, not Halieutic, even with fishermen, nor Cinegetic, even with hunters. Because none of these is an adequate subject to be treated, either alone or with the other subjects. But because it introduces all those referred to, it has to be said that it is a Poem. The Poem admits and accepts them all, whichever they are. It is without any doubt Melic or Lyric, called so because they are chants, this is Melos, to the sound of the lyre. (quoted by Vilanova 1952: 425)[2]

The abbot explores all the genre possibilities and cannot find one that fits the poem, the only exception being the obvious fact that the poem is a poem, a lyrical poem, and what gives unity to it is the figure of the young pilgrim:

> [Jáuregui] would only be able to complain about this Poem being longer than the lyric poems left by the ancients and about not having one action but many. Regarding the length, you know that it does not matter because it does not change the genre. Regarding the plot or story, it can be sustained because it is the journey of a young shipwreck victim, but we like them to be many and diverse: because without any doubt pleasure comes from diversity instead of from unity. (1952: 426)[3]

What gives unity to the poem is the *mancebo*, the young man. Córdoba thinks that the protagonist is like the hero of the Byzantine novel; but to follow this pattern we need to think in terms of four solitudes: having a story with a closed end, reuniting the two lovers, naming them, and giving full account of their lineages. We do not have four solitudes, however. The trip of the young man is not an adventure in the sense that it lacks meaning; he is not pursuing a goal and is not overcoming difficulties. Vilanova tries to associate the young man with the literary figure of the pilgrim of love and provides a good number of these in the literary tradition. The problem is that these pilgrims do not help to explain the figure of the *mancebo*, and they are not related to the characteristics of this pilgrim. Góngora's *mancebo* is not worried about his fate as a lover. He is not trying at the present moment to regain his beloved. The Christian tradition of the pilgrim does not help either, because there is no religious connotation in Góngora's poem. Vilanova cannot convince the reader that Góngora's *peregrino* is following the Petrarchan tradition.

Another important attempt to analyze the impact of *Soledades* is Nadine Ly's "Las *Soledades:* . . . 'Esta poesía inútil' . . ." (The *Solitudes:* . . . "This Useless Poetry" . . . , 1985). She quotes Francisco Cascales, who wrote in 1634:

> And I demonstrate this poetry to be useless. It is not good for heroic poetry, nor lyric, nor tragic, nor comic . . . A good job would be *Ulysses* or the *Aeneid* written in that enigmatic language! . . . Oh diabolic poem! So, what has our poet pretended? I will tell you; to destroy poetry . . . How? Returning everything to its original chaos; making neither comprehensible thoughts nor words that can be known in the confusion and disorder. (1985: 10)[4]

To Cascales, don Luís is destroying poetry. It is interesting to notice that critics of the baroque period were aware that they were dealing with a new genre. Ly calls the new genre, based on the *silva* as a poetic form, the *soledad-texto* (textual solitude; 1985: 19). She also notes the continuity of the genre during the twentieth century, explaining how Spanish writers like Antonio Machado, Federico García Lorca, Jorge Guillén, and Rafael Alberti, among others, wrote *soledades*. This is key to understanding the impact and influence of the *Soledades* on the *modernista* and avant-garde writers of Spain and Hispanic America. Ly's conclusion is that "this poem, which does not fit in any preexisting mold, is, from my point of view, the first 'modern' poem, that is to say the first poem whose only possible definition is to be a poem" (1985: 19). As we already saw, this was also Francisco de Córdoba's conclusion, once he noticed that he could not use any genre to explain the poem.

The ambiguity of genre was extremely difficult in a period when literate people were used to thinking and reading in terms of genres, which is also the norm today. This is why *Soledades* is so important in the configuration and redefinition of modern poetry and poetic prose. One of the most interesting answers to the question about the functioning of this new modernity is given by Thomas R. Hart (1977): "I suggest, that the pilgrim's presence in the first *Solitude* is essential not only because it makes clear the perspective from which the rural scene is to be viewed but also because the pilgrim's limited perception enables us to judge the limitations of the courtly view of experience" (218–219). The point of view of the wayfarer is limited, and its limitation is deconstructed by the reading of the poem. First, the poetic voice is not omniscient; second, it is enclosed in limited ideological borders, like any modern man in his relationship with any of the ambits he inhabits.

What I want to make clear is that this young, gayish man was a literary tradition known to the avant-garde writers of the Hispanic tradition. To these writers—Luis Cernuda, García Lorca and Novo—among others, this young man was gay, in the modern sense of the term.

In this section I relate the neo-baroque and homosexuality. The point of departure is an article by Paul Julian Smith, "Barthes, Góngora, and Non-Sense," which is helpful to link these cultural paradigms. Smith writes (citing Barthes):

> Pleasure, difficulty, intertextuality, discontinuity—these are general areas that Barthes and Góngora seem to have in common. There is one point, however, at which Barthes refers explicitly to Góngora in his own writing. It is a fragment in *Roland Barthes par Roland Barthes* entitled "Actif/passif": "Virile/nonvirile: this famous couple, which reigns over all the Doxa, comprehends all kinds of the play of alternation: the paradigmatic play of meaning and the sexual play of the parade (all well-formed meaning is a parade; coupling together and putting to death)" (136). (Smith 1986: 82; his translation)

> There remains, nevertheless, the possibility of escape, both sexual and textual: "However, once the alternative is refused (once the paradigm is scrambled), utopia begins: meaning and sex become the object of free play, in the midst of which polysemic forms and (sensual) practices, freed from the binary prison, will reach a state of infinite expansion. In this way there can be born a Gongorine text and a happy sexuality" (137). (Smith 1986: 83; his translation)

"The transgression that will transcend transgression itself and free the subject from the binary prison is thus given a name: happiness, or Góngora." (Smith 1986: 83; his translation)

"Pleasure, difficulty, intertextuality, discontinuity": the first key word is "pleasure." It means to put into practice the *carpe diem* ideology. Pleasure is also the possibility of writing poetry of the body without the constraints of romantic love. It is aristocratic pleasure too — Góngora and Novo, as members of a privileged and conservative caste, vindicate for themselves the privilege of pleasure. They take poetry (pleasure) from the domain of the people, the popular, and bring it back to the aristocracy of the blood and the intellect. The poststructuralist and more physical Barthes understood Góngora, the gay Góngora, who could destroy the rigidity of sexes and introduce the reader to an orgy of words and bodies, outrageous and daring synecdoches of the body, especially the male body, the untold body of courtly love. Góngora destroys the paradigms of literary genres, to be able to create a character who could desire and be the object of desire at random, free of the literary and moral restrictions of his time and any other time in history. The pilgrim had to represent what could not be represented; the pilgrim had to say what could not be uttered. It is homosexuality (*sic*), of course, but it is also the beginning of a new social class and a new age group, the idle teenager, the new Peter Pan (always performed, not by chance, by a woman). Difficulty and intertextuality are the moral justifications of this unending right to pleasure; these authors represent the true aristocracy, that of the intellect. That is why they can desire other men, make love to them, be penetrated by them. This is the influence of Gide, although at the very last moment the triumph belongs to Proust and Joyce.

Salvador Novo, in the satire "La Diegada" (quatrain 26), paraphrases the beginning of *Soledades:*

Del año en la fértil *saison* esplendente
— mentido de Europa raptor, como dice
don Luis el de Argote —, la luna en la frente
se afirma en los patrios terrenos que pise.   (1978: 15)

[At the splendid and fertile season of the year / — the feigned bull that stole Europa's love — as said / by don Luis de Argote, the moon in his forehead / and his feet firm in the fatherland he treads.]

This is a direct reference to Góngora. The beginning of *Las Soledades* is as follows:

Era del año la estación florida
en que el mentido robador de Europa
— media luna las armas de su frente,
y el sol todos los rayos de su pelo —,
luciente honor del cielo,
en campos de zafiro pace estrellas.   (1993: 75)

[It was the florid season of the year / when Europa's feigned raptor /
(the half moon the arms of his brow, / and all the sun's rays his hair), /
lucid honor of the heavens / grazing upon stars in the sapphire fields.]

As Smith says, "when tossed naked by the waves onto the island in
the opening lines, [the pilgrim] is defined with reference to the most
common of homosexual myths, that of Ganymede: 'el que ministrar
podía la copa / a Júpiter mejor que el garzón de Ida,' 'fitter cup bearer
than Ganymede / For Jupiter' " (1986: 86). In this stanza Góngora
writes one of the best scenes of (homo)erotic desire in the history of
Spanish literature:

Desnudo el joven, cuanto ya el vestido
    Océano ha bebido,
restituir le hace a las arenas;
    y al sol lo extiende luego,
    que lamiéndolo apenas
su dulce lengua de templado fuego,
lento lo embiste, y con süave estilo
la menor onda chupa al menor hilo.   (1993: 77)

[The youth then stripped, and all that they had quaffed / Of Neptune's
humid draught / Back from his garments to the sand he wrung, / Then
spread them out to meet / The sun, whose gentle tongue / Licked them
with gradual and temperate heat / And mild insistence, till his kindly
aid / Sucked the least moisture from the tiniest thread; 1968: 9]

In a footnote Beverley writes: "El sol 'lame' (seca) su ropa porque
es Júpiter-Taurus, el toro celestial" (1993: 77). The Sun as Jupiter,
Taurus the bull, licks the clothes/body of the naked young man, who is
more handsome than Ganymede and more gay than Ganymede?
Ganymede had been at the center of the representation of homoerotic
desire since Ovid. Benvenuto Cellini and Michelangelo Buonarroti
among others continued this tradition, epitomized by the baroque
painter Caravaggio (who portrayed the most daring male Lolita of
Western culture).

What is more—if the tmesis is done, and Beverley's advice is followed, the results are impressive. "Góngora rarely misses in his poetry the opportunity to suggest an erotic allegory" (Beverley 1980: 46). Beverley is very polite; he could have said that the reader always has to make the reading of any given text by Góngora obscene (this tradition from baroque wit has continued in the popular *albur*). Very close to the naked young man we find a reference to the *ano*, the young man's anus (the paronomasia in *Océano*). Let us not forget in this context two of Quevedo's favorite insults: *italïano* and *sicilïano*, the dieresis being the mark and the stigma of the homosexual.

It does not matter if Jupiter is really licking the clothes of the young man, because the desire is obvious; and the *lo* of "lo embiste" can be either the *vestido* or the young man. If Jupiter is really licking the young man's clothes, there is no doubt about their fetishistic nature: "dulce lengua de templado fuego," "lento lo embiste," and "süave estilo" make of this stanza a beautiful erotic enjoyment, and the play of nasal and fricative sounds of the alliteration illustrates the sensuality of the caress. But the key here is Ganymede (see Barkan 1991), because he represents the homoerotic mark.

It is in this context that the words of Barthes and Smith have to be understood. The baroque tradition creates an open space of canonical literature that escapes the rigid moral and aesthetic norms of previous literary movements where the individual had not yet been defined in modern terms. The baroque could become and became a space where freedom of creation and sexual freedom could be explored, because a new language, new combinations of words, and new words from the classical tradition were put together for the first time. This is why the avant-garde movement put the baroque at the forefront of the new possibilities to write the literature of the twentieth century. A clear example is *Poeta en Nueva York* by Federico García Lorca, where, among other existential problems, Lorca used neo-baroque techniques to explore his homosexuality and his position as a gay man in society.

The key text to understand the importance of connecting the baroque and avant-garde is García Lorca's lecture "La imagen poética de don Luis de Góngora" (The Poetic Image of don Luis de Góngora, 1987 [1927]), where Lorca says: "Hoy su obra está palpitante como si estuviera recién hecha" (Today his work is alive, as if just made; 223). And, of course, he comments on the stanza of the young palpitating man naked on the beach:

How wise is the touch to bring into harmony the Ocean, that golden dragon at which the Sun is probing with his warm tongue, and the wet clothes of the young man, where the blind head of the Sun "sucked the least moisture from the tiniest thread"! There are more shadings in these eight lines than in fifty stanzas of the *Gerusalemme Liberata* by Tasso. Because all the details are studied and felt as with a precious jewel. There is nothing that gives the sensation of the Sun falling, weightless, like the lines: "hardly licking it/him . . . probing it/him slowly . . ." Since Góngora ties the imagination, he can stop it at will, and he is dragged neither by the dark, natural forces of inertia nor by the fleeting mirages where unwary poets are killed like butterflies in a lamp. There are moments in the *Soledades* that turn out to be unbelievable.[5]

It is not always easy to understand what García Lorca means, but there are enough clues here to make sense of some of the double entendres of Lorca's closeted text. It seems that he warns the writer of homosexual literature not to be explicit but to depend on the aesthetics of the "shading" (*matiz*) to express homosexual desire. *Mariposa* is a coded term for homosexual. Angel Sahuquillo has studied different butterflies in the poems and plays of Lorca (see 1986: 215–217); although Sahuquillo does not mention this one, Lorca's warning to those gay poets who do not follow the model of Góngora is obvious: they will die if they go very close to the light. The reader interested in the internalized homophobia of Lorca can read Jaime Manrique's study (1999). Lorca was killed because he was gay and because of his political and artistic ideas—and this was the interpretation given by his murderers when they shot him in the anus. But the best part is Lorca's reading of Góngora's scene: Jupiter is licking the youth or his clothes with his "ciega cabeza" (blind head), which is the penis; Jupiter, according to Lorca, is sodomizing the young man. "Oscuras fuerzas naturales" (dark, natural forces) and "espejismo" (mirage) as codes for homosexuality have been studied by Sahuquillo in another of Lorca's (con)texts. The corresponding quotation is part of the lecture read by Lorca in Granada to commemorate the tercentenary of Góngora's death. Lorca wrote a closeted text that only those very close to him could understand fully. The gay poets of the avant-garde of Spain and the Americas were ecstatic with this lecture. This became the law of the father: two of the greatest poets in Spanish literature allowed these writers to write gay poetry.

García Lorca (1987 [1927]: 241) also found a second homosexual reference in the *Soledades*:

He proceeds by allusions. We get the side-view of the myths, and sometimes he only provides a feature hidden among other different images. Bacchus endures in mythology three passions and deaths. He is first a ram with twisted horns. Because of the love of his dancer Ciso, who dies and turns to ivy, Bacchus, to be able to continue the dance, becomes a grapevine. At the end, he dies to become a fig tree. Therefore, Bacchus is born three times. Góngora mentions these transformations in a *Soledad* in a delicate and deep manner, but only comprehensible to those who know the secret of the story:

Six poplar trees, embraced by ivy, stand
Like thyrsi of the twice-born Grecian god,
Who twines his brow with vine-leaves, that the wreath
    May hide the horns beneath.   (GÓNGORA 1993/1968: 99)

The Bacchus of the bacchanalia, close to his lover, stylized in embracing ivy, *denies*, crowned with vine-leaves, his old lewd horns.[6]

But, again, this is only comprehensible for those who are in on the secret of the story; those who are not are intended to miss the homoerotic interpretation. The literary critics who were in on the secret and were friends of the writer were supposed to abide by a code of honor and not mention homosexual references or cover them with a heterosexual patina (e.g., make references "a la amante," the female lover, even if there are no marks of gender in the text).

Lluís Fernández (1990: 6) says that in the realm of pop culture, gay subculture is baroque because it generates instability and social distortion thanks to a decentered aesthetic and sexual practice. This statement rings some bells in the Latin American realm. Severo Sarduy (1972), based on Lezama Lima, understands the (neo-)baroque as a cultural and textual phenomenon, opposed to Alejo Carpentier's ideal of a text analog to nature. Sarduy's baroque is that of a text whose context (the referent) is made of other texts (Méndez Ródenas 1983: 24). It is not that we cannot reach nature; even nature is so mediated by texts that it is impossible to have access to it without going through an unending maze of texts. This is also to say that the romantic ideal of nature read as a nationalistic epitome is false. Sarduy is so comfortable in this world of words that he prefers metaphor over metonymy. Metonymy has a remnant of reality not needed in the metaphor, where the literary creation can overshadow reality.

Now that the literary origin of the wanderer is established (this sort of clueless young man), I am going to comment briefly on Rosa María

Acero's fine analysis (1998) of *El joven.* She begins by stating that it is very difficult to put this text into a specific literary genre (141). Following Novo, who called *El joven* a novel, she prefers the label "brief novel" (*novela breve*). Acero quotes Villaurrutia, who says he considered this text a total novelty not found in contemporary authors like Edouard Dujardin or James Joyce. According to Acero, *El joven* is a novel about the city and the homosexuality of the protagonist. She goes into detail about the content of the book then offers an analysis of the homosexual aspects of the text:

> In *El joven* the author deals with homosexuality in three different ways: first, naming the places in Mexico City where homosexuals meet on a regular basis; second, quoting texts and authors who are related to the homosexual topic; and third, when the protagonist talks about the discovery of his own sexual orientation. (1998: 166)[7]

What has to be added to Acero's analysis is an explanation of the genuine novelty of *El joven.* This text breaks with the nineteenth-century idea that modern life represented a coherent whole, especially within the context of the invention of the Mexican nation by romanticism. The new Mexico, according to Novo, is not based on the cult of ethnic values, the fatherland, and the epic battles of the Revolution but on breaking some of the taboos of the cultural tradition:

1. Recuperate the tradition of disruption, denying the a posteriori spontaneity of an uninterrupted cultural tradition that goes from the Mexica to the Revolution, via the romantic liberals of the Reforma.
2. Convey the new vocabulary. If romanticism brought *ceibas, palmeras, papagayos, huacos, caimanes, maíz, hamaca, zamba* (Blanco 1983: 28), in *El joven* Novo introduces *camión, shampoo, teléfono, dentista, cine, drogas, checar, automóvil, semáforo, machetear, copyright, Sanborn's, discos.*
3. Recuperate the homoerotic subtext of the *Soledades* to mark a change in the cultural, social, and literary paradigms. The new changes are not social but individual, and the right to live new forms of sexuality is at the heart of the attempt by Novo to define the postrevolutionary society. The virulent attacks against the Contemporáneos defending the need for a patriarchal nation explain how right Novo's choice was. The conservative forces (both from the right and from the left) felt the state could be threatened by a collection of texts with homoerotic subtexts, which shows how weak was the official definition of the state-nation given by the Revolution. The new state had to be patriarchal and heterosexual. But this time there was going to be resistance. As many

Mexican intellectuals have explained (José Joaquín Blanco, Héctor Aguilar Camín, Carlos Monsiváis, Octavio Paz . . .) Mexico was the invention of different elites, creoles, liberals, and so forth. But the twentieth century was going to be different: little by little and in an unending transition to a more democratic state and nation, Mexicans started to define their own nation(s) in their own terms. Again, this is an extremely slow process and far from being finished.

Salvador Novo and Federico García Lorca

Novo was working at the Ministry of Public Education in 1933 and was sent to Buenos Aires to represent Mexico. There he met Federico García Lorca, and the encounter had a very deep impact on Novo for the rest of his life. It also made him write some of his best texts: *Continente vacío, Canto a Teresa, Décimas en el mar, Seamen Rhymes,* "Romance de Adela y Angelillo," *El tercer Fausto, Espejo, Poemas antiguos,* and *Nuevo amor* (Alderson 1994: xxxi–xxxii). It seems that this union brought the best literature out of Salvador Novo, including his finest book, *Nuevo amor.* He told the story of this encounter in *Continente vacío* (Empty Continent).

> Federico García Lorca is right now the idol of Buenos Aires . . . Pedro invites me to this performance [*The Shoemaker's Prodigious Wife*]; maybe it will be possible to introduce me to Federico. He has lectured, has played and sung, he is adored by everybody and the newspapers are full of his pictures. I very much admire him, but I would not like to be just another admirer, and maybe there will be no way to be his friend. (1935: 188) [8]

No one could have accused Novo of being shy or not open about his homosexuality/gay persona. But he was shocked by the display and performance of Lorca in Buenos Aires. Novo realized that a gay man could render different roles: as intellectual, entertainer, and celebrity. This new kind of man could change society's perception of homosexuality. Novo also realized that the correct use of the new mass media could liberate the artist, who could make money and write with freedom. He was struck by Lorca's performances and the lavish display of his pictures. At the core of *Continente vacío* is their first meeting:

> Federico was in bed. I remember his pajamas with black and white stripes . . . Federico imposed his voice, somewhat hoarse, nervous, alive, and to explain things he helped himself with his arms, which he

waved, and with his black eyes that glowed or laughed. After he got up, while he was taking his bath, he would turn every once in a while to say something, because he had taken the conversation with him; I sat on his bed . . . Federico came and went, looking at me surreptitiously, telling anecdotes, and little by little I noticed that he was talking directly to me; that all those illustrious admirers of him were fancying him, and at the same time making me uneasy, and that I should wait for them to leave, and then he and I would have a true embrace. At that moment, he had to attend the rehearsal of *The Shoemaker's Wife*, because that same night was the opening. I would see him there, after the play, if possible to chat, if not, the next day I would go look for him and we would have lunch together, just the two of us. (1935: 198–199) [9]

The only important study about *Continente vacío* is by Mary Kendall Long (1995). In "*Continente vacío:* Un-writing a Continent" (the last chapter of her dissertation, "Salvador Novo, 1920–1940: Between the Avant-Garde and the Nation") she does a very fine job of reading *Continente* as a deconstruction of and challenge to the Iberoamerican movement of José Enrique Rodó, José Vasconcelos, and Pedro Henríquez Ureña.

In this context Novo can sneak in a queer moment of homosexual play, desire, and seduction. Federico is presented in his pajamas and then naked in the bath or maybe half-naked in the room. A fetishistic scenario is shown: the pajamas, the bed, the hoarse voice, and the eyes. In a writer with a perfect command of the language like Novo, the anacoluthon "me senté en la cama" produces the poetic effect of estrangement and brings the attention of the reader to the bed. The next step, after the power of the voice, is the gaze: "de reojo"; and little by little Novo notices that Federico has isolated the two of them among the small crowd in his room. Both know that as soon as they can be left alone they will meet with a true embrace. Novo is a master of introducing gay moments into his mainstream literature, subtle enough not to annoy the heterosexual reader but with enough textual markers to be recognized by more sympathetic readers.

When they meet at last, Novo introduces one of the key poems in the history of gay literature in the twentieth century, "Oda a Walt Whitman": "I had fresh in my memory his 'Ode to Walt Whitman,' virile, brave, beautiful, which in a limited edition had just been published in Mexico by the people of *Alcancía*, and which Federico had not yet seen" (1935: 201).[10] To Luis Cernuda, the *Oda* is at the core of *Poeta en Nueva*

York (Cernuda 1957: 216). This is a key text in understanding the development of gay literature in the Hispanic world in the twentieth century. The Alcancía edition is "limited" (i.e., closeted, available only to those who belonged to the intellectual gay group of Mexico City) and serves as an ideological validation of the gay way of life. According to John K. Walsh,

> the first printing—the only complete publication of the *Ode to Whitman* before Lorca's death—was a special edition of fifty copies, run off by a private press called Alcancía in Mexico City and released on 5 August 1933. The issue was small enough to make it immediately exclusive, but every care was taken in the reproduction. The sponsors of the "Alcancía" issue were a distinguished group of young Mexican intellectuals, led by Edmundo O'Gorman [later a renowned professor of history] and Justino Fernández [the celebrated art historian], both in their late twenties. There is reason to believe they took on the project as a kind of private anthem for a small and elitist liberal circle with strong social sympathies toward homosexuals, or even—though this would veer from Lorca's gesture—as apologia for a discreet or ennobled coterie. In this early context, the *Ode* was clearly a piece taken as justification, one that would not offend; it included for this special original audience an ethic that would elevate or redeem. Here, Lorca would be something of a spokesman—one speaking within the circle, knowing his voice would be understood exactly, and not taken as the troubled, tangled, or ranting voice that has been heard by later readers beyond the circle. (1995: 258–259)

Like André Gide's *Corydon* or *Si le grain ne meurt* (see Pollard 1991: xi), the *Ode* establishes the importance of virility for gay men. According to an important group of writers of modernity: "effeminacy is not the mark of a 'normal' homosexual" (ibid., 28). Lorca's poem vindicates Whitman's virility as a model. It is easy to understand the success of the poem in the intellectual gay circles of Mexico City at a moment when they were suffering several waves of homophobic attacks by different organizations in and outside the government. Whitman in the poem is "hermosura viril" (virile beauty) and "macho" (masculine), and he is denounced by the *maricas* as one of them. The *maricas* represent to Lorca the effeminate homosexuals, who are "turbios de lágrima" (grimy with tears; 121), with "saliva helada" (freezing saliva; 123) and "curvas heridas como panza de sapo" (contours, split open, like the belly of the toad; 123). And most of all:

¡Maricas de todo el mundo, asesinos de palomas!
Esclavos de la mujer. Perras de sus tocadores.
Abiertos en las plazas con fiebre de abanico
o emboscados en yertos paisajes de cicuta.   (GARCÍA LORCA 1994: 223)

[Perverts of the world, dove-killers! / Toadies of women, dressing-room bitches, / brazen in squares in a fever of fans / or ambushed in motionless landscapes of hemlock. (García Lorca 1994/1983: 125)]

Of the many studies about homosexuality in Lorca, like those of Paul Binding and Sahuquillo, Jaime Manrique's is the most challenging. He puts together traditional literary criticism, gossip, and personal experience, and the result is extraordinary: the reader can recreate the deep impact the homosexual (also homophobic) and gay poetry of *Poeta en Nueva York* had upon gay writers and gay people in general. Manrique also tells in detail the impression the gay and black culture of New York had on Lorca. There is a continuum of testimonies, of literatures in different languages that helped develop a gay culture and allowed men of different background, countries, and languages to fight for their individual freedom and right to live their sexuality without the unwanted interference of others.

Novo, of course, continued dealing with homosexuality throughout his life. A more mature, rich, powerful, and conservative Novo at age forty-seven tackled the issue again in *La vida en México en el período presidencial de Miguel Alemán*. The entry corresponding to March 10, 1951, is key to understanding the evolution of Novo's position on homosexuality (1967: 585–589): "I started reading Gide in 1920, and since then I have read all his books. Gide was very fashionable among the youth of that time, which is why we were scorned and criticized" (586).[11] Novo does not explain who the "we" behind the "nos" in Spanish were, but the importance of the testimony is transcendent because it tells about the literary history of the moment. Novo also tells how Jaime Torres Bodet translated some essays by Gide: *Los límites del arte y algunas reflexiones de moral y literatura* (The Limits of Art and Some Reflections on Moral and Literature, 1920), indirectly bringing Torres Bodet out of the closet (Paz 1994). The same thing happened with Xavier Villaurrutia when Novo told the anecdote about Villaurrutia giving him a raincoat in exchange for his issue of *Si le grain ne meurt*. Of course, this was Novo's second copy of the 1924 first edition. He explains:

In a certain way, *Si le grain ne meurt* caused more scandal than *Corydon*. This was a treatise in the form of a dialogue, one more exposition of already known even though abstract sexual conclusions. While in *Si le grain* Gide confessed to practicing what he was preaching, he said when and how it started, and he described and remembered in gruesome detail his first and satisfactory Bedouin suffocation in the hot sand of the desert. (587) [12]

Novo adds humor to his description of the event, juxtaposing a comic summary to what is a highly poetic and serious depiction in the original. Then he explains why the scandal was very trivial when compared to what happened to Oscar Wilde twenty-five years before:

> But in that quarter of a century, two circumstances of the intelligentsia, besides those of society, had helped to adequately dispel hypocrisy: one in science, the other in literature: Freud and Proust . . .
> The topic of "l'amour qui n'ose pas dire son nom" had been rarely, if at all, touched by the novelists of the 19th century. (587–589) [13]

Novo now traces the history of the subject of homosexuality in French literature, beginning with Honoré de Balzac's *Vautrin*, which is dominated by euphemisms. Novo details the importance of Proust and his character Charlus and how Proust gave way to other novels: Francis Carco's *Jesus-Caille*, Henri Deberly's *Un homme et un autre*, Maurice Duplessis's *Adonis Bar*, Abel Hermant's *El proceso de Lord Chelsea*, and translations into Spanish like *La muerte en Venecia* by Thomas Mann. Novo then turns to science and the Kinsey report, translated into Spanish as *La conducta sexual del varón:*

> [*The Kinsey Report*] imparts unadorned scientific authority (depriving it of any artistic singularity or its esoteric character) to the simple zoological fact of what is artificial and therefore weak, debatable, and invalid, all conventional pigeonholes attributed to orgasm. This is what all men try to get and look for, and it is found in any of the forms, occasions, and modalities that are mediated by the opportunity of the moment.
> Of course, say good-bye to all reverence for the sacred and fictitious roles of paternity and maternity, which are the unforeseen side effects of a simple orgasm. But also, farewell to the taboo against its search and procurement in forbidden forms or territories, not by nature but by decency [*buenas costumbres*]. Neither one hundred percent chemically pure A nor one hundred percent chemically impure B is a given among men. Some more, others less, some once, some before, and others later, others still, appear tabulated in the *Kinsey Report*, included by

choice in some of the percentages of the different columns, neither 100 percent black nor 100 percent white.

Gide's life had the fortune to reach an age in which science and its influence over morality would erase the scandal which, moreover, he never incurred. Fortune thus favors the purity of light, once the stupid taboo is eliminated which in another age might have exterminated him, that enables the admiration of his work. (588–589) [14]

As early as 1951, Novo defended in a mainstream publication the scientific character of bisexuality and the naturalness of the so-called paternal and maternal instincts. This is an important qualitative and quantitative step; Sigmund Freud and Proust had opened the possibility of creating a homosexual space in society, but the new scientific discoveries coming from the United States gave the green light to begin vindicating the possibility of demanding a status of normalcy for homosexual behavior. It is interesting to note that Novo follows two of the truisms about modern sexuality: that it is conditioned by medical discourse, as would be theorized by Michel Foucault among others, and the reality of sexuality being defined by the mass media. As a relevant member of the media he is trying to educate his public and convince them to accept the new social reality.

Novo and Lorca

Previously in this chapter we left Novo and Lorca in the same room. After the homoerotic moment that Novo creates in *Continente vacío* to recount their first meeting, he continues with the story of the encounter. He begins by summarizing the conversation and imitates the Andalusian accent of Lorca at a trivial and anecdotal level, then suddenly, in a very (melo)dramatic fashion, changes to the present and develops a nostalgic passage. Novo tells about a letter that Federico never answered because he was always in a hurry; he evokes that evening of intimacy, the fire of the conversation, and the admiration of the "little Mexican Indian" for the great poet. There are several key words, including *carta* (letter): now the addressee is not the reader but García Lorca himself. The public is invited to enter the intimacy of the two new friends; *intimidad* and *fuego de la conversación* are words with enough strength to open gaps in the imagination of readers and enable us to imagine the love scene. But the most important word of Novo's recreation is to refer to himself as an "Indian" using the diminutive form: *indiecito*, the humblest possible form. In *Poemas proletarios* (Proletariat Poems, also of 1934; in Novo 1955), he has a realistic portrait of the "Indian" and denounces the acculturation problem, the illiteracy, and the demagoguery of the revolutionary government (lines 153–197). Other poems in *Espejo* (Mirror, 1933) address the problem of ethnicity, especially "La historia" (History) and "La escuela" (School), in which Novo problematizes his own position as a Creole or at best a mestizo, as opposed to the otherness of the Indian, and his new position of self-confrontation after the Revolution. These are poems about Novo's childhood, about events that happened during those turbulent times.

Novo was conscious of the real position of the Indian in contemporary Mexican history. This is not a romantic posture: my first reaction was to establish a parallel between a medieval ballad where the daughter of the emperor tells a count, "I am a 'morica,'" and now that I am in an inferior position, you can rape me, I am the other, la *chingada* [the one who gets fucked]." Because Novo could not tell the love story in an open manner, he devised the following textual strategy: to write a ballad à la García Lorca, imitating (parodying) the style of the Andalusian ballads that made Lorca the most popular poet of his age. The love poem is heterosexual; Angelillo, a bullfighter from Málaga who represents García Lorca, and the Mexican Adela (see Herrera-Sobek 1990: 104–108). The poem is dedicated to "Federico García Lorca": Novo wants to make it clear that the poem is related to the Spaniard. Carlos Monsiváis, in his article about the influence of Lorca in Mexican literature, notes that this poem is one of the few exceptions of quality to what became an unending number of literary texts full of pseudo-Andalusian imagery (1986: 250–251). Novo's poem is very sober, precisely to avoid the *españolada*. It says that Adela was leaving a love in Mexico and that Angelillo was a 22-year-old bullfighter from Málaga; because the Virgin Mary wanted it, they met in Buenos Aires:

> Porque la Virgen dispuso
> que se juntaran sus penas
> para que de nuevo el mundo
> entre sus bocas naciera,
> palabra de malagueño
> — canción de mujer morena —,
> torso grácil, muslos blancos
> — boca de sangre sedienta.
>
> PORQUE la Virgen dispuso
> que sus soledades fueran

como dos trémulos ríos
perdidos entre la selva
sobre las rutas del mundo
para juntarse en la arena,
cielo de México oscuro,
tierra de Málaga en fiesta.
¡Ya nunca podrá Angelillo
salir del alma de Adela!

[Because the Virgin wanted / to put their sorrows together / to make
the world / be born again in their mouths, / the vow of a malagueño /
and the song of a dark woman, / graceful torso, white thighs / mouth
thirsty for blood. // BECAUSE the Virgin wanted / their solitudes to
be / like two trembling rivers / lost in the rainforest / among the paths
of the world / to join in the sand, / the dark sky of Mexico, / land of
Málaga in fiesta. / Angelillo will never be able / to leave Adela's soul!]

Angelillo's body is displayed in the poem: his torso, his thigh, his
mouth, and the desire he provokes in Adela. The last two lines are very
romantic, which is not characteristic of Novo's poetry; he usually uses
the last lines to destroy the ontology of the poem. The main difference between avant-garde poetry and its romantic predecessor is that in romantic literature there is no separation between literature and life. Avant-
garde literature introduced irony into romantic poetry and separated life
from literature. The absence of irony in this poem allows for a romantic
reading, where Novo can fantasize the idea of a life together with Lorca.

Lorca's answer was to draw pictures for a limited edition of *Seamen
Rhymes*. Drawings 21, 22, and 23 in the *Obras completas* (1947–1949)
represent three sailors, are dated Buenos Aires, 1934, and were
(re)published in a 1953 edition of *Títeres de cachiporra* (The Slapstick
Puppets). Drawing 22 is the most important because the title is "Amor
novo"; I think the right title should be "NOVO AMOR" because these
are the two words in the picture, in capital letters, forming a pun on
Novo's most important book, *Nuevo amor*. The drawing is on page 7 of
Seamen Rhymes. Rosa Acero interprets one of the drawings in the picture
as a phallus with two arrows pointing at what could be a seed (Acero
1998: 76). When Novo saw *La casa de Bernarda Alba* (The House of
Bernarda Alba) in Mexico, he had the fantasy that Adela had been
named in his honor—which was not true because a real Adela existed—
but one of the symbols of free love in the drama is Maximiliano. Perhaps
Lorca had Novo in mind when he chose this name.

It is obvious that both Lorca and Novo helped to create a space for freedom and struggled with the rigid norms of conservative societies. García Lorca paid with his life, and Novo with different ostracisms throughout his life. But in the end they imposed their choice thanks to the quality and the strength of their texts.

After I had already written this part of the book, a new article by James Valender (1996) filled in some of the gaps in the relationship between Lorca and Novo, using three letters Novo had sent to Lorca. Novo wrote the first one, dated December 11, 1933, from Montevideo, asking Lorca for the drawings he later used in his private edition of *Seamen Rhymes*. He requested that Federico draw a sailor or a nautical penis (*verga*). The letter shows a high degree of intimacy, and there are references to a fantastic day of love between them. The second letter, dated December 25, 1933, reveals a Novo deeply in love. He tells Lorca that he wrote the "Ballad of Angelillo and Adela" in his honor and reminds the Spaniard of his promise to visit Mexico. Novo also says that he is sending his *Seamen Rhymes* to Gerardo Diego, Manuel Altolaguirre, Luis Cernuda, Rafael Alberti, and Pedro Salinas. The third letter, dated January 3, 1935, is more important. Novo had suffered political persecution during the Cárdenas administration and had intended to leave the country. In fact, he stayed in exile in the United States for several months. In the letter Novo asks Federico for help and for advice on how to earn a living in Spain. He says he could take five thousand pesetas with him. Valender reminds us that Novo at that time was living with his secretary, Rafael Rodríguez Rapún. It is clear that Novo's one-night stand with Lorca marked him forever; he fell in love and treasured the memory of Lorca for the rest of his life.

Seamen Rhymes *(1934)*

Seamen Rhymes is a closeted text printed in Buenos Aires by A. Colombo, a private edition of one hundred copies (ten in Whatman paper, fifteen in parchment paper, fifty in antique, and twenty-five in pergament) to be given to friends of the author. The cover of the book has a picture by García Lorca: what looks like a sailor with blank eyes, with two other faces superimposed; one face only contains the mouth, and the second is like the drawing of a child with the tongue sticking out. The sailor's hat has two ribbons, with two inscriptions: "amor" and "love" (in English in the original). The second page has another sailor, this time with eyes, with both hands emerging from his mouth; the left hand is on his head and looks like the roots of a plant. Tears or drops fall on him. The most sophisticated drawing is on page 7, just before the beginning of the text. It represents the torso of a sailor emerging from a platform. His eyes are closed, with feminine eyelashes. His hands are disproportionately big. The platform has the inscription "NOVO AMOR." The picture is signed "Federico García Lorca." It includes two more objects, a hanging last-quarter moon with one eye and a glass close to the right hand of the sailor. The last drawing represents the bust of a dead sailor with roots instead of throat and lungs. Four arrows come from the body of the figure.

These sailors, especially the main one, link *Seamen Rhymes* and *Poeta en Nueva York,* which contains at the front of the book the picture of a sailor very similar to the ones found in Novo's book. With these drawings these texts are part of the tradition of homosexual/gay seamen that has been part of Western culture for centuries.

Novo's poem has two parts. The first is in Spanish and describes the sea with a technique similar to that of *poesía pura;* the second is the sailor telling his story to a passenger, who is presumably the poetic voice of the first part of the poem. What is interesting, and was highly criticized, is that the second part is entirely in English. With this estrangement Novo achieves two important goals. The first one is to underline again the change in the cultural paradigm, from France as beacon of Western civilization to the United States, with all its consequences. This explains Novo's work in mass media: publicity, radio, cinema, the syndicated press, and television. The second one is to declare English a postcolonial language. English and Spanish are languages rich enough to allow different nations and cultures to use them as their own. There is no longer a cultural center in those languages — Buenos Aires and Mexico City are as culturally challenging as Madrid or Barcelona. Moreover, the Spanish literature of Spain of the twentieth century could be transformed by two American writers like Darío and José Martí via Góngora, completing a circle, which is from now on a spiral (not by chance symbol of the baroque). Novo wrote his best Mexican literature thanks to the help of the Argentinean Lorca, heavily influenced by a Cuban and a Nicaraguan, who had read well a libertine Andalusian priest of the seventeenth century.

Neo-Baroque Villaurrutia

Nostalgia de la muerte (Nostalgia for Death, 1938; in Villaurrutia 1991) is Villaurrutia's most famous collection of poems. One of the best in the collection is "Nocturno amor" (Nocturne Love), a very original poem because it develops a new corpus of images in Spanish (the armpit, ear, and artery as synecdoches of the body and the mouth as metonymy of sex) to tell a story of passion and absence between lovers. "Nocturno de los ángeles" (Nocturne of the Angels) is a poem about the sailor's gay world in Los Angeles. Other important poems are "Nocturno Mar" (Nocturne Sea), "Nocturno de la alcoba" (Nocturne of the Bedroom), and some of his epigrams. In prose a key text is *Variedad* (ca. 1930; in Villaurrutia 1991), where Villaurrutia used Gide as the model to verbalize homosexuality.

According to my own reading, there are fourteen neo-baroque poems in Villaurrutia (I understand other readers will come up with a different list). My list includes "Ya mi súplica es llanto" and "El viaje sin retorno" from *Primeros poemas;* "Poesía" from *Reflejos;* and "Nocturno en que nada se oye," "Nocturno amor," "Nocturno eterno," "Nocturno muerto," "Nocturno de los ángeles," "Cuando la tarde . . . ," "Estancias nocturnas," "Décima muerte," "Décimas de nuestro amor," "Deseo," and "Soneto del temor a Dios" from *Nostalgia de la muerte.*

The best starting point is provided by two articles by César Rodríguez Chicharro, who has studied Villaurrutia's use of the pun. Chicharro begins by juxtaposing two comments: the first one from Pedro de Valencia to Góngora telling him not to please common people (*el vulgo*) with puns, and the other by Alí Chumacero, who thinks Villaurrutia's puns undermine the depth and seriousness of his message (1964: 249). Rodríguez Chicharro uses the following examples, among others (250, 251):

Góngora:
Cruzados hacen cruzados,
escudos pintan escudos,
y tahures muy desnudos,
con dados ganan condados;
ducados hacen ducados
y coronas Majestad,
          ¡verdad!

Villaurrutia:
En Boston es grave falta
hablar de ciertas mujeres
por eso aunque nieva nieve
mi boca no se atreve
a decir en voz alta:
ni Eva ni Hebe.

From "Nocturno en que nada se oye" (254):

Y con el jugo angustioso de un espejo frente a otro
cae mi voz
y mi voz que madura
y mi voz quemadura

y mi bosque madura
y mi voz quema dura.

Rodríguez Chicharro finds examples of *disemia, paronomasia* (para-nomasia, double entendre, heteronym, polypteton), *correlación,* and *paralelismo* (symmetry). Another trope found is the *calambur* (when Góngora says: "a este lopico, lo pico"). To Rodríguez Chicharro these poetic choices are, of course, legitimate. Ignacio Navarrete reminds us that paronomasia was already found in Juan Boscán y Almogáver's translation of *Il cortegiano* (1995: 51). Boscán himself was very fond of wit (52). It is interesting to observe how prominent paronomasia and *calambur* are among contemporary Mexican comedians.

"Sor Juana Inés de la Cruz" is the title of one of the most important lectures compiled in the *Obras* (1991: 773–785); in it Villaurrutia explains why Manuel Touissant, Ermilo Abreu Gómez, and he decided to edit the sonnets and the *endechas* (laments). Sor Juana is a classic of Mexican letters, as expressed by don Marcelino Menéndez y Pelayo and Karl Vossler—thus *foreign* critics had declared the importance of the Mexican writer in obtaining a more complete picture of Western culture. Villaurrutia declares that Sor Juana is a poet of intelligence (wit) and labels her a *conceptista,* using Menéndez y Pelayo's terminology. A second characteristic is her *barroquismo,* "tan característico del espíritu mexicano" (so typical of the Mexican spirit; 779). The third characteristic is the most influential for Villaurrutia himself:

> She is a poet of intelligence, concept, reason. If you examine her series
> of sonnets about love, for example, you will find a key to this topic.
> These sonnets may appear cold, if this term is admitted to describe
> intelligence, *an idea that I do not share.* But Sor Juana is not just a poet
> of reason; she is also a poet of feeling. Predominant in her literature is
> what I called in my previous lecture the logical power of the word.
> (779) [15]

Another important lecture is "Introducción a la poesía mexicana" (764–772), a very interesting document for studying Mexican poetry. In this lesson Villaurrutia explains the aristocratic component of Mexican literature. He reworks the process followed by Boscán and Garcilaso de la Vega at the beginning of the government of Emperor Carlos I, as explained by Navarrete (1995). After the Comuneros war Boscán and Garcilaso took poetry away from the *people* (the servant poet) and created the figure of the courtesan poet, the knight who was also a writer of lyric poems. Villaurrutia says that Mexico's poetry is not popular (of the people) as it is in Spain, Ireland (*sic*), and Germany. He is asserting that the avant-garde writers are not going to allow popular forms like the melodramatic bolero and the epic ballad (*corrido*) to define Mexican poetry.

One of the most interesting poems by Villaurrutia is "Mar," published posthumously in 1953 (see Forster 1976: 100). It can be assumed that Villaurrutia considered it very personal (closeted) when he decided not to publish it.

Te acariciaba, mar, en mi desvelo;
te soñaba en mi sueño, inesperado;
te aspiraba en la sombra recatado;
te oía en el silencio de mi duelo.

Eras, para mi cuerpo, cielo y suelo;
símbolo de mi sueño, inexplicado;
olor para mi sombra, iluminado;
rumor en el silencio de mi celo.

Te tuve hirviendo entre mis manos,
caí despierto en tu profundo río,
sentí el roce de tus muslos cercanos.

Y aunque fui tuyo, entre tus brazos frío,
tu calor y tu aliento fueron vanos:
cada vez te siento menos mío.   (FORSTER 1976: 100)

[I caressed you, sea, in my vigil; / I dreamt you in my unexpected dream; / I breathed you in the quiet shadow; / I heard you in the silence of my mourning. // You were my body's sky and ground; / symbol of my unexplained dream; / scent for my well-lit shadow; / a murmur in my silent zeal. // I had you boiling between my hands, / I fell, awake, into your deep river, / I felt the close touch of your thighs. // And although I belonged to you, cold in your arms, / your warmth and your breath were in vain: / every time I feel you less and less mine.]

According to Forster:

The careful and extended personification in this poem suggests strongly a symbolic interpretation. The sea might symbolize physical love, in which the poet finds diminishing meaning, or perhaps even poetic inspiration, which becomes progressively more difficult. The sea could even represent the source from which all life comes, and in this way the sonnet becomes a search for metaphysical meaning. (1976: 101)

The stormy sea as a metaphor for emotions belongs to the Petrarchan tradition (see Navarrete 1995: 217), and the poem is a classical sonnet. Garcilaso de la Vega, Lope de Vega, Fernando de Herrera, Luis de Góngora, and Francisco de Quevedo wrote love poems based on the sea metaphor. It is clear, then, that Villaurrutia wanted to insert himself into this tradition; Octavio Paz has noticed how Villaurrutia and his group were preoccupied with the idea of continuity and tradition in literature (1991: 14). The sonnet form and the metaphors used in the sonnet, mainly the sea and the antithesis *calor/frío*, emphasize a standard emotion, which Villaurrutia has decided to develop with overused tropes.

The difference, which is also a *différance* in the Derridean sense of the term, is in the homoeroticism of this particular love, especially the last two tercets: line 9 can be read as the poet having in his hand the lover's semen. The image of the river as a place of erotic encounter is found in Garcilaso's eclogues; and in a poet of the body like Villaurrutia the thighs as synecdoche of the lover are very important. Line 12 is critical, because it places the poetic voice in a position of passivity as a lover: "fui tuyo," — the poet is taken sexually by a lover who has cold arms, although this lover with his warmth and his breath tried vainly to warm the poet. This last piece of information is implied by the last line of the sonnet: "every time I feel you less and less mine." The rhyme between "frío" and "menos mío" is essential to establish a logical relationship between these two concepts. And, of course, there is a metaphysical dimension: this is not just the eternal fight between lovers but a forbidden love fiercely attacked by a homophobic society. In the tradition into which Villaurrutia is inserting himself there are homophobic poems written by Miguel de Cervantes, Quevedo, and Góngora — poets who also included homosexual moments in their literature.

The poem is based on three concepts: the semiotization of "water," "shadow/light," and "cold/hot." It would be interesting to explore how Villaurrutia's use of "water" corresponds to Garcilaso's and to Garcilaso's animism and to compare Villaurrutia's use of "shadow" to San Juan de la Cruz's religious animism instead of the lay animism of Garcilaso. This is because the bourgeois mentality of Villaurrutia could not accept the anachronistic substantialism that the Council of Trent brought to baroque art (e.g., the honor plays). Let us remain with the cold/hot metaphor. Merlin H. Forster called his book on Villaurrutia's poetry *Fire and Ice* (1976), indicating that this is the most important metaphor in Villaurrutia's poetry.

Forster does not explain the metaphor's semiotic process, but Eugene Lawrence Moretta has traced its origin:

> The epigraph of the first group of *nocturnos* is a line from the poetry of the English writer Michael Drayton (1563–1631) which reads, "Burned in a sea of ice, and drowned amidst a fire." (1971: 5–12)

Moretta notes that the metaphor appears in other poems and that Elías Nandino in a study about Villaurrutia paraphrased the metaphors but did not explain them. Moretta limits himself to displaying the metaphor without deciphering it. But the "fire and ice" poet in Spanish is Fernando de Herrera (1534–1597). In Herrera, as in Villaurrutia, the lover is the Absolute, and the poetic voice is always aiming to become one with it/him/her. And in both Herrera and Villaurrutia this union can be either bliss or death. The fire of the lover melts the ice of the beloved to become one, but this same fire can destroy the object of desire. This is the poetic logic of Herrera, which is borrowed by Villaurrutia (cf. Rodríguez 1974): the awkwardness of Herrera's lover can help him develop the awkwardness of his own love(r). "Nocturno amor" is a fine example of the new writing of the gay body in modern poetry:

> Guardas el nombre de tu cómplice en los ojos
> pero encuentro tus párpados más duros que el silencio
> y antes que compartirlo matarías el goce
> de entregarte en el sueño con los ojos cerrados
> sufro al sentir la dicha con que tu cuerpo busca
> el cuerpo que te vence más que el sueño
> y comparo la fiebre de tus manos
> con mis manos de hielo
> y el temblor de tus sienes con mi pulso perdido
> y el yeso de mis muslos con la piel de los tuyos
> que la sombra corroe con su lepra incurable.
> Ya sé cuál es el sexo de tu boca
> y lo que guarda la avaricia de tu axila
> y maldigo el rumor que inunda el laberinto de tu oreja
> sobre la almohada de espuma
> sobre la dura página de nieve
> No la sangre que huyó de mí como del arco huye la flecha
> sino la cólera circula por mis arterias
> amarilla de incendio en mitad de la noche
> y todas las palabras en la prisión de la boca
> y una sed que en el agua del espejo

sacia su sed con una sed idéntica
De que noche despierto a esta desnuda
noche larga y cruel noche que ya no es noche
junto a tu cuerpo más muerto que muerto
que no es tu cuerpo ya sino su hueco . . .

(VILLAURRUTIA 1991: 49–50)

[You keep the name of your accomplice in your eyes / but I find your eyelids harder than silence / and before sharing it you would kill the pleasure / of giving yourself over to a dream with your eyes closed / I suffer when feeling the pleasure you are looking for with your body / the body that conquers you more than sleep / and I compare the fever of your hands / with my icy ones / and the trembling of your temples with my lost pulse / and the plaster of my thighs against the skin of your thighs / that the shadow is rotting with its insatiable leprosy. / I already know the sex of your mouth / and what is hiding in the greed of your armpit / and I curse the murmur that inundates the labyrinth of your ear / over the foam pillow / over the harsh page of snow / This is not the blood that left me as the arrow flees the bow / it is but the anger circulating in my arteries / yellow like flame in the middle of the night / and all the words in the prison of my mouth / and a thirst that quenches its thirst with the water of the mirror / quenching it with an identical thirst / During the night I wake up to this naked / long and cruel night that is not a night anymore / beside your body more dead than dead / it is not your body but its void . . .]

Like the poem which has just been discussed, this one belongs to Garcilaso's animism, constructed in terms of the function of the eyes. It is impossible not to remember the eighth sonnet of Garcilaso, where live, incandescent spirits leave the eyes of the loved person and pass through the body of the lover, who cannot retain those spirits and can only behold the absence of love. In Villaurrutia's case the beloved, after being loved, still retains the lover's spirit in his eyes. This is Garcilaso. Villaurrutia takes as his point of departure a break with the poetic tradition because he has to utter a love story which has not been told before, that of two men. He cannot describe the body of his male counterpart using the same metaphors that have been used for the last five centuries (lips, the neck, the bosom, etc.). A new body has to emerge: eyes, hands, temples, thighs, skin, mouth, a sexual mouth, ear, blood. And, then, as in Garcilaso, the absence.

3)Ξ *Satiric Poetry*

Introduction

Gay and baroque poetry converge in Salvador Novo's satire. It is baroque because it follows the conventions of Golden Age literary models; it is gay, even in those poems where the topic is not mentioned, because in this genre Novo comes out of the closet. In his other works, depending on the genre, Novo may or may not be closeted; as an editorial writer he is definitely closeted, even if he is writing anonymously. He is moderately out of the closet in his love poetry, where he plays with ambiguous gender markers or develops a new imagery to describe the desire for the male body. He is definitely out of the closet in his autobiography. Because he did not intend to publish it until his death, he could be very graphic in the sexual details and explicit in the names of the protagonists.

Novo takes a different approach in his satiric poetry. He is conscious that his homosexuality makes him an easy target for his enemies and that this is the first attack he is going to receive. The only way to preempt it is by acknowledging his homosexuality, making fun of it, and deconstructing homophobia.

In his ground-breaking study on satire, Dustin Griffin dedicates a chapter to the politics of satire (1994: 133–160). He discusses why there are historical moments and places where satire flourishes and why at other times it vanishes. Griffin notes that the first precondition is to have a significant number of writers who know the conventions of the genre. During the Renaissance and the baroque, satire thrived because classical satire was being republished and discussed on a regular basis, so the writers had models to study and imitate. It is not a surprise, then, that the same phenomenon occurred during the times of the Contemporáneos, when baroque poetry was being rediscovered and Góngora became one of the points of reference of the avant-garde movements. It does not make any difference whether the *modernistas* were first in their interest in baroque poetry, because the new knowledge of the 1920s was based on the scientific studies of the *estilística* (Leo Spitzer was writing his dissertation in 1910; Dámaso Alonso and Amado Alonso would follow soon); these analyses and editions confirmed the modernity and pertinence of baroque literature ("Introducción," in Buxó 1960).

The second component according to Griffin is tolerance and taste for ridicule (1994: 136). We need to bear in mind that this is the golden age of the double entendre and the paronomastic speeches of the *carpas*, the popular theaters where stand-up comedians like Cantinflas, Adalberto Martínez Resortes, and Palillos developed a popular baroque language of the people. These humorists created a taste for wit and competed to satiate the unending demand for new and more daring puns. The most revered form of humor was the *albur*, the (homo)sexual pun of the *carpas*. In this context, Novo's satire is no more than a highbrow version of the *albur*, but without the element of improvisation of this genre, although his punch lines try to recreate the pleasure listeners feel after a good *albur*.

The most important element for satire is the presence of a modest but homogeneous reading audience of the ruling class who live in the political capital (Griffin 1994: 137). The people writing for this audience must be writers who know each other and are active in the political life of the city. A key characteristic of this audience is that they have to be interested in gossip (cf. Chapter 6), because gossip empowers these dandies by making them feel part of a crowd that stands higher than those who do not share the same knowledge. This "elite" is formed by either the café society or those who enjoy following it, even if their pleasure is only vicarious. This audience must be able to understand the in-jokes, the indirect references, and the sly remarks. An element of performance is also involved; Novo read his poems at parties and social gatherings, and the listeners could get copies of the poems (printed in pink) and distribute them among other friends. These satirists, Novo included, had to be either members of the café society or social climbers in the process of becoming part of it. This explains the contradictory condition of marginality and, at the same time, membership and belonging present in satire.

The last element necessary is some kind of censorship. When there is total freedom of speech, press, and opinion the direct route is taken, and satire is not needed. Griffin writes:

> The most inventive satire arises when the artist is seeking simultaneously to take risks and escape punishment for his boldness, and is never quite certain himself whether he will be acclaimed or punished. In proportion as you remove these conditions of danger, by liberalization, satire becomes arbitrary and effete. (1994: 139)

I have already commented on the letter Novo sent to García Lorca about the possibility of going into exile in Spain; moreover, Novo's trip to Hollywood in 1940 had the double function of doing business and getting him out of the country for a while. Satire has always had its peaks at times like imperial Rome or the French, English, and Spanish Renaissance and baroque during the *ancien régime*, the "culturas dirigidas" as studied by Maravall. Some of the great satirists of all times wrote during the seventeenth century in France and Spain: Savinien de Cyrano de Bergerac, Molière, Nicolas Boileau, Góngora, Quevedo, and the Conde de Villamediana. In the case of Spain, other moments for satire were the reigns of Enrique IV (fifteenth century), Carlos I (sixteenth century), and Carlos IV (eighteenth century). Julie Greer Johnson (1993) has studied the following satirists as the most relevant in colonial Spanish America: Cristóbal de Llerena and Mateo Rosas de Oquendo (sixteenth century); Juan Rodríguez Freile, Sor Juana Inés de la Cruz, and Juan del Valle y Caviedes (seventeenth century); and Alonso Carrió de la Vandera, Esteban Terralla y Landa, and Francisco Javier Eugenio de Santa Cruz y Espejo (eighteenth century). The best of them all are the baroque writers Sor Juana and Valle y Caviedes.

Mala carmina: Opprobriis dignum

As explained in Chapter 1, in the mid-thirties Novo was immersed in the political and artistic controversies of Mexico City. A hidden blessing brought by these culture wars was his forced departure from the administration, because it led him to embark on a very successful career in the private sector. Novo started working as a publicist for Augusto Elías (1936) and then began writing successfully under his name and anonymously in newspapers and magazines (*México al Día*, 1935; *Síntesis*, 1936; *Lectura* and *Ultimas noticias*, 1937; *Hoy*, 1938). Both as a journalist and as a publicist he received high salaries that allowed him an economic independence that few writers before him had enjoyed in Hispanic countries. He had a small team of young journalists to help him with the documentation and even ghostwrite some of the editorials. Little by little, he became one of the most prominent voices of the incipient Mexican urban middle class, especially those opposed to the Marxist rhetoric of President Cárdenas. He soon was the scourge against the abuses and the demagoguery of this administration.

Satiric poems were easily distributed in cafés, *tertulias,* and newspaper and government offices. Censorship and decorum prevented the official publication of these witty insults, but they were widely read and even memorized. There was definitely a pragmatic reason to distribute these lampoons. Like the satirists of the Austrian and Elizabethan courts, these young men like Novo were courtiers looking for a position in the city, competing to enter a small world with few posts open. In Habsburg times the job could be as the secretary or the diplomatic aide of a nobleman; during the Cárdenas presidency the appointments were in the mass media or the administration. Mexican historians have on different occasions compared the revolutionary presidencies since Cárdenas to the viceroys of the colony and have found a continuum, because many traditions and vices of the *ancien régime* have survived until present times.

Octavio Paz says that Mexican baroque culture was mostly oral (1982: 84). These satiric poems have an oral dimension in the sense that they did not belong to the published corpus of their authors. In Novo's case, he did not publish his satiric poetry until late in his life. This was not a literature to be read alone at home but aloud among friends to celebrate the "bad faith" of the attacks against the enemy. Spanish émigrés helped to revitalize the oral tradition with the social gatherings known as *tertulias* in the cafés. Octavio Paz says: "The liberal republican and democratic ideology was a historical superimposition. It did not change our societies, but it distorted our consciences: it introduced bad faith and lies in our political life" (1982: 30).[1] I have decided to replace Paz's label "bad faith" with *mala leche* (bad milk), because it is the popular expression used in Mexico to explain evil intention, the aim to hurt someone's feelings and/or status viciously. In my view Paz is wrong here, because this new, "liberal" tradition only revitalized the classical one of *mala carmina* opposed to the Horatian *bona carmina*. Hispanic culture followed the most important theorist of satire in the seventeenth century, the French Isaac Casaubón, who belonged to the Juvenalian tradition instead of the more moderate and "good" variation of Horace.

Let us begin with Novo's sonnet "Un Marof," chosen because of its quality and also because Marof reappears in Chapter 5 (dedicated to Lupe Marín). Marof wrote extensively in negative terms about female and homosexual writers; this made him *opprobriis dignum* (deserving of abuse). Marof (the Bolivian writer Gustavo Navarro) was the quintessential misogynist and homophobe (García Gutiérrez 1999: 104).

Here we follow the school of criticism alert to the workings of wit and imagery, but we are also trying to reconstruct as much as possible the historical context of the poems:

¿QUE PUTA entre sus podres chorrearía
por entre incordios, chancros y bubones
a este hijo de tan múltiples cabrones
que no supo qué nombre se pondría?
Prófugo de la cárcel andaría
mendigando favores y tostones;
no pudieron crecerle en los cojones,
en la cara la barba le crecía.
Bandido universal, como la puta
que el ser le dio, ridícula pipilla
suple en su labio verga diminuta.
Treponema ultrapálido, ladilla
boliviana, el favor de que disfruta
es lamerle los huevos a Padilla.

[What whore could drip that pus, / that son of so many cuckolds, / who didn't know how to name himself, / [born] among pests, chancres and buboes? / He must be a fugitive from prison, / asking for favors and money; / [they] couldn't grow in his balls, / his beard grew on his face. / Universal bandit, like the whore / that gave birth to him; ridiculous little smoking pipe / in his lips, replacing a tiny cock. / Most pallid treponema, / Bolivian crab, the position he enjoys / is because he sucks Padilla's balls.]

"A Marof" is a poem of *ingenio* (ingeniousness) and *concepto* (concept), "palabras que definen la poesía barroca" (words that define baroque poetry; Paz 1982: 80). Although Novo is a poet of the canon and has been widely anthologized, critics have not paid attention to his neo-baroque poetry. The situation is not unique, according to Octavio Paz (in a different context): "By a double contagion, one neoclassic with an excess of correction, another romantic with an excess of spontaneity, it became habitual to scorn these wordplays: echoes, acrostics, alliterations, retrograde poetry, cento, paronomasias, and other puns. Unfair criticism: these are legitimate resources of poetry" (1982: 83).[2] This is a key remark: Novo's sarcastic and obscene poetry is as good and at times as perfect as the poems of *Nuevo amor* or *XX poemas*. The same phenomenon occurred during the seventeenth century: many of the satiric poems by Quevedo, Villamediana, or Góngora are among their best.

In this sonnet, Tristán Marof is the pseudonym of a Bolivian Communist political activist. In 1934 Marof published a book in Buenos Aires, *México de frente y de perfil* (Profile of Mexico), intended to be a comprehensive portrait of Mexico's intellectual life. In one part of the book, "Literatos afeminados" (Effeminate Literati, 123–127), he says: "su prosa [Novo's] es movible, acrobática e insignificante" (his prose is fickle, acrobatic, and insignificant; 123); "Salvador Novo es autor de un libro sedante, jactancioso y para ciertas mujeres lesbias" (Salvador Novo is author of a sedative and boastful book for lesbian women; 124); "narcisos y petronios familiares, literatuelos de alcoba como los perritos de agua, asustadizos ante el menor gesto viril . . . la burguesía en su irremediable decadencia no tiene otros productos intelectuales. Para sobrevivir, este género de literatura se escuda en el arte puro . . . En México constituyen una minoría delincuente y despreciada" (narcissists and familiar Petronios, irrelevant literati, always in their beds like poodle dogs, frightened of the slightest virile gesture . . . the bourgeoisie in their irremediable decadence have no other intellectual products. To survive, this kind of literature is shielded in pure art . . . In Mexico they are a delinquent and despised minority; 126). Marof also ghostwrote articles against the Contemporáneos group signed by Diego Rivera.

As has already been said, these literary wars meant that the menial jobs held by the writers in the state bureaucracy were put in jeopardy; this is why Novo underlines the fact that Marof was under the protection of Ezequiel Padilla, the presidential candidate who lost to Miguel Alemán. Because these poems circulated widely and were very famous, they brought the attention of readers to the press articles written by Novo and reinforced the power he was acquiring as a well-known, respected, and feared opinion writer.

Novo's sonnet could be part of the anthology *Picardía mexicana* (Mexican Obscenities, 1960) by A. Jiménez, a collection of obscene jokes (*charras*), puns (*albures*), and eulogies (*caravanas*), most of them as old as the Revolution. From Jiménez's book a popular appetite for these literary games, especially obscene wit and concept, can be inferred. My 1970 edition of *Picardía* is the forty-third printing in ten years. Mercedes

Etreros in her book *La sátira política en el siglo XVII* (Political Satire in the Seventeenth Century, 1983) demonstrates how almost everybody, including illiterate people, enjoyed and understood satiric poetry read aloud in seventeenth-century Spain.

The next step must be to try to understand what is behind the use of obscenity and smut. Why do we derive pleasure from it? Peter Michelson in his book *Speaking the Unspeakable* (1993) has a reasonable answer:

> An aesthetics of obscenity implies a perceptual alteration whereby the obscene, a species of the ugly, is reconstituted to a function akin to that of the beautiful. In that sense it is a *contemplation* of the unspeakable and counterpoints traditional aesthetic assumptions. Traditionally the beautiful is associated with an idealist synthesis or transcendental revelation. The obscene counters by redirecting attentions from the ideal to the material nature of human being and doing. (xi)

The obscenities gathered by Jiménez aim at the material nature of the human being; for most people everyday life is material, and idealism only exists in the mythical melodrama of the soap operas.

Novo's obscene language also puts us in contact with this materiality. Juan Goytisolo (1977) and Malcolm K. Read (1984) have noticed the democratic dimension of scatology. Novo's answer to Marof subverts the idealism of both Communist ideology and more conservative idealism (for instance, acritical nationalism or the sentimentalism of Mother's Day). Novo had been accused by Marof of being a pure poet. He answers by using the language of the body; but at the same time, he has to go beyond this boundary. Novo turns to writing neo-baroque literature and deliberately decides to add more layers of difficulty to the poem. He achieves this goal by using cultured language, in this case, the semantic field of venereal maladies: *Treponema* is the bacteria that produce syphilis. He also inserts himself in the baroque tradition of satiric poetry depicting illnesses. For instance, Valle y Caviedes's poem "A una dama que paró en el Hospital de la Caridad" (To a Lady Who Ended Up in the Hospital de la Caridad) describes in graphic terms the venereal disease of a lady in colonial Lima.

Read's article (akin to that of Goytisolo) "Language and the Body in Francisco de Quevedo" explains the importance of bringing the body to the realm of literature and all the problems implied by this process. Quevedo gave voice to the body and to realities like buggery. He brought the anus, feces, and farts ("ruiseñor de los putos" [the nightingale of the faggots]) to his literature, even if it was to deny or condemn the practice. Quevedo saw, tasted, listened to, smelled, touched, and wrote the body. This had an important influence on modern gay writers who wanted to bring the body, the gay body, to the *idealistic* realm of poetry (from Benedetto Croce to Dámaso and Amado Alonso, the best-known theoreticians of literature were implying the truism of idealism as the only possibility for writing true poetry). This is why, when poets like Novo or Villaurrutia bring the male body as object of desire to their poetry, the critics of the sixties and seventies, heavily influenced by New Criticism and *estilística,* rushed to indicate that the love gay poems were just platonic or should be read as idealized versions of love.

To balance Marof's homophobia, Novo portrays him as a pathetic homosexual. Instead of enjoying love and sex, Marof is more like a prostitute selling his services and body in the same miserable and humiliating manner he used to sell his pen.

As a bridge between this chapter and Chapter 5 (dedicated to Lupe Marín) and as a link to Chapter 1 (on the neo-baroque), we may pause to consider the longest and most sophisticated piece of satiric poetry developed by Novo: *La Diegada.* This is a cultured ballad composed of twenty-eight quatrains with consonant rhyme, thirteen sonnets, seven *décimas* (ten-line stanzas), and one *quintilla* (five-line stanza). The twenty-sixth quatrain starts with the parody of the *Soledades* already mentioned in Chapter 1. The choice of form is no accident, because it links *La Diegada* to the best baroque tradition.

La Diegada tells the life of Diego Rivera. More interesting than the particulars of the conflicts between Novo and Rivera is the confrontation of their visions of Mexico. Both have been very successful in imposing their views; it is impossible to think about Mexico and not have as one of the predominant images the murals by Rivera, who made universals from Mexico's particulars. Like Novo, Rivera used Mexico's popular culture to make his high art, as in the use of the engravings of José Guadalupe Posada and the murals painted on the walls of *pulquerías.* Novo and Rivera also shared the same fascination for the United States and in general had a very positive attitude toward Spain (seen, for instance, in the influence of Pablo Picasso and Ignacio Zuloaga on Rivera until he found his personal style). Both used their knowledge of universal art to create a true Mexican art, independent of the forced Spanish art during colonial times and the always artificial import of French culture during the nineteenth century. Both also shared the vision of a dark side of adulation of power.

In *La Diegada* Diego Rivera is a bull, but not the constellation of Taurus as a symbol of sexual potency as in classical literature. Rather it is a creature with horns, a cuckold or *cornudo*. Amphiboly (sentence construction that allows two different meanings) and expolition (repetition of the same argument) are the main rhetorical devices in this series of poems. Amphiboly is used to open the text to confusion and begin the unending play of puns. Expolition satisfies the need for redundancy and creates gradations to exaggerate the negative attributes of the victim. This rhetorical apparatus is the framework of specific rhetorical figures like tmesis, the separation of the elements of a compound word, as in "Cuerna-vaca," transforming one of Rivera's masterpieces, the painting of the mural at the Cortés Palace in Cuernavaca, into the place where he is being cuckolded. Another pun, close to tmesis, is the *calambur*, in which two different words when pronounced together create a new one; in this case "ve-cerro" ([he] sees the hill) becomes *becerro* (calf), which adds one more layer of reference to the portrayal of Rivera as a bull. To augment the intensity of the attack, Novo uses catachresis (the violation of semantic rules): "aquel cuya panza tomaron por frente." Here Novo makes fun of Rivera's belly, which because it is in front (*frente*) becomes the forehead (*frente*) where we put the horns.

These devices are supported by attacks to enrich the effect: (1) dilogy, the use of a word with two different meanings at the same time: "la diestra, siniestra," where *diestra* means right hand and the hand used to bullfight, and *siniestra*, the left hand and sinister; (2) epanalepsis, the anaphora when each line starts with the same words: "dejemos a Diego que Rusia registre / dejemos a Diego que el dedo se chupe"; (3) paranomasia: "recluta, retreta, retrata y retrete." This entire rhetorical arsenal is placed at the service of the political *mentideros* of Mexico City, places where people gossip.

Lines 85–112 play with U.S. popular culture. There are references to baseball (the San Diego Padres) and fast food: Rivera's favorite food is corn (*cuerno*) flakes. Rivera becomes Buffalo Bill, pronounced and written *Vil* (vile). New York's skyline, with its *rascacielos* (skyscrapers), also reminds us of the part of the temples where Rivera grows his horns. The poems taken together form a collection of hilarious puns that have as their intention a deformative parody of the public image of Diego Rivera. There is a brutal blasphemy (37–40) in which Guadalupe Marín (see Chapter 5) becomes the Virgen de Guadalupe and (Juan) Diego is impotent. Novo also uses closet imagery to make his *albur* clearer. If the *albur* has a homosexual component, Novo stresses the masculinity of Guadalupe Marín and the (baroque) monstrosity and femininity of Diego's body (e.g., his large breasts). The climax of this part is the union of Marín with the bisexual poet of the Contemporáneos, Jorge Cuesta.

Ego mecum *(With Myself)*

We now focus on the auto-satiric poems of *Sátira* (1970), reprinted in 1978 under the title *Sátira: El libro ca . . .* (Satire: The Son of a . . .). The poem "Prólogo" (9) opens the book:

> Escribir porque sí, por ver si acaso
> se hace un soneto más que nada valga;
> para matar el tiempo, y porque salga
> una obligada consonante al paso.
> Porque yo fui escritor, y éste es el caso
> que era tan flaco como perra galga;
> crecióme la papada como nalga,
> vasto de carne y de talento escaso.
> ¡Qué le vamos a hacer! Ganar dinero
> y que la gente nunca se entrometa
> en ver si lo cedes a tu cuero.
> Un escritor, un gran poeta . . .
> Desde los tiempos del señor Madero,
> es tanto como hacerse la puñeta.

[To write just because, to see if by chance / one more worthless sonnet is made; / to pass the time, and to get / on its way the compulsory consonant. / Because I used to be a writer, and this is the case / I was as thin as a greyhound bitch; / my jowl grew like a butt, / vast of flesh and scarce of talent. / What are we going to do! Make money / and to have people not meddling / in seeing if you yield your skin. / A writer, a great poet . . . / Since the times of Mr. Madero, / this equals being in big trouble.]

Novo wrote (or published) this poem at the age of sixty-six, four years before his death. The first quatrain is conventional and reminds the reader of "Un soneto me manda hacer Violante" by Lope de Vega, which inserts the poem in the tradition of baroque poetry. The second quatrain is more interesting and is based on the following axiom: literary talent and fat are proportionally reversed. This is *laudatio* and *vituperatio*, praise to the poetry he wrote in his youth and criticism of his late poetry, this poem included. Then Novo inserts his decrepit body—his old, gay, and decaying body—into the poem. The key here is the rhyme between *galga* and *nalga*. He is a bitch and an ass. He was known by his enemies as "Nalgador Sobo," the fondler of asses. One more time the baroque reading has to be done: we have to ask ourselves why Novo chose the term *galga*. One possible answer is in the *Tesoro de la lengua castellana o española* (1987 [1674]: 622) by Sebastián de Covarrubias. He explains an enigma that says:

> Lo mismo que un galgo valgo,
> su retrato soy y amigo,
> y si por el campo salgo
> las liebres mato y persigo;
> y es cierto que no soy galgo.

> [I am as worthy as a (male) greyhound, / I am his portrait and friend, / and if I go to the field / I kill and chase the hares; / and it is true that I am not a (male) greyhound.]

A first reading could evoke the easy explanation that Novo had feminized himself to make a reference to his public homosexuality. Novo agreed with Lorca about the need to make clear the virility of the homosexual man and that homosexuality and femininity were not synonymous (see Chapter 2). This is the reason why Novo chose the word *galga* (the female greyhound), which is one of the very few domestic animals in which the abilities of the male and female cannot be distinguished when they are performing in the field. By the same token, when Novo was doing literature he was in control of the gender and sexual orientation of the poetic voice. As the *galga* can pass as a *galgo*, he could pass as a heterosexual writer if that was his intention.

As early as 1924 Novo had answered a question about Mexican literature in this way: "Existe una literatura mexicana moderna cuya buena reputación de muchacha fresca y viril han querido opacar las lenguas doloridas" (Sheridan 1985: 257). It is extraordinary that so early in his career he understood that gender was a key issue in the process of modernizing Mexican literature. Novo mocked the interviewer with this funny metaphor of modern literature as a virile young woman with a lot of nerve. Peter Roster says categorically: "el Novo de 1970 se ve ya en el de 1920" (1978: 80), which is true, at least in this case. It seems that from very early in his career Novo realized there was a dimension of performance in the job of a writer and decided to be in command when acting his role. This is why he acknowledges with the rhyme his object of desire in the *nalga*.

The rest of the poem draws the reader to notice many similar examples, such as the pun with *cuero* (meaning "skin" and "hunk") and the fact that the beginning of the new literature is during the Madero presidency, which is to say that it coincides with the beginning of the Revolution. It is obvious that a new historical period demanded new ways to do literature, like the realism of the novel of the Revolution and the avant-garde literature of the Contemporáneos.

The second autobiographical poem in *Sátira* is "A mi queridísimo compadre don Agustín Arroyo Ch. para desearle muy feliz año nuevo, después de leer su salutación a 1967 en la 1a. plana de *El Nacional.*" As in the previous poem, Novo is a man in his sixties; and in this case he links his name and his fate to that of don Agustín Arroyo Ch. (1891–1969), the well-known politician: governor of Guanajuato (1927–1931) and secretary of labor (1940) under Cárdenas. In 1967 he was editor-in-chief of the government newspaper *El Nacional.* Arroyo Ch., one of the most skilled "plumbers" of the revolutionary parties, was a hawk disguised as a dove. His main function for the party had been to censor the press for thirty years, but without losing the appearance of a free press in a democratic society. For many years he had controlled the distribution of paper to the newspapers. Paper, a scarce commodity, was used widely by the PRI as a tool to censor the press.

> EN ESTE comienzo de año
> que sus misterios alberga,
> rememoro al ermitaño
> que no vestido de paño,
> sino envuelto en pobre jerga,
> solo desciende cada año
> a que le pelen la verga.
>
> ¡Compadrito! ¡Vaya carga!
> Me llena de sobresalto
> ir "con el pendón en alto
> y en el brazo, con la adarga."
> ¡Mire si será monserga
> lo mismo aquí que en Pisuerga!
> Pues es mi esperanza amarga
> que nos halle el Año Nuevo

con decadencia de huevo
¡y abatimiento de verga!

¿Enfrentarnos con la adarga?
¿No es errata por aderga?
¡No me la fiéis tan larga!
Voy — como el buen ermitaño
lo hacía año con año —
a ver quién jijos me asperga
lo que usted llama la adarga
y el diccionario, la verga.

[At the beginning of this year / harboring mysteries, / I remember the hermit / not dressed in clothes, / but dressed in poor jargon, / he who descends every year / to have his cock jerked off. // Buddy! What a burden! / I'm getting a fright / from going "with the banner raised / and the shield in my arm." / This is tedious / here and in Pisuerga! / It is my bitter hope / to enter the New Year / with ball decadence / and cock depression! // To fight with the shield? / Is not that a mistake? / Don't trust me! / I am going — like the good hermit / to do it just once like every year — / to see who the hell jerks me off / what you call the shield / and the dictionary, the cock.]

Both men are presented with decaying bodies, with little sexual activity; their only goal is to get someone to masturbate them and to achieve their only orgasm of the year. But from the point of view of the neo-baroque, what is interesting to us is the reference to Don Quijote: "un hidalgo de los de lanza en astillero, adarga antigua, rocín flaco . . ." as he is introduced in the first sentence of the novel. Don Quijote does not own a flying banner, and his lance is on the wall in its sheath; his old shield means he belongs to a noble family. The joke of Novo's poem is based on the mistake made by Arroyo when he thought *adarga* meant spear instead of shield. Novo used this mistake to make of them both two old Quijotes. According to Daniel Eisenberg (1999), Don Quijote is a fifty-year-old man, virgin, not married, and fond of the all-male world of the chivalric books. In the first chapter he has a *mozo* (young servant) who soon disappears and ends up linked to a fat, middle-aged man with stinking buttocks (1999: 48), a good deterrent for Don Quijote's bad thoughts. Don Quijote was the perfect metaphor for Novo's purpose: to characterize the lives of the two of them as aging homosexual men with very few sexual expectations left.

Final Reflections

In *Generaciones y semblanzas* Octavio Paz alludes to Novo's satiric poetry:

> Salvador Novo showed up, a master of the [satiric] genre. He had a lot of talent and poison, very few ideas, and a total lack of morality. Loaded with lethal adjectives and light in scruples, he attacked the weak and praised the powerful. He did not serve any idea or belief but his own passions and interests. He did not write with blood but with shit. His best epigrams, written in a moment of shameless cynicism and lucidity, are the ones he wrote against himself. This saves him. (1987: 524)[3]

I wanted to introduce Paz's comment at the very end of the chapter to demonstrate how unfairly and how badly Salvador Novo has been read. There are exceptions, but in general the literary criticism written while Novo was still alive could not distinguish between the writer and the literary texts. Novo attacked powerful people and less mighty people, but he also had to endure attacks, as in this quotation by the patriarch of Mexican letters, who could not or did not want to read Novo's poetry analytically. Paz's perspective is clear in the following quote:

> While Novo always rather flaunted his sexual leanings, Xavier defended his private life. I do not think it was hypocrisy. He did not hide away and was able to cope with public condemnation. He was discreet in real life and in literature. (Villaurrutia 1991: 16)[4]

Let us juxtapose these words by Paz with what Rosario Villari has to say about the baroque *Rebel:*

> What made the figure of the rebel of the baroque age tragic — his eagerness to avoid being branded as a rebel, even in contradiction with his own acts and his own goals; his attempts to connect himself at all costs to a constitutional legality and an established tradition — depended largely on the conviction that rebellion was fated to fail. Although the Protestant reformation suggested that successful revolution was possible, on the more strictly political and social plane failure was the rule. (1995b: 107)

The poets of the Contemporáneos group were unhappy with the Revolution because of the lack of real changes brought by the revolutionary process and at the same time — in what only seems like a contradiction — because of the magnitude of the revolutionary change, especially in the development of a nationalism with fascist overtones. Some of these poets (Novo, Villaurrutia, Cuesta) are rebels as defined by Villari, at times conservative, more along the lines defended by Maravall in his thesis that baroque culture is "a government culture working in the interests of political stability and public tranquility that managed to impose itself and gain common acceptance, drastically thrusting aside (more than had been true in past times) notions of opposition, protest, or subversion, whether open or clandestine" (Villari 1995b: 101). Villari disagrees with Maravall because she thinks his theory is too radical. Even if she is right, one cannot put aside the presence of a culture descending from the institutions of power (e.g., Diego Rivera!). In the introduction to *Baroque Personae* Villari notes how figures like Giordano Bruno, Galileo Galilei, Francis Bacon, René Descartes, and Baruch Spinoza — and I would add Juan de Mariana (1536–1624), the theoretician of the people's sovereignty, and Diego de Saavedra Fajardo (1584–1648) — have been read as precursors when in reality they were people of their time, the period of baroque artifices. Twentieth-century avant-garde writers turned to seventeenth-century individualism because there they found the origin of their ideological premises — individualism in the context of an aristocratic society in spite of the dominant substantialism of that society.

The new dogmatic and authoritarian ideologies of the twentieth century presented their own challenges, and the baroque and satire were good models to overcome them. The Contemporáneos were not revolutionary in the utopian sense of the term. But their individualisms, combined, challenged the status quo and ended up changing the canon of Mexican literature. They did not intend revolution but evolution.

≋ *Agustín Lazo (1896–1971)*
Xavier Villaurrutia's Shadow

Introduction

Agustín Lazo was born in Mexico City into a wealthy and well-known family. This is one of the main reasons why he is so different from many of his contemporary writers and painters. While the others were fighting to get a position in the administration or in the mass media, Lazo could choose where and what to study, write, and paint. When he decided to work in theater, he also chose his own terms and was able to do what he liked and to continue his career without the pressure of short-term success. By the same token he stopped working when he decided he did not have the challenge, the love and presence of his companion of many years, Xavier Villaurrutia.

Lazo studied in the Escuela Nacional Preparatoria and in the Escuela Nacional de Artes Plásticas (San Carlos). In the Art School one of his classmates was Rufino Tamayo, who was very influential in Lazo's development as an artist. Of all the great Mexican masters of the twentieth century, Tamayo is the closest to the sensibility of the Contemporáneos. According to Villaurrutia, he belongs to the group (1991: 1035). Villaurrutia says Tamayo uses colors as Góngora manipulated words, not because of their logical content but because of their capacity to create provocative allusions. Tamayo preferred the easel to the mural, which in the Mexican tradition has important ideological consequences. He favored non-nationalist, avant-garde painting instead of the social realism of most of the mural paintings. Tamayo's murals are compositions of colors and forms, in contrast to the revolutionary visions of Rivera and José Orozco. Tamayo also catered to the idea of the

Mexican Revolution as a reevaluation of the position of the Mexican middle class instead of a real revolutionary process. In his paintings he gives similar treatment to personalities like Zapata and Cantinflas, in a huge contrast to the cubist vision of Zapata by Rivera.

Lazo spent two years in Paris (1928–1930) working as a painter and learning from the international community of artists who flocked to Paris in the period between wars; he had already traveled briefly to Europe in 1922. He visited museums in France, Italy, Germany, and Belgium. Agustín Velázquez Chávez has explained Lazo's 1926–1929 period as follows: "The coloring of these productions is a city-gray that embraces the seven primary colors of the rainbow. Parlors, the bourgeoisie, city maidservants, and robust serious children are the usual themes of these pictures" (1969: 125). MacKinley Helm describes Lazo's late 1930s painting as "a personal style of crosshatching, in which fine crossed lines, instead of dots of paint, secure the effect of vibrating light and color. Lazo uses this stroke with telling effect in his water color" (1941: 172). As a painter Lazo had his first solo exposition at the age of thirty (1926). Helm was deeply impressed by the aristocratic manners of Lazo when he visited his study (ibid.).

In Paris Lazo became interested in theater, learning set design and stage machinery with Charles Dullin (L'Atelier). While in France he was already living with Xavier Villaurrutia. In *La estatua de sal* Salvador Novo tells the story of how they first met and became lovers. When they returned to Mexico, Lazo taught drawing in La Esmeralda School and in the Instituto Nacional de Bellas Artes (cf. Rehbein 1992; Novo 1982). He was one of the key members of two of the most prominent theater developments in twentieth-century Mexico: Teatro Ulises and Orientación.

A[lma] L[ilia] R[oura] and J[ulia] S[oto] provide this valuable information in the only existing biographical account of Lazo:

> He worked as a set designer and clothes designer for the "Orientación" group under the direction of José Gorostiza in plays like *Antigone, Macbeth, Requesting Her Hand*, in [Cervantes's] interlude *The Jealous Old Man*, Gogol's *The Marriage*, Molnar's *Liliom*, and in other plays by Mexican authors like *Ifigenia Cruel* by Alfonso Reyes, *Parece mentira [entremés* by Alberto Cosín] and *En qué piensas* by Villaurrutia, and *La escuela del amor* and *Ser o no ser* by [José] Gorostiza. He also translated (almost always with Villaurrutia) and adapted the following plays: *Le secret* by Henry Bernstein; *The Daughter of Lorio* by [Gabriele] D'Annunzio; *Each in His Own Way* by Luigi Pirandello; *Trojan War Will Not Take Place* by

[Jean] Giradoux; *Nostra Dea* and *Minnie la candida* by Massimo Bontempelli; *La nueva Eloisa* [*Femme de luxe?*] by Alfred Savoir. (1982: 13–14)[1]

To this list we should add, for the season at Teatro Hidalgo in 1932, *The Brothers Karamazov*, *The Double Mrs. Morli*, "and the scenery and costumes for the Greek Theater productions staged by Julio Bracho in 1936 at the Palace of Fine Arts" (Velázquez Chávez 1969: 125). Lazo "also did the set design and costumes for *Asia* by H. R. Lenormand and *La hiedra* by Villaurrutia . . . As a set designer, his contemporary critics stressed his 'stylized' work, thanks to the economy of the elements on stage and very simple scenography using only the essentials" (R[oura] and S[oto] 1982: 13).[2] In 1982 the Museo Nacional del Arte paid homage to him with an anthological exposition of his pictures.

Lazo's vast knowledge of set design surfaced in his plays. It becomes very clear when reading his plays that he views theater as a primarily visual production instead of a combination of dialogues. Words are important, but they are just one more component of the whole.

El caso de don Juan Manuel *(The Case of Don Juan Manuel)*

In 1985 Eve Kosofsky Sedgwick published *Between Men: English Literature and Male Homosocial Desire*, a useful study that helped us to understand how some specific patriarchal structures worked in literature. This was an important step in the right direction because at that time feminist and gender research was still in the preliminary stage: labeling cultural products as patriarchal. But there was a developing need to go beyond that naïve stage of mere recognition of patriarchal structures: to start explaining the cultural texts that were reproducing the patriarchal system. Sedgwick's thesis was that in many examples of literature (especially nineteenth-century British novels) the reader could find the erotic triangle of homosocial desire. She based her discovery on the pioneer studies by René Girard, Claude Lévi-Strauss, and Gayle Rubin. She found that English literature is full of instances of male bonding and that for this union to be possible a woman was needed to serve as indispensable intermediary between the two men. The only function of the woman in many of these cultural instances was to serve as a bridge between two men. This did not mean that those men were homosexual; but the presence of the woman introduced an element of heterosexuality, which somehow legitimized the bonding between the two men she was helping to join together.

It is logical to infer from Sedgwick's discovery that similar examples are found in other literatures. One example is Agustín Lazo's *El caso de don Juan Manuel* (1948).

Let us start with Salvador Novo's account of the staging of the play as he described it in a newspaper article of November 5, 1948. At that moment Novo was the theater director of the Instituto Nacional de Bellas Artes, under the presidency of Mexican composer Carlos Chávez, during the Alemán Valdés administration. It was very important for the Mexican process toward democratic normalization to have for the first time in a long while a president who did not come from the military sector (see Chapter 1).

Novo's review is important for us to learn about the public who attended these sophisticated dramas. The director of the play was Cipriano Rivas Chérif (Aguilera and Aznar Soler 1999: 416), one of the most prominent members of the community of Spanish exiles; he had been secretary to the president of the Spanish Republic, Manuel Azaña (1936–1939), who was also his brother-in-law. Rivas Chérif was one of the principal members of both the upper-class and gay communities of Mexico City. He was a real gentleman, one of the dandies in charge of establishing high fashion and culture. Novo writes:

> Last week the Group of Friends of Theater, under the direction of Cipriano Rivas Chérif, staged *Don Juan Manuel* by Agustín Lazo at La Posada del Sol. They had not invited me to their previous plays, and I could not attend this one. Apparently this is an association of very rich people. To be a member the associate has to contribute 5,000 pesos, and this is a nonprofit organization. The spectators have to wear tuxedos when they attend the plays.
>
> Three of the actors of *Don Juan Manuel* come from the [INBA's] school [of theater]: Beatriz Aguirre, Agustín Sauret, and Mario Muratalla. Agustín Lazo came today to see me because he wanted to discuss the possibility of producing the play at *Bellas Artes*, so that more people could see it. (Novo 1967: 260–261)[3]

After this play critics considered Lazo a major playwright like Rodolfo Usigli or Villaurrutia. But the sudden death of Xavier Villaurrutia in 1950 sent Lazo into a state of despair. According to legend he never wrote or painted again. Salvador Novo summarized the situation:

> He died, slowly, twenty years later — overwhelmed by his own wealth that he was inheriting from all his relatives. He was the last descendant

of one of the most long-established and distinguished Mexican families. (1982: 8) [4]

The action of *El caso* is set in Mexico City in colonial times, when a mass murderer is killing young criollo men. The main love triangle in the drama consists of don Juan Manuel Solórzano, his wife, doña Isabel, and their nephew, Esteban Solórzano. *El caso* expresses the tension in representing a homosexual man in the patriarchal, civilian, virile, and revolutionary Mexican society at the end of the 1940s. The homosexual male is perceived as a sexual predator because of the so-called homosexual panic. Sedgwick notes that in Great Britain, where homosexuality had been made illegal again in 1885 (now from a scientific point of view, instead of the previous religious one), the popular imagination of the middle classes associated extreme violence with homosexuality (1985: 177). But the same phenomenon can be found in the Hispanic world; for instance, historian Gaspar Escolano tells of an incident that is closer in time and culture to the plot of *El caso de don Juan Manuel* than one referred to by Sedgwick, which occurred in 1611. Escolano says that during a famine in Valencia in 1519 the Franciscan preacher Luis Castellolí told the people that foreigners had brought sodomy to the city of Valencia, and this was the reason for the shortage of food. The mob found four sodomites and burned them on July 29, 1519 (in Tomás y Valiente 1990: 52–53).

Lazo staged his play in 1948. His challenge was how to reveal the epistemology of the closet (see Sedgwick 1985: 68) to the upper-class Mexican society in a manner palatable to this public. This was a society that at the time had as one of its master narratives the ideologeme of revolutionary virility. It was a commonplace of official discourse to refer to the revolutionary virility of the Mexican political system, with the obvious meaning that the regime was patriarchal and heterosexual. Because staging the closet is a very difficult task, Lazo needed some devices to help him represent what should not be represented in a patriarchal society. At the same time, the closet never ceases to reproduce itself, because outings are always partial; there is always one more person who does not know about the homosexuality of the people who are trying to live their own lives free of social pressures to conform.

The first device Lazo uses is to situate the action in the colonial period, the beginning of Western and Christian Mexico. Second, the pathological homosexual, don Juan Manuel, is a married man. He complies with one of the basic norms of heterosexual society, maintaining at least the appearance of being heterosexual. The play is very Freudian; the title says we are confronted with a "case." It should be remembered that according to Olivier Debroise: "Lazo is probably the most direct introducer of Surrealism in Mexico" (1983: 129).[5] It is a well-known fact that of all the avant-garde movements surrealism is the most influenced by Freud. The play addresses, as mentioned, a very sophisticated public familiar with modern psychological and psychiatric theories. An example in the text itself is don Juan Manuel's sword (an "actant-object" in A. J. Greimas's terminology), with an obvious phallic meaning. All the acts start with an indication of the exact position of the sword, which has a symbolic meaning that matches the development of the plot in the act. The play ends when don Juan Manuel renounces his (badly used) patriarchal phallus and gives it to his nephew so that the family surname and the masculine tradition of the clan can survive. Don Juan Manuel has to disappear because his homosexuality does not allow him to represent his role in the (at least according to Freud) "normal" Oedipal process of his nephew. Moreover, don Juan Manuel almost commits incest when he stabs/penetrates his nephew and nearly kills him. This incident is the high point of his criminal career, because the murder assault is attempted against Oedipus—it almost prevented the Oedipus process from running its course.

In the first scene don Juan Manuel has just returned home, and his wife is waiting for him. Because she can no longer stand the uncertainty of their marriage, Isabel reminds him:

> Our conjugal life never existed . . . We are not a husband and a wife. On our wedding night you suddenly left the bedroom without saying anything to me. I never tried . . . I do not try now to know what happened in your soul. It is a mystery . . . We live behind a façade, we could say . . . like two friends, because after that inexplicable night you never returned to my rooms. (Lazo 1948: 17)[6]

Theater theorists have explained that "the topic of a play [any play] is the *tension* surrounding a confrontation, not the plot of that confrontation" (Bobes 1987: 177).[7] The initial situation is a marriage that has not been consummated. This circumstance reappears in *La mulata de Córdoba* (The Mulatto Woman from Cordoba), where the reader or the spectator confronts another unconsummated marriage. It is at the core of patriarchal society that in the institution of marriage the heterosexual couple must have sexual relations to guarantee the continuation of the species and also the perpetuation of the family lineage, especially in the upper classes like those represented in the plays by Lazo. Spanish and Creole women were a scarce commodity in the first years of the colony. This is why there was very strict control over their sexuality.

Don Juan Manuel tells his wife: "[H]as comprendido que *mi desvío* era más amargo que tu decepción. . ." (you have understood that *my deviation* was more bitter than your disappointment; Lazo 1948: 19; emphasis added). She answers: "[T]us palabras son más *oscuras* que tu silencio" (your words are *darker* than your silence; 19; emphasis added). Don Juan Manuel responds: "¡Hay cosas de las que un hombre no puede hablar! (Alejándose) Hay *palabras que no se deben pronunciar*, que es preciso suplir" (There are things a man cannot talk about! [Walking away] *There are words that cannot be uttered*; it is necessary to fill them in; 22; emphasis added). He is trying unsuccessfully to explain to Isabel (and their upper-class audience) in 1948 terms how difficult is to confront his own homosexuality. Don Juan Manuel is not only a closeted character; he has not yet conceptualized the closet as a social institution. He uses key words that are commonplace nowadays and are very useful to understand later developments in gay literature. Don Juan Manuel is a homosexual character, but the author is a homosexual writer in the transition to becoming a gay writer. "Deviation" is not a word in need of further explanation, like the "*words that cannot be uttered.*" These have been well-known heterosexual labels to talk about homosexuality. It is different with *oscuro amor* (dark love) to indicate homosexual love between men and even gay love. A good example is the *Sonetos del amor oscuro* (1935–1936) by Federico García Lorca, especially the sonnet "¡Ay voz secreta del amor oscuro!" (Ay, secret voice of the dark love!; 1996: 27). In the impressive last line of the sonnet —"¡que soy amor, que soy naturaleza!" (That I am love, that I am nature) — García Lorca justifies the notion that gay love is natural.

In the play Isabel does not understand this situation very well but is conscious that she has a role to fulfill and demands a son, a logical request considering the lack of Europeans in the colony and the societal pressure to fulfill her position as a wife and mother. The discussion ends when the butler and a bailiff interrupt. They bring the body of a young man, Esteban, mortally wounded. He will survive miraculously.

With Esteban's arrival the triangle is closed. We learn eventually that the murderer is don Juan Manuel, who has the urgent need to penetrate male victims with his scalpel. Because he does not know how to channel his homosexuality, he has to kill young men. This is very pedestrian Freudianism, but let us not forget that the play is from 1948. Then don

Juan Manuel and doña Isabel confess their love for each other. This is important because it gives a heterosexual patina to the story. Everything works "well" for don Juan Manuel: he can channel his sexuality by murdering young men, and he has a loving wife waiting for him at home: the perfect alibi. But the whole system collapses when he commits "incest," the day he — without realizing it — tries to kill his brother's son. It is interesting to observe that on this occasion, for the first time, he fails. He is impotent to kill his own blood. When all the clues begin to lead to don Juan Manuel as the murderer, he calls a priest for confession. He tells the Franciscan: "Love — true love — kept me from its pleasures, but not without leaving me convinced that there was no error in me from Nature" (96).[8]

This conversation between the priest and don Juan Manuel is a psychodrama, thanks to the skillful questions asked by the priest. Don Juan Manuel starts psychoanalyzing himself, until he reaches the root of his problems. He could not deflower his wife because of the memories he had of his mother — that is, he could not avoid establishing a relationship between his mother and his wife. This is a naïve pattern, and don Juan Manuel is happy because he is convinced that he has achieved the real anagnorisis and has provided a plausible explanation for his behavior. He is a virile man, but his mother somehow castrated him. At this moment, however, the play takes a sharp turn. The priest does not buy the "logical" explanation and don Juan Manuel's tears:

> Go ahead and cry . . . From now on, your tears will run freely. Feelings will not stop them. And consider, for your own consolation, that for a long time those confusing feelings were considered nefarious. Remember the exempla made by the poets of antiquity. (105)[9]

The priest does not accept don Juan Manuel's oversimplification and diagnoses the problem (the "case") with the euphemism "poets of antiquity" (i.e., homosexuals). Don Juan Manuel accepts the priest's explanation and confesses his crimes. Once we are in the third act, don Juan Manuel's sword is very visible on a piece of furniture. In one drawer don Juan Manuel hides the handkerchiefs stained with the victims' blood. In the Hispanic tradition, blood-stained sheets are the required proof of the bride's virginity, now yielded to her husband. Likewise, the handkerchief is often associated with masturbation and sperm: the folklore motif of the young maiden and her teenaged boyfriend. The motif of the handkerchief as representative of masturbation and homoerotic sexuality is common in the work of a poet contemporary with

Lazo, Emilio Prados (1899–1962), who lived in Mexico in exile from Spain from 1939 until his death (Oropesa 1999).

After every homicide don Juan Manuel would return home, get comfortable, clean the weapon, and fall asleep contemplating the stained handkerchief. When the priest asks for the meaning of this ritual, don Juan Manuel answers unabashedly that this is what satisfied him sexually. He calls this ceremony his "tesoro" (treasure; 121); it is his fetish, which Robert J. Stoller has defined as "a story masquerading as an object" (quoted in Garber 1992: 209). This is the reason why don Juan Manuel could not consummate his marriage. He had displaced his sexuality by a monstrous behavior. Lazo portrays the homosexual as he is seen by mainstream heterosexual society, associated with extreme violence. At the same time, don Juan Manuel is presented sympathetically and shielded by his social position.

Don Juan Manuel is not punished at the end of the play. Also, as one notices in the scene of the confession, he does not consider himself guilty of a crime because his *avant la lettre* Freudianism has provided him with an explanation of his behavior and an alibi. At the end of the play he gives Esteban the final instructions:

> I need you now to keep the secret the three of us established earlier. They all think, you heard them, that I am just going for a trip; you are the only one who knows that I will never come back. (155) [10]

Don Juan Manuel then gives Esteban his sword. As he goes to put on his hat, he notices that it has an ornamental feather, which he takes off and throws away (161). His final joke is to remove the last symbol of heterosexuality he had with him. Once he has left, he can say: "[M]y house will have standards and dignity" ("mi casa guardará una norma y una dignidad"; 155), which he can not provide with his criminal homosexuality. Marjorie Garber, quoting Eugénie Lemoine-Luccioni, says that "if the penis was the phallus, men would have no need of feathers or ties or medals" (1992: 119): the penis is an organ; the phallus is a structure. This is the explanation of the feather as a symbol of heterosexuality.

Let us review the play again to compare my a posteriori analysis with one done when the play was staged. Novo reviewed the play on November 27, 1948. I intend to demonstrate that a well-educated spectator like Novo was able to appreciate the play in all its details, although it has to be noted that Novo uses humor to tone down his sharp criticism:

It was eight-thirty when I arrived at the theater in the belief that *Don Juan Manuel* by Agustín Lazo was going to start soon. But on stage we had the exams of the opera school. Señoritas in formal gowns and gentlemen in tuxedos were trilling melodic songs before a pleasing audience in front of the orchestra that Lalo Hernández Moncada was conducting. The exam had started one hour late, and the play was also late . . . *The Case of don Juan Manuel* is a Freudian play where don Juan Manuel is psychoanalyzed until he discovers the neurosis that makes him kill men at a fixed time. The gloomy shadow of the Oedipus complex is what drives him away from his wife. He sees Jocasta in her every time he tries to perpetuate the Solórzano surname. A Franciscan does the analysis, which is what really happened in Catholic countries through confession, long before medical analysis was widely available. All the Freudian symbols are in the play: a bloody handkerchief fetish that don Juan Manuel kept in a little box after each crime. This was the symbol of the unhealthy, truly sick satisfaction he got because he was not having sex with his wife. (1967: 276) [11]

Lazo chose the topic of homosexual panic and the closet in 1948. His thesis is that homosexual panic exists because the gay person is not allowed to express himself. Once he knows he is gay and accepts himself as he is,[12] he will not be a menace to society; if society represses him, however, he will be a threat to the social order.

To gain a better understanding of the dissemination of Freudian thought in society and in literature in the forties and early fifties, let us move to the next dramatic text.

La mulata de Córdoba *(The Mulatto Woman from Córdoba)*

The edition of the complete works by Xavier Villaurrutia has two versions of this play: one is an opera libretto, and the second redaction is a movie script. Agustín Lazo is given credit only in the opera version. The movie script is analyzed here. I have no proof that Lazo should receive credit for the movie script, but there is no evidence to the contrary except for the omission of his name as co-author. There are plot developments in *La mulata* that are similar to *El caso de don Juan Manuel;* and Lazo and Villaurrutia always worked together when they adapted and translated plays, which is the main reason for my speculation here. One possibility is that Villaurrutia was unionized; therefore, only his name could appear in the credits. Novo's entry of December 5, 1945, does not confirm my hypothesis. It says that Xavier Villaurrutia is dedicated exclusively to the movies: he had two in the movie theaters (*La mujer legítima* and *La casa de la zorra*), and *La mulata de Córdoba* was forthcoming (1965: 438).

Frank Dauster's seminal analysis of Villaurrutia (1971) is a good starting point to analyze *La mulata*. Dauster very kindly explained in a letter to me that the Mexicanists who worked with members of the Contemporáneos group while they were alive had a gentlemen's pact with the writers not to write about homosexuality in their criticism. This may explain many heterosexual readings of texts that had gay overtones. About *La mulata* Dauster says:

> The basic story is that of a woman in league with the Devil, who destroys the families which have rejected her by enslaving the men, father and son, and forcing the latter to abandon his bride. (1971: 110)

Our reading is going to be different than Dauster's because instead of concentrating on the evil woman of the *Doña Bárbara* or *La vorágine* tradition we are going to pay more attention to the men of the play and how they interact with each other. One of the male protagonists is don Juan Reyes, who is a don Juan and a *rey* (king) and patriarch of his dynasty. The object of his affection is the mulatto woman, Sara:

> Her servants, trembling, call her "La Niña Sara." She inherited wealth from her deceased father. Regarding her mother, who is never mentioned at her house, it is known she was a black woman. Her father belonged to the San Juan family. He was don Carlos's brother, one of the richest men in Rincón Brujo. Don Juan Reyes later bought from him the sugar mill and the sugar refinery. Sara's father died two years ago. Sara is the product of Luis San Juan's sensuality. One night, when he was drunk, he ordered that he be sent a black woman, a sensual woman, because he wanted to have a son with her. That son turned out to be a daughter: Sara. Nobody in Rincón Brujo likes her. Nobody receives her. Sara, proudly, challenges this situation. She is bitter, even if she is made of honey and the intoxicating liquor made from sugarcane. She has promised revenge on the San Juans, because they do not recognize her as their relative, and also on the inhabitants of Rincón Brujo, who despise her . . . The antecedents of this *drama of love and mystery* are old, but they are going to crystallize now, in 1910. (1991: 192; emphasis added) [13]

Sara's characteristics are archetypal: she is doubly "natural," first, because she is a woman; second, because she is black. Both don Carlos and the anonymous black woman share the same sensuality. At the same time, Sara's *illegitimacy* is double; because she is not considered part of the clan of the San Juans and also for an unexpected reason: because she is a woman. Carlos's brother, for unknown reasons (besides the patriarchal), wanted to have a mulatto son.

The plot of the script moves to the day of the wedding between Emilia San Juan and Pedro Reyes. They are rich and Creole; most importantly, their marriage is going to bring back to the San Juans the fortune that is now in the hands of the Reyes family. According to don Carlos, the Reyes are no more than *advenedizos* (social climbers; 197). The San Juans represent the Creole aristocracy of the Porfiriato and the Reyes the new money, the new bourgeoisie that is going to triumph with the Revolution. At the wedding party the uninvited Sara shows up. Although don Juan and don Pedro move quickly to expel her from the party, it is the bridegroom, Pedro, who walks her home. Later we learn that after a fortnight the marriage has not been consummated. Pedro has been absent from his house for eight years; when he returns, the presence of his father, stirring up his Oedipus complex, prevents him from fulfilling his duties as a businessman and as a husband. He accepts marrying Emilia, but this does not help to solve his real problem: how to relate to his father. At last, he can resolve his manhood problem when he makes Sara his lover. He soon finds out, however, that his father had also been Sara's lover.

According to Gilles Deleuze and Felix Guattari (1977), the Oedipus process is at the center of Western civilization because it is the unifying element in the nuclear family, the base of modern capitalism. Jane Gallop summarizes this process:

> In the oedipal moment the boy gives up possession of the mother and gains identification with the father. According to a structuralist, Lacanian reading, the boy loses the imaginary dyadic relation and is inserted into the symbolic order, into the circuits of exchange which constitute (male) society. Lacan's symbolic order is based upon Lévi-Strauss' understanding of the incest taboo which exposes the supposedly heterosexual institution of marriage as actually an exchange for the purpose of creating and strengthening bonds between men. (1988: 33)

> The Oedipus is good: one loses the mother but gains entry into the world, into the exchange between men. (1988: 34)

> Men exchange women for heterosexual purposes, but the real intercourse is that exchange between men. The heterosexual object is irre-

trievably lost in the circuits, and the man is consoled by the homology, the temptation of the analogy points to the homosexual, the anal. (1988: 37)

Whereas the homosocial is the realm identified with the father, the realm of power, the homosexual is associated not with power but with humiliation. Identification with the father equals patriarchal power; desire for the father equals castration, humiliation . . . Exposing the homosexual desire hidden behind the homological identification may operate in the psychosexual realm like exposing the class exploitation hidden beneath the ideology of equality and democracy. (1988: 38)

Let us add one more quotation, by Marina Pérez de Mendiola:

It is not much the idea of same-sex desire that Mexican culture questions. It is the idea that men could actually degrade themselves by acknowledging femininity within their homosexuality, forcing them to cross the boundaries between genders and collapse gender divisions. (1996: 197)

I do not expect the reader to take Gallop's words at face value. What interests me is not the question of their validity but rather what is shared by Lazo, Villaurrutia, and Gallop: the belief that the homosocial relations among men can sometimes have homosexual overtones and that at times heterosexuality and homosexuality are indistinguishable. For instance, an interesting secondary character named "El Cuadrado" should be analyzed; he is the administrator of the house and bodyguard of the family: "In the patio, Cuadrado, administrator of the house, strong and grossly sensual, gives orders in the name of the master" (198).[14]

It is interesting to note that for the author the strong orders given by Cuadrado are gross but at the same time sensual. In the key scene when Sara arrives at the wedding party he is the first person to confront her:

CUADRADO: No, I will not let you in. The master would never forgive me for it. (A wave of gross sensuality reaches his head, like the alcohol he has been drinking) . . . No, Sara. You will not enter. (Getting close to her, confidentially.) You'd better come with us, with me, outside, under the trees . . . (201)[15]

Cuadrado experiences a Freudian slip when in the same sentence he says "come with us" and then says "with me." He first has the idea of sharing her with other men (one single man?) in what will be a bisexual relationship where part of the pleasure will derive from seeing other men making love to her. But Sara cannot have relations with Cuadrado because her function in the play is to be the go-between for the father and the son; thus Cuadrado cannot create a new triangle that could put him in a relationship with the son. The author of the play has mentioned the gross sensuality of Cuadrado twice; obviously, the beauty of the character shocks him. Later in the script we find Cuadrado again. He is drunk, which is a literary convention to indicate that he is a reliable narrator at this point; the alcohol is making him tell the truth (only children and drunkards tell the truth). By the way, Cuadrado is at the billiard parlor, where gay men go to see the poses of handsome straight men. He is telling the other men what happened on the wedding night.

> CUADRADO.—What you do not know is that the same night [of the wedding], Pedro spent it getting drunk with us, with me. He did not go to see Emilia. And for one reason or another, it has been the same since then . . . (208) [16]

What are these reasons? Why again the same mistake between "with us" and "with me"? Filling in the gaps in the plot, it is implied that Pedro makes love to Sara; then he finds out she has been his father's lover. After this he does not feel the need to consummate his marriage with Emilia, since both Emilia and Sara are San Juans. Putting Oedipus at the center of the plot, Lazo and Villaurrutia can play with the blurred border between the socially permitted homosocial and the homosexual taboo. The end of the drama is significant. Sara flees the town, breaking the triangle and letting the Oedipus process work, putting together father and son. It should also be noted that Sara is not the only woman who disappears, because both Pedro's and Juan's wives disappear from the plot. In the case of Emilia, as in the previous play, the bridegroom cannot consummate the marriage. The end of the play is as follows: "Veremos a Pedro y a don Juan, mudos, erguidos, con las armas dispuestas, avanzar enérgica, pausadamente, sin ocultarse del posible enemigo invisible" (We will see Pedro and don Juan, mute, standing, with weapons ready, advance, energetically, slowly, without hiding from the invisible enemy; 226). Pedro and don Juan, speechless, walk with their erect phalluses to confront the invisible enemy: homosexuality? They reach the house, which is now empty, so that they can find each other, where they both made love to the same woman. And, of course, "entran en la casa a cuyas puertas se queda, vigilante, el 'Cuadrado' " (they enter the house, and at the door stands Cuadrado, vigilantly; 226).

Segundo imperio *(Second Empire)*

Segundo imperio is one of the forgotten plays in the history of Mexican theater because there is a more popular play with the same subject and written at the same time, *Corona de sombra* by Rodolfo Usigli.[17] Usigli wrote the play in 1943 during the presidency of Manuel Avila Camacho, and the drama was first staged on April 11, 1947, during the presidency of Miguel Alemán Valdés (Beardsell 1992: 167). Lazo wrote *Segundo imperio* in 1945 and published it in 1946.[18] It seems very probable that Lazo had the opportunity to read *Corona de sombra*.

Segundo imperio is a very fine drama in five acts, as good as Usigli's. It is an expensive play to produce, although more easily produced than Usigli's and not as expensive as *Corona de sombra*. *Segundo* is a didactic play to teach the public, the bourgeoisie of the Alemán Valdés presidency, about a part of their past that they may ignore or know in a distorted way. Maximiliano and Carlota's story had been incorporated into Mexican historiography, but always considering Benito Juárez at the center of nineteenth-century Mexico. Porfirio Díaz had been set on popularizing Juárez as the true founding father of Mexico. For instance, during this period Emperor Agustín de Iturbide was "demoted" by historians as one of the founding fathers of Mexico, in favor of more republican figures.

Segundo imperio's first act is perfect and beautiful; the action takes place on the deck of the *Novara*, the ship that is taking the emperor and empress to Mexico, at the crucial moment when they are crossing the Strait of Gibraltar. Because everyone knows the outcome, it is very dramatic: the audience is aware that Emperor Maximiliano is seeing Europe for the last time in his life. This helps to construct the dramatic tension already mentioned at the beginning of this chapter. The set is green; because the sunset is approaching, it soon slowly turns to gold. Carlota is beautifully dressed in gray pearl, and Maximiliano wears his uniform as admiral of the Austrian Navy. A play of customs is still fascinating for the bourgeoisie, as the success of the movie *Titanic* (1998) shows so well. The British tradition epitomized by James Ivory movies or the adaptations of Jane Austen's novels has influenced the whole world. In the case of Mexico we have *telenovelas históricas*, from the first *Los caudillos* series to more recent ones like *La antorcha encendida* and *La Constitución*. Ernesto Alonso, the father of Mexican historical soap operas, worked in his youth with Novo, Usigli, and Villaurrutia.

The audience knows the end of *Segundo imperio;* so what is important is how the story is told, how the tension is developed and revealed. This first act, visually beautiful, is also full of historical information that will feed the audience the necessary background to understand the historical process. We learn that Great Britain's attitude about the imperial experiment in Mexico is lukewarm. We also discover that the most important contradiction of the imperial experiment is that the Conservative Party supports the emperor, despite the fact that Maximiliano is a liberal. The emperor and empress are also conscious that they have been chosen by Napoleon III and Pious IX, their sponsors, as a means to try to resolve their disputes in Mexico, although Napoleon and the pope are not sure if this will be the solution. The emperor's ignorance about the Mexican people and the frivolity of the enterprise are also made evident. A reference is made to the United States as the referee in everything concerned with the Americas.

In spite of all the information communicated in this act, it is not verbose but rather the opposite. It is fast, interesting, and very beautiful to watch (read). What is more, Maximiliano makes reference to the theatricality of power and the court, which imparts metatheatricality to the play because it is also teaching the spectator about the important role that representation plays in politics. The act finishes as a sailor explains to one of the ladies how vultures (*zopilotes*) devour their victims, a clear prolepsis of what is going to happen in the rest of the play.

Act 2 is a succession of intelligent conversations at Chapultepec Palace in Mexico City. The spectator understands the precarious situation of the monarchy, its lack of popular support, the strength of President Juárez, and the fact that the European advisors are at the service of their masters instead of being at the service of the Mexican monarchs. The act concludes with the decision to name as heir of the Mexican Empire the grandson of Emperor Iturbide. This is important and helps to explain the title of the play, *Second Empire*, because it reminds the spectator/reader of the first empire of Iturbide. Iturbide, as stated earlier, is the forgotten father of Mexican independence, for reasons that are not difficult to understand. Independence is based on the Creole elites' fear of the consequences of the Spanish liberal constitution of 1812, and Iturbide is the quintessential Creole. Maximiliano represents the last attempt by the Creole conservative Mexican party to hold power. President Benito Juárez (a Zapotec Indian) and President Porfirio Díaz (Mixtec-blood mestizo) were not Creole; but they did not institute the mestizo as national character, something that did not happen until the Revolution.

The third act is the most political part of the play and explains the problem of the liberal monarchy that accepted the Reform laws (authored by Juárez) and that was unable to sign a concordat with the Vatican (Krauze 1994: 249–274). The conversation between Carlota and the pope's ambassador is at the core of the act and the play. Fernando Ramírez, secretary of foreign affairs, says:

> The arrival of those generals [Miramón and Márquez] would increase the animosity between the social class to which Minister Lares refers and the middle class, the mestizo race Your Majesties want to bring to the [imperial] cause. (66) [19]

This is the main topic of the play, the transition from the *ancien régime* to the new one, from the Creole elite to the new middle class first of the Reforma and later of the Revolution. It is also the change from white European groups to mestizo culture, an opportunity to remind the audience watching *Segundo imperio*—the elite of the new Alemán Valdés presidency, the first civilian president since the Revolution—where they came from. The fourth act is also superb; the action is in a small boudoir by the Chapultepec Palace Ballroom at the moment before the final crisis of the empire, when the French troops abandon Mexico and the emperor and empress cannot stop the republican offensive. The ladies are dressed in their elegant gowns and the gentlemen in their spotless uniforms. This act features the youthful and authentically Mexican Creole beauty of María José, the Mexican bride of General Achille-François Bazaine, commander-in-chief of the French troops in Mexico. It is the act in which the fate of the empire is sealed, but it is also when the theatricality of power is at its peak. When there is an attack on the castle/palace, the monarchs keep their poise. The act ends with María José, Bazaine, and the emperor and empress entering the ballroom to start a special dance.

The fifth and final act closes the drama very well. The action takes place in a room in the port-city of Veracruz. The assistants work until the very last moment to try to give an imperial elegance to the room; but everything is half done, and the result is a disaster. The juxtaposition of sumptuous objects and ordinary things forms a peculiar disorder that epitomizes what the empire has been. At this time we have the first glimpse of Carlota's madness; we understand the futility of her trip to Europe and know that she is never going to return to Mexico.

It is sad that this play has been overshadowed by Usigli's *Corona de sombra,* because as in Usigli's play the blend between the micro-history of the protagonists and the history of Mexico is perfectly achieved.

La huella *(The Trace, 1946)*

La huella is the logical step after *Segundo imperio,* because it studies Mexican society after the Reforma process and the dictatorship of Porfirio Díaz. According to the brief bio-bibliography in the edition of *La huella,* this play was written at the beginning of 1946, a few months after *Segundo imperio.* If *Segundo imperio* portrays the crisis of Creole society, *La huella* represents the problems of mestizo society as it configures itself as the authentic Mexican society. The political background of the play is the Revolution of 1910; the setting (as stated on the cover of the book) is "En una vieja hacienda de la Altiplanicie Mexicana, hacia 1910" (In an old hacienda in the Mexican highlands, circa 1910); the hacienda is presented as a synecdoche of Mexico. The Revolution is accepted as necessary because Mexican society has reached a dead end in a number of personal and social situations that can only be overcome by radical changes in social paradigms.

The play is the story of two relationships; at the core of both is Guadalupe, an unmarried Creole traditional and old-fashioned woman who is a second synecdoche of Mexico. She is the object of desire of two very different men who want to create the new, modern Mexico. Guadalupe is the last generation of a Mexico that is fading and cannot survive. For these reasons she is single, and she has to die. She represents a Mexican fantasy that the Revolution is going to demystify: that of a true Mexican aristocracy, the gilded era when the masters were kind to their servants and everybody lived happily in the peace and harmony of the hacienda (a myth very similar to that of *Gone with the Wind*). Lazo is very subtle in his deconstruction of this myth. The landlady is a widow, señora Laura. To have this version of a *pax mexicana,* a matriarch is needed. Everything has been perfect until the beginning of the play, when bandits destroy this fictitious tranquillity by assaulting the *raya* of the hacienda (the payroll).

The antagonist to doña Laura and first suitor of Guadalupe/Mexico is Ernesto Arvide, a 52-year-old *gachupín,* a Spaniard born in 1858 at a moment when the Old Regime was collapsing in Spain. It has already been mentioned that one harsh reality of Mexican independence is that it was an attempt by the Creole elite to bypass the liberal constitution of 1812 and maintain the status quo of the *ancien régime.* There was a slow but inexorable process in both countries toward the triumph of the middle class, which culminated in the Revolution in Mexico and the Restoration in Spain.

Spain: The Motherland

In my own research regarding the presence of Spain in the prerevolutionary period in Mexico, I studied the case of one of the paradigmatic novels in Mexican literature, *Santa* (1903) by Federico Gamboa. The first principle of my own study of *Santa* is that the character Santa is a synecdoche of Mexico. This reading coincided with those made by Ana María Alvarado (1980: 57), Rosa Bernardina Fernández in her dissertation (1989: 86), and also John Brushwood (1966), who provided a good summary of this position. The so-called golden age of the haciendas had been the time of the *dictablanda* (the soft, liberal dictatorship) part of Porfirio Díaz's dictatorship. It is not by chance that the play starts with a reference to trains and the railway that crosses the hacienda. During Díaz's tenure Mexico went from 638 kms of railways in 1876 to 19,280 kms in 1910 (Krauze 1994: 309). But by 1900 the country had entered into an economic crisis that brought inflation, a reduction in salaries, and a more repressive government. Díaz always tried to impose consensus policies and to give something to the different groups, but the beginning of more organized opposition parties against the regime brought the abrupt change from the so-called *dictablanda* to the *dictadura*, the hard dictatorship (cf. Katz 1992).

History books explain the foreign affairs of the Díaz period as an attempt to guarantee Mexico's independence from the United States. In order to neutralize the neo-colonial policies of the Republican administrations of presidents William McKinley (1897–1901) and Theodore Roosevelt (1901–1909), Mexico tried to expand its relationships with Germany and Great Britain. The cultural model, in spite of the wars against it during the nineteenth century, was still France. It is surprising, then, that Gamboa does not contrast Mexico with France or other European countries that according to the history books were the governments with strong investment potential in Mexico. Instead, *Santa* represents Mexico in relationship to Spain. Joaquina Navarro has noted that in Gamboa's novels the only foreign character is the Spaniard (1955: 290) and that there is a lack of Mexican and indigenous vocabulary in all his literary works (1955: 301), not just *Santa*. What is more, the first edition of *Santa* appeared in Barcelona.

These traits are very similar in *La huella;* Guadalupe's fiancée is a Spaniard, Ernesto Arvide. We learn that Guadalupe, now forty, broke her engagement a few days before the wedding and did not give an explanation to her relatives as to why she made that drastic decision. But what is interesting is that both texts make Spanish immigrants an important presence in Mexico. History books have the tendency not to register this because they are written in macroeconomic terms. They only explain the existence of foreign monopolies and trusts in Mexico. One of the reasons why the Spanish influence is not detected is because many Spaniards ended up establishing themselves in Mexico, becoming Mexicanized, like Ernesto in *La huella.* They became Mexicans in a process very similar to that of Jewish immigrants, creating communities of mutual support and filling gaps in commerce and manufacture. The second reason is that the Porfiriato in general did not regard Spain very highly. For example, this testimony is given by Jonathan Kandell:

> The new aristocrats [of the Porfiriato] were masters in their own
> nation, and had a government of which they could be proud . . . They
> disdained the heritage of Spain — a country viewed as being in utter
> decline, politically and economically weak, all too immersed in a rigid
> Roman Catholicism. (1990: 372)

Enrique Krauze (1994: 295–296) has noted that one of the main characteristics of Porfirio Díaz's ideology was to consider the centuries before independence irrelevant.

Pilar Cagiao in 1992 studied the presence of Spain in Mexico. In 1875, before the Porfiriato, immigration laws were implemented to attract European immigrants to Mexico. In spite of the efforts of the Mexican state, the country was left out of the massive immigration currents. Mexico never had the same numbers of immigrants from European countries as did the United States, Argentina, Chile, Uruguay, Brazil, and Cuba. According to the 1900 census there were only 15,000 Spaniards in Mexico, although the numbers should be higher because deserters from the Spanish army did not register in the consular census. Cagiao says:

> According to the investigation by V. González Loscertales (1976)
> regarding agriculture in Mexico between 1882 and 1911, Spaniards,
> dispersed throughout the country, ended up owning 27 percent of the
> arable land in Mexico. They also practically monopolized some indus-
> trial sectors (especially in clothing and foods). They had an important
> presence in commerce and had control of some of the most important

banks. Together, in this period they were the most influential foreign group in Mexico . . . In Mexico City, as in cities in other states within the country, the Spanish practically dominated the *abarrotes* stores [foodstuffs and other general items]. They imported from Spain oil, canned food, and wines. The *abarrotes* sometimes doubled as pawnshops. According to M. T. Jarquín . . . the storeowners included "modest storekeepers to large-scale businessmen." The movement of capital allowed these merchants to make investments in other sectors. The social mobility of this group was sometimes very high; they helped other Spaniards to establish themselves in Mexico and they formed a closed group, which allowed them to gain experience and to earn capital. (1992: 307) [20]

In Mexico City Spaniards dominated the cotton and wool clothing industries, tobacco, matches, tiles, and iron beds.

La huella is subtitled "Drama romántico" because a love story is used to reveal a social conflict, which is a standard procedure in today's cinema and literature. As mentioned above, Ernesto Arvide is a *gachupín*. We first hear about him through Remedios and Señora Laura, Guadalupe's sister and mother, respectively:

REMEDIOS. — My sister declared that she wouldn't marry because she had made a mistake.

SRA. LAURA. — Absurd words! . . . We know Guadalupe loved Ernesto. Nobody influenced her to respond to his prolonged attention.

REMEDIOS. — No indeed, we all agree, until the day she unexpectedly changed her mind my sister looked like she was in love. And no one can say that other factors influenced her, because from the social point of view her marriage was not brilliant. Ernesto was not yet the well-to-do man he became later.

SRA. LAURA. — He was only one of many entrepreneurial foreigners who just came to the country. Neither his name, nor his position . . .

REMEDIOS. — Corresponded to our name and position? . . . Of course not. But Guadalupe said when she made the decision to accept him that he was a decent man . . . (7) [21]

In *Santa*, where we find an archetypal melodramatic/romantic scenario in which a love story is used to relate more complex social problems, the central love story is between Santa and Jarameño, the Spanish bullfighter. Santa falls in love with the Spaniard precisely because he is a Spaniard and can provide her with a public life to which she aspires. Jarameño falls in love with her because she is desired by the high-class society of Mexico City. Before being famous and rich, Jaramillo was poor. This is a perfect combination for disaster, because they both are trying to find in the other what they lack and are never going to have. In *Huella* we have a similar scenario: the Creole decent Mexican woman falls in love with a Spaniard, a social climber, because he represents mobility, dynamism, and modernity. She, in contrast, is static. My hypothesis is that these factors play an equal role in attracting Guadalupe's attention. Guadalupe realizes that the status quo is not valid anymore, the Porfiriato is dead, and something new will have to replace it. Her first attempt fails; Ernesto is not the model needed for the new Mexico of the twentieth century. The answer may come from considering Ernesto more closely. Who is Ernesto? What is the appropiate model for modern Mexico?

The stage directions say:

> The landlord of the Satueña hacienda is almost fifty, and he does not look bad. Nothing should call attention to his appearance, except that he dresses too elegantly to be in the countryside. His moustache is too dyed. He also keeps remnants of a foreign accent in which the s sound is too stressed. (46)

> GUADALUPE.—You [Ernesto] have bought land and more land, all the available land and that which was not available. Your land on the plateau spread like oil. Your paths reach the border of the desert, waiting to extend their tentacles everywhere, haciendas, ranches, the nearby *ejidos*. Everywhere there is land to grasp, sorry, I should say, buy. The more your hacienda grows, the more hatred is spread. The hatred of those robbed, oppressed, exploited. Because you not only grab the land but the people living on it . . . Little by little hatred is entering your golden hacienda, and it is threatening to drown us all. It is the hatred that grows every day, cheating, racketeering, stealing. You are a bird of prey incubating hidden, anonymous hatred that does not distinguish between guilty and innocent. (53)[22]

Guadalupe's position is complicated. When she first decided to marry Ernesto she was infatuated by the possibility of change. Ernesto was the person who could modernize the semifeudal, anachronistic institution of the hacienda. But what she wanted was *decency*. Let us not forget Remedios's statement: "Guadalupe said when she made the decision to accept him that he was a decent man . . ." Decency is the modern, nineteenth-century, middle-class concept that replaced the Old Regime's concept of honor, and it brought a great change to the structure of the family. The feudal, patriarchal family changed profoundly. The new goal was domesticity, but the situation of exploitation did not change. Benito Pérez Galdós in *Tormento* (1884) defined decency perfectly:

> Let's say it clearly. Amparito did not have ambition for luxury but for decency. She aspired to a life with order, comfort, and without ostentation. (1979: 130)

> This is why Amparito aspired to family and marriage and wanted her home firmly based on moral laws. Religion, as an element of order, also seduced her. (1979: 131)[23]

Stephanie Coontz has described a more accurate picture of the decent family:

> For every nineteenth-century middle-class family that protected its wife and child within the family circle, then, there was an Irish or a German girl scrubbing floors in the middle-class home, a Welsh boy mining coal to keep the home-baked goods warm, a black girl doing the family laundry, a black mother and child picking cotton to be made into clothes for the family, and a Jewish or Italian daughter in a sweatshop making "ladies" dresses. (1992: 11–12)

Of course, Coontz is referrring to the United States; but if we change the terms "Jewish," "German," and "black" to "Indian," the situation is very similar. The idea is to leave the feudal structure of the hacienda, where there is a family (in the Roman sense of the term) tie between the servant and the master, to change it to a more capitalist system where the relationship is that of salary. Again, this has been an unending transition in Western civilization, and the reader can return to *La Celestina* to see the feudal and the protocapitalist systems fighting against each other. What decency does — establishing as a limit the invisible ceiling of excess — is to hide the exploitation. The function of honor was to naturalize a system of inequality based on the substantialism of blood; in modern terms, decency naturalizes the exploitation process of modern capitalism. What Ernesto is doing — monopolistic capitalism — is totally unacceptable, and Guadalupe rejects this possibility for her and for Mexico. She only wanted Ernesto while he could be the true representative of the Spanish, Victorian (Isabelina/Alfonsina), massive middle class as depicted in the novels of Pérez Galdós.

The Mestizo Identity

Once the Ernesto model is rejected, the new alternative is more daring. The stage directions say:

> Luis is a dark-skinned young mestizo, with very black and straight hair. He is wearing black, tight, woolen trousers without buttons. He also wears a chamois jacket and a wide felt hat, which is right now in his hand. (15) [24]

In the description of the character at the beginning of the play we are told that Luis is twenty-four years old. He is a foreman (*mayordomo*) at the hacienda. In act 2 the moment of anagnosiris occurs when Guadalupe and Luis realize they are in love with each other:

> LUIS. — It is reality, it must be reality. We were looking at each other without knowing each other, among silent things. We looked at each other until that day when, not knowing how, . . . we discovered in each other the same feeling about life. I was alone. Who was I? Where was I headed? What was I looking for? . . . My life through the paths, on stone blocks, among magueys, among the people of my own race, was just a huge, unsuspected loneliness. People, sun, land; what I thought I loved and understood was just an illusion, created by my own solitude to help me live. This is reality, this love that soothes, that fills, the loneliness I experienced. (31) [25]

As in *Santa,* both lovers are looking in the other for what they lack. Guadalupe says, "I belong to a past age" ("pertenezco a una época pasada"). Luis Madrid (let us pay attention to his last name because it stresses his mestizo condition) could provide Guadalupe with youth and "Mexicanness." Guadalupe could give Luis class and legitimacy. But, again, the union is not going to be possible.

> GUADALUPE [talking to Remedios]. — The night you saw me with my arms around him, I was not asking anything, that night on which I stopped with my white veil the blood coming from his forehead; that same night I gave myself to him, I was all his. Our union, because it was hopeless, was complete. (61) [26]

Because of the class difference between the lovers their relationship is impossible; this is why the Revolution is necessary, because it is the only solution for the country. The power of the old aristocracy had to be destroyed; the power based on race had to disappear. Thus the lovers have to die at the end of the play, to deconstruct the social paradigms that make their love relationship impossible. They shut themselves in the old playhouse by the big house of the hacienda, burning the house and themselves with it. It is interesting that this ending is very similar to the ending of a contemporary novel that has captivated the imagination of Mexicans and people all over the world, Laura Esquivel's *Como agua para chocolate* (1989). In this novel Tita burns herself and the body of her lover Pedro, who has just died, and with the fire she destroys the hacienda. After their destruction it becomes a place of wealth. Literary critics were puzzled by this end where love did not triumph, but what is important is the destruction of the hacienda in order to create a new Mexico. Tita and Pedro are products of the hacienda system; this is why they cannot create the new Mexico. I do not know if Esquivel had read *La huella;* but if so she did an excellent reading of the play, incorporating the burning of the lovers and the hacienda as a symbol of the sterility of the hacienda system and its end as the basic social structure of the country.

5 Guadalupe Marín
The Madwoman in the Murals

Introduction

Guadalupe Marín is one of the most fascinating women of twentieth-century Mexico. She is most famous because she was Diego Rivera's first or second wife (depending on whether we include Angelina Beloff) and by far his most important muse. After her Catholic marriage to Rivera (they never had a civil, legal marriage in Mexico), she wed Jorge Cuesta, a writer of the Contemporáneos group and one of the most complex personalities in Mexican artistic circles. Marín was more than anything else a celebrity (see Chapter 6). When she decided to publish two novels, no one took her seriously. She was Lupe, the scandalous woman with the beautiful body; but she was not an intellectual and could not be considered a serious writer. The fact that her first book contained autobiographical material helped neither her reputation nor her book's reception. The "decent" society of Mexico thought it was in bad taste. She had never been a high-class lady, and her books corroborated this idea.

In her article "Rosario Castellanos: 'Ashes without a Face' " (1992), Debra Castillo says: "Let me begin with what is only a slightly hyperbolic statement: Latin American women do not write autobiography" (242). Lacking an autobiographical tradition, Marín resorted to the form of the novel to tell her version of a series of events which were mainly personal, although most of them had taken place in the public domain. From her perspective, we can better understand the development of the meaning of the Mexican patriarchy at the end of the *caudillo* period and the transition from Lázaro Cárdenas to Alemán Valdés, as the radicalism and rhetoric of the Mexican Revolution were diminishing and leaning toward a *pax* of the bourgeoisie. Sylvia Molloy writes:

> One might say that, whereas there are and have been a good many autobiographies written in Spanish America, they have not always been read autobiographically . . . filtered through the dominant discourse of the day, they have been hailed either as history or as fiction, and rarely considered as occupying a space of their own. (1991: 2)

This becomes an interesting statement once we begin the analysis of Guadalupe Marín's *La única* (1938), because although it is a novel with significant autobiographical elements, in the end it has to be considered fictional. Marín neither dared nor knew how to write an autobiographical account about the part of her life that she felt had to be told. When a literary or artistic tradition does not exist, it is very difficult to be the first to create one. Frida Kahlo's diary provides another good example of the difficulties Mexican women encountered when writing their autobiographies. Many people were disappointed when they first read Kahlo's journal, which was not available until forty years after her death. They expected juicy gossip, lesbian affairs, and scandalous relationships but were instead confronted with pain, anguish, loneliness, scarce glimpses of happiness, and very few names. Kahlo became Diego Rivera's wife after he divorced Guadalupe Marín. Evidently, Rivera was the seminal inspiration of female discourse. Beloff also wrote an autobiographical account about her years with Rivera (*Memorias*), a story that is also told by Elena Poniatowska in *Querido Diego, te abraza Quiela* (1987). The last chapter of this saga is *Diego el Rojo* (1997) by Guadalupe Rivera Marín, daughter of Rivera and Marín.

When Guadalupe Marín entered the literary world in 1938, she was already a very famous and controversial woman, especially after her separation from Rivera in 1929. Later she married and then divorced the Contemporáneos poet Jorge Cuesta. At that time divorce was legal in Mexico but still carried a stigma for the divorced woman. Cuesta's suicide did not help Marín's cause. José Agustín writes: "Jorge Cuesta died in 1942, and his horrific death still terrifies the reader. The maestro emasculated himself, after having made sexual advances toward his sister (according to Elías Nandino)" (1990: 1:28).[1] *La única* deals with this issue of incest, among other controversial topics.

Lupe Marín's presence was a must at many upper-class parties in Mexico City, particularly in artistic circles. She hosted *tertulias* at the beginning of the Contemporáneos movement, when the members found themselves low on money and at the periphery of Mexican culture. Furthermore, Marín never ended her relationship with Diego Rivera, because he was her two daughters' father and main provider. She oscillated between friendship and animosity with Frida Kahlo. But Marín was famous because her naked body was in some of the most important Rivera frescoes.

My thesis is that Lupe Marín decided to write her autobiographical novels in order to give her version, because her life and her body were being painted, photographed, reproduced, told, and represented by others. She felt compelled to add her own voice to that choir of voices.

The section on *La única* examines the idea (shared by Bertram Wolfe, Salvador Novo, and Edna Coll) that Marín's novels are situated between fiction and autobiography, neither being satisfactory. This coincides with Molloy's hypothesis concerning the difficulty Latin American readers have in accepting a hybrid genre, halfway between nonfiction and fiction. I have to agree, for example, that of all Poniatowska's novels I find *Tinísima* (1992) the most disturbing, because her account of the life of Tina Modotti is neither a novel nor a biography.

Wolfe, Novo, and Coll disliked Marín's subjectivity.[2] Using fiction, Marín did not claim for herself the category of textual truths, while at the same time her texts denied the privilege of truth to other accounts. For instance, in light of Marín, Wolfe's authorized biographies of Diego Rivera are exposed as heavily edited, and the same can be said of Novo's witty articles about Mexican social life. It is the roughness, the (edited) sensation of spontaneity in Marín's books, that deconstructs the truisms of her contemporaries.

Visions of Lupe

Wolfe says that Marín wrote her books because she wanted to give her version of the story, a fairly obvious statement. But before moving to what Marín said, we have to visit the cultural construction "Lupe," the collage of diverse texts that ended up being the Lupe Marín we all know. Only with the knowledge of how she was represented by others can we see how those visions contrast with her own story. Wolfe describes her in the following manner:

> The model [Guadalupe] obsessed him [Diego Rivera], was to obsess him for years, as the incarnation of exuberant feminine form . . . She continued to haunt his vision, reappear in his frescoes, serve for portraits and sketches, model most of his nudes, inspire the best and stron-

gest of his feminine figures . . . Guadalupe Marín, when Diego met her, was the wildest and most tempestuous beauty in Jalisco. (1963: 182–183)

Long of limb and tall of body, graceful and supple as a sapling . . . hair black, wild, unkempt, curly . . . dark olive skin, light pea-green eyes . . . high forehead and nose of a Phidian statue, full lips ever parted by eager breath and by lively, disorderly, and scandalous chatter . . . a body so slender as to suggest a youth rather than a woman — such was Lupe when Diego met her. Part of her beauty lay in her wildness . . . wayward of thought and speech and action . . . primitive as an animal in her desires and her readiness to scratch, bite, and slash to attain them . . . clever, spontaneous, untutored, cunning with animal cunning . . . as absorbed in herself as a spoiled kitten, with the same toleration of those who serve and pet and feed her, the same aloofness . . . the same claws too, hidden in deceptive softness . . . capable of giving blow for blow in her bouts with her mammoth husband, making up for what she lacked in physical strength by the long nursing of her wrath and the wild tongue . . . capable of slashing his sketches and fresh-painted canvases before his eyes as an act of vengeance . . . threatening once to shoot his right arm off so that he might never do another painting — a hell-cat when aroused, a graceful, splendid, purring, feline creature when contented. (1963: 184)

Wolfe has observed that Rivera never painted Angelina Beloff or Frida Kahlo in the nude (1963: 251).

This is Marín's portrait in Poniatowka's *Tinísima*:

Lupe sang corridos and ballads. Diego really loved her *Borrachita me voy, El quelite,* and *La barca de oro.* Concha Michel accompanied her. Tina Modotti did the same. Even Antonieta Rivas Mercado, with her wide hat covering her face, in the latest fashion from Paris, parted her thin lips to follow them. The most astonishing of them all was the panther. Her black hair was tied back in vain, because her strong curls escaped, like a mane in the four winds. Lupe was a formidable character. Her long, crossed legs extended in front of her, revealing her shapely and noble thighs; her big hands with her nails all in red, placed on her knees; her head thrown back; her proud chest always with a necklace of jade and silver and a pre-Columbian rattle. Diego admired her, stared at her full mouth, her moving lips, her big white teeth. She was his girl, breathtaking all in red, with golden scallop trim and big, tinkling earrings. (1987: 155)

Modotti remembered Dr. Atl's definition: "Lupe is a fury born before the Flood" (174).[3] Frida Kahlo called Marín "the eternal bomb" (1995b: 118).

Louis Panabière, who has written the most complete biography of Jorge Cuesta, adopts a very hostile attitude toward Marín and declares her to be the guilty party in the failed marriage: "In her book *La única* (a barely disguised autobiography, pitiful because of its hatred and malignancy) she gives Cuesta a particularly repulsive role . . . If Jorge was a refined intellectual in his ivory tower, Lupe was passionate and exuberant . . . Cuesta was fascinated by this vivacious, sensual, and frivolous woman, totally incomprehensible to a personality such as his. More than passion, she inspired curiosity in him . . . Lupe would abandon his son almost immediately and demand a divorce" (1983: 51–52).[4]

Feminists such as Mary Ann Doane and Teresa de Lauretis, grounded in Lacanian psychoanalysis, have studied the generic properties of the gaze and the fact that the traditional view of women is one seen through men's eyes. In Marín's case, the reader can add to the testimonies already given the photographs by Edward Weston (Wolfe 1963: pictures 61, 62, 63, 64) and, of course, the frescoes by Rivera. Marín had become something of *la encuerada nacional,* the most ubiquitous naked body in Mexico, and representative of the new and strong Mexican woman. Of all her portraits, one of the most relevant is the one at the Chapingo chapel. This is how Poniatowska saw it in *Tinísima:*

> At the Chapingo chapel Diego had finished tracing the main character: Lupe, with a bulging abdomen, breasts swollen from a recent pregnancy, and thick hair. "What I like the most are my tits," Lupe had commented. "But, *gordito,* what are the people going to say in Guadalajara when they see that I am completely naked in the middle of a chapel? Let's be fair: my tits are better than Diego's chile." (1987: 193)[5]

Diego Rivera has explained this picture:

> On the bottom of the wall [of the chapel] is fertilized soil. The wind is behind her like the maternal force, like water and fire, that produces energy: almighty electricity at the service of humankind. (Torriente 1959: 237)[6]

When Marín was writing her two novels, Mexican women had not yet achieved the status of citizenship, which occurred in 1946 (Castillo 1992: 244). The love relationship between Lupe and Jorge Cuesta was

portrayed in *La Diegada,* a series of satiric poems written by Salvador
Novo (discussed in Chapter 3). This is another type of representation
of Lupe Marín. Horacio Espinosa Altamirano has explained the book
jacket of *La única* and how it is related to *La Diegada:*

> *La Diegada* is a foulmouthed and festive series of quatrains and sonnets,
> which among other corrosive topics celebrate the love relationship
> between Lupe and Jorge Cuesta. The events had a tragic and truculent
> end. Rivera took revenge on the cover of the novel *La única,* a sort of
> autobiographical novel written by Ms. Marín. Diego, with a seraphic
> innocence, illustrated the cover. In the picture two heads emerge from
> a hermaphroditic torso. The head on the left is that of an ambiguous
> adolescent with a small nipple, resembling Jorge Cuesta. The head on
> the right is Lupe Marín with big earrings and a huge nipple as a phallic
> symbol. The hands by the waist hold a tray on which lies the head of
> the decapitated important poet of the Contemporáneos group, recalling
> the story of Salome and St. John the Baptist. To give the picture more
> ferocity and cauterization the letters of the title form a circulatory sys-
> tem or communicating vessels. (1985: 42)[7]

In 1934 a Bolivian Marxist intellectual, under the pen-name Tristán
Marof, wrote a curious book about Mexican cultural life, *México de frente
y de perfil.* Among other topics he analyzes Mexican women's literature:

> Between the faggot group [*grupo "jotista"*: the Contemporáneos] and
> women there is really little difference. Although women of any age and
> circumstance are always more pleasant! . . . Women of talent are in
> general ugly . . . Mexican women writers are nice . . . I cannot under-
> stand why such charming ladies have chosen the hard work of writing
> to please the bourgeoisie. (127)[8]

An initial reaction to this quotation would be to label it sheer stupidity;
but upon a second reading we may notice that it contains interesting ob-
servations. The first one is that the Contemporáneos group, one of the
most important avant-garde movements in Western literature, is
equated with women writers. That is to say, women are creating literature more akin to the avant-garde than to the more "official" realism of
the writers of the Revolution (e.g., Mariano Azuela). It is also interesting for us as modern readers to see how women's literature came to be
considered a minor and secondary, although nice, activity. Marof is correct when he declares that literature in general belonged to the bourgeoisie. The most important of these ideas for us, even if it is stated in

an odd manner, is that Marof perceived literature like Marín's as part of the Contemporáneos movement.

La única *(The Unique Woman, 1938)*

Edna Coll had a strong reaction to *La única* in her 1964 analysis:

> This is the story of a woman with an unbalanced mind who analyzes her crazy life. This is an absurd and annoying book with pretensions of erudition based on the paradoxical contradiction of having a mad-woman reasoning . . . Marcela is a deceived woman in her love life, her two marriages, and her maternal feelings. The novel is overwhelmed by pessimistic and closed-minded romanticism. At times the language displays a nauseating naturalism. (75) [9]

Wolfe, Diego Rivera's official biographer, comments: "The novel [*La única*] allows Lupe to revise life so as to improve the light in which she was viewed" (1963: 192). Coll called *La única* a "novela confesión" (1964: 75; the ideologeme of confession is discussed in Chapter 4).

La única is an autobiographical text in which, through the character of Marcela, Lupe Marín tries to explain her version of the truth to the public. In this novel she denounces what she perceives to be the most important problems in Mexican society: homosexuality, communism, machismo (including battered wives), state misogyny, underdevelopment, lack of a real division between political powers (legislative, executive, and judicial), the arbitrary nature of justice, and the lack of citizenship for women. To resolve or at least describe these problems, she had to employ a "nauseating naturalism." Sylvia Molloy writes:

> Spanish American autobiography, at its inception, is basically a public story: public in the sense that it tells what can and should be told, and public because, more than satisfying the individual's need to speak of himself, it serves the public interest. There is little or no room in these texts for the petite histoire and a great desire, instead, to become part of a more important History in the making. Indeed, in some cases, what is announced as the story of an individual soon becomes, by metonymy, the story of an emerging country. (1991: 82)

As a litmus test for *La única,* the reader may use Angelina Beloff's *Memorias* (Memoirs, 1986), in which the author/narrator annuls her persona when she compares herself to the greatness of Diego Rivera. It is paradoxical that one finds a better defense of Beloff in Elena Poniatowska's *Querido Diego*. Lupe is not as easy to please as Beloff is, and she claims her right to be part of the cultural and symbolic space of the fatherland. She adds her voice to those of Cuesta and Novo in order to deny Mexican nationalism a monopoly on Mexican discourse. For instance, take this example from Lola, Marcela's girlfriend:

> Nobody works except in politics. It is the only way to get an automobile. This is why there are changes in politics, although they are not substantial. Everything stays within the family, "the revolutionary family." The change of president is just for show. The only change is from one office to the other. They always keep the same salary and more or less the same category. It does not matter if they go to the Department of Education, Agriculture, War, or the Interior; what is important is to have the same status and the same salary. God only knows how long this is going to last. My opinion is that the present situation is going to break the record of the Porfiriato. (1938: 201) [10]

These are very impressive words if the reader considers that they were written more than sixty years ago and that the regime did not change until 2000. But *La única* deals with other important topics: communism/socialism (e.g., 95, 122, 166, 185, 186, 246), desire (e.g., 218, 232), disease (e.g., 61, 64), divorce (e.g., 6, 24, 79, 113, 193), drugs (e.g., 233), exhibitionism (e.g., 54, 244), the female body (e.g., 46), female madness (e.g., 37, 40, 57, 237, 251), feminism (e.g., 90, 102, 138, 141, 155, 188, 215–216), fitness (e.g., 204, 249), hermaphroditism (e.g., 106, 107, 163, 164, 213), homosexuality (e.g., 7, 8, 19, 33, 81, 87, 94, 95, 120, 140, 173, 203, 241), incest (e.g., 7, 228, 230, 231), lesbianism (e.g., 126, 160, 161, 247), masturbation (e.g., 83, 86), and spousal abuse and battery (11, 12, 13).

This is not your typical "feminine" novel. Marín's boldness and sincerity as she deals with her topics compensate for what she may lack in narrative skills. The common denominator of *La única* and *Un día patrio* is the presence of desire (especially feminine and homosexual desire) and how it is perceived by society at large. Chapter 4 discusses the wide dissemination of Freudian theories and of the public's knowledge of how to read and/or watch the new psychological texts. For instance, the vulgarization of Freud is already present in the movies of Alfred Hitchcock, who started his career as a filmmaker in 1925. A good example is *Rebecca,* filmed in 1940, between the publication of Lupe's two novels.

The novels *La única* and *Un día patrio* are full of references to psychiatrists and madness because the practitioners of psychiatry are the new experts in charge of determining normalcy. *La única* can also be described as a hodgepodge of perversions. As already noted, this is a novel with autobiographical elements. Marín/Marcela hides her own perversion(s) in the cluster of perversions presented in the novel. For instance, the references to exhibitionism are unnecessary and apparently do not add anything to the novel. But in reality they constitute another layer of abnormal sexual mores. The pervert who goes to the city park to show his genitalia represents the necessary contrast to the woman who, for artistic reasons, has been portrayed in the nude in many of the most important pictures of twentieth-century Mexico. Her artistic exhibitionism seems sanitized, normalized, when compared with the "sick" version.

Teresa de Lauretis takes a specific reading of Freud as the basis of her own theory of sexuality and perverse desire (1994: xii), saying in effect that "normalcy" does not exist or that it lies in the eyes of the beholder. I understand that this is not the same as saying that normalcy is strictly social and, therefore, not natural. But this is a very important step, especially for the first generation of Mexican women to come from the sexual revolution of the twenties (cf. Coontz 1992: 193–196). Marín understands that sexuality goes beyond the social and the personal. Lauretis (who follows Catharine Mackinnon) perceives womanhood in sexual/social terms:

> Since one "becomes a woman" through the experience of sexuality, issues such as lesbianism, contraception, abortion, incest, sexual harassment, rape, prostitution, and pornography are not merely social (a problem for society as a whole) or merely sexual (a private affair between "consenting adults") or within the privacy of the family . . . for women, they are political and epistemological. "To feminism, the personal is epistemologically the political, and its epistemology is its politics [Mackinnon]." (1984: 184)

There is not a big difference between the topics chosen by De Lauretis in 1984 and those chosen by Marín in 1938. I understand that I am asking the reader to accept in good faith this social reading of gender in which women are supposed to internalize their identity according to how they are seen by men, but Marín presents a very obvious case. Marín's novels are so interesting for a social reading of the feminist movement in Mexico because she was able to perceive the political content of sexuality as early as 1938. She also understood that for women at that moment, when they were not even citizens, the novel was one of the very few arenas/theaters for politics. Angeles Mastretta explained this process perfectly when she wrote the "biography" of Catalina, the wife of Maximino Avila Camacho, the governor of Puebla. As in the case of Tina Modotti (the protagonist of *Tinísima*), Mastretta wrote a novel in order to tell the story of a woman in the precitizenship period. Don Maximino was governor of Puebla during the Cárdenas presidency, when Marín published *La única*. In Mastretta's novel, Catalina uses her sexuality as the only weapon she has left to fight against her *caudillo* husband's tyranny at home and in office. In my own study of this novel, *Arráncame la vida* (1985), I have analyzed how this text subverts the nineteenth-century tradition of the novel of adultery in order to represent the new dynamic in the relationship between genders after the first sexual revolution (Oropesa 1996b: 137–164).

As noted at the beginning of this chapter, Debra Castillo and Sylvia Molloy indicate that there are problems in the autobiographical genre in Latin America, especially for women. This leads me to the conclusion that Marín tried to invent a genre that did not exist at the time she wrote the book — and this is the reason why most critics consider her novels to be failures. Today autobiographies of celebrities are very common, but this is a genre that slowly took shape in the twentieth century. Publishing companies pay fabulous sums for this kind of gossip. Perhaps Marín anticipated the existence of the genre but was not perceptive enough to shape it. This, in essence, is what Sandra Gilbert and Susan Gubar have found in the study I am using as a critical subtext, *The Madwoman in the Attic*: "Many of the most distinguished late eighteenth-century and nineteenth-century English and American women writers do not seem to 'fit' into any of those categories to which our literary historians have accustomed us. Indeed, to many critics and scholars, some of these literary women look like isolated eccentrics" (1984: 72).

Let us return to the quotation by Molloy concerning the manner in which the metonymic process operated in the Latin American autobiography and how very quickly writers tried to forget the trivial events of their lives so that their work became the story/history of their country. We must understand that Molloy is writing mainly about nineteenth-century literature; but with Marín we are dealing with a post–1920s text, after a culture of celebrity has begun to develop. Marín understands that she belongs to the new urban pop culture. She realizes that there is an exertion of power in the deployment of gossip, typical of neobaroque culture, in which the boundary between high and low culture is difficult to establish. Some of the satiric sonnets by Novo are excellent examples. The impeccable form and technique are classic, but the content is the most rabid gossip anyone can imagine. What Marín attempts, then, is to control some of the gossip about her; but she fails because she uses the form of a "serious" novel to convey her share of the gossip. Nevertheless, the experiment has some brilliant moments. One is the aforementioned sorting of desires and perversions, which makes her novel one of the best examples for exploring the urban sexual revolution of the twenties. Also successful is her vulgarization and understanding of Freud, not as the father of a normative sexuality but quite the opposite, as the person who opened the Pandora's box of multiple sexualities and the possibility of exploring the social politics of sexuality.

Even the somewhat homophobic passages of the novels are sympathetic to the homosexual characters. For instance, in *Un día patrio* one of the characters attacks Marañón, the leader of normative, conservative Freudian interpretation in the Hispanic world (cf. Keller 1977: 19, 43–44; Laín Entralgo 1969: 167–170):

> Marañón's theory about Don Juan is wrong. I think that his theory is just consolation for asexual people and a refuge for those who are exhausted. It can also be useful for those who are not part of the present time. Nowadays it is miserable, very miserable for a man to be trapped by just one woman. (1941: 118) [11]

Marín links this pulp Freudianism to the power of gossip:

> [Jorge Cuesta's] first passion, which he secretly fostered for a long time and from very early in his youth, was for his younger sister. One day, out of desperation, he entered her bedroom. When she realized her mad brother was trying to rape her, the young woman yelled furiously, asking her parents for protection. (1941: 7) [12]

The best parts of the novel are those in which, instead of doing "serious" literature, Marín lets the characters speak like ordinary people. Perhaps the most interesting passage, from the traditional political point of view, is the following:

> I went there with Lombardo Toledano, his wife, and Diego Rivera. When the young women at the market saw me with them, they asked me why I was going out with a gringo and two foul-mouthed pigs. Lombardo's wife and Diego are fat and white. [13]

Marín is writing about the Tehuantepec market. According to her characterization, she is the only one who belongs to the *pueblo*—the other three do not fit in, especially since they are not mestizos. Lombardo Toledano (of Italian and Mexican origin) was one of the most important representatives of the Cardenista left, and Rivera was a well-known member of the Communist Party.[14] These are the same people who were attacking everyone who was not considered Mexican for being exotic (see Chapter 1). According to Marcela, however, the real Mexicans — the *campesino* Indians of the Tehuantepec market — see them as foreigners. These are some of the more fortuitous examples of *La única*, which still reads very well in spite of its defects. It reads much better, for example, than the avant-garde novels of Torres Bodet, which the canon considers first-class literature.

Male Homosexuality

As we can see in *La única*, Lupe Marín was able to grasp the political dimension of sexuality. Because homosexuality is a subtext that runs throughout this literary analysis, it is interesting to see how Marín, the epitome of heterosexuality and female splendor as she is painted in the Chapingo chapel, views it. At the same time, this shows how important homosexuality had become — if there is a need to attack a behavior this is because it has attained a certain relevance. As often noted in this work, some of the Contemporáneos writers were part of the first generation of gay men in Mexico, gay in the contemporary meaning of the term. But from the 1920s to the 1940s the discussion of the topic was carried out in homosexual terms, according to which homosexuality is an aberration or abnormal behavior that threatens the status quo: the normative heterosexual sexuality characteristic of the Catholic tradition.

This is a centuries-long custom. From very early in the colonial discourse on the Indian as other,[15] one of the ways of stigmatizing the Indian was to proclaim him a sodomite. As early as 1521 Diego de Ordaz, a supporter of Cortés, explained in a letter to Fr. Luis de Figueroa that the Mexica were all sodomites (Thomas 1995: 471). The so-called revolutionary virility of the official discourse of the regime adopted this attitude as its own: the Mexican Revolution was by definition associated with masculinity within the parameters of a strong division between the genders. The common denominator of both discourses is the same: homosexuality can be used at any given time as a stigma to separate the discourse of power from that of the other. Homosexuality as a challenge to the orthodoxy of the Revolution can be better understood by the reader who has followed Octavio Paz's thoughts concerning eroticism and sexuality, developed over a long period. Although Paz's discourse is heterosexual, he has always seen the liberation of "el hombre nuevo" (the new man) in a free sexuality that will cast aside the constraints of Western civilization, especially the Protestant Puritanism of the North and Latin Catholicism of the South. According to Paz — and he has been adamant on this point — it is through the individual use of sexuality that a new society will be able to emerge.

It is common to juxtapose the names of Karl Marx and Sigmund Freud as the two late-nineteenth-century men who shaped the twentieth century, and this is true of the postrevolutionary period between the world wars. What should be evident in the study of Lazo and Marín is the vulgarization of the discussion. This debate is not for the most part intellectual but instead enters the realm of popular culture: for example, celebrity gossip as a common way to psychoanalyze the object of attention and/or of desire.

The first reference to male homosexuality in *La única* occurs when the narrator, Marcela, is explaining the personality of the Jorge Cuesta character, Andrés, in the already discussed quotation concerning gossip. Here homosexuality is represented very much in line with André Gide, who sees homosexuality ("pederasty" in Gide's terms) as a superior level of relations between men, based on Greek (Socratic) love. In this reading of the classics, wise older men are expected to educate younger men, cultivating their intellect and teaching them about love and culture. Most of the homosexual literature of the end of the nineteenth century holds to this plot line. The narrator Marcela understands that homosexuality is something learned and similar to a cult — the key word used is *gremio* (guild) — where homosexuals convince other young, educated, and sophisticated men to enter their *círculo mágico* (magic circle). *Círculo mágico* has two meanings: in a general sense it refers to men who have same-sex sexual relations; but it also means the group of gay intellectuals protected by Narciso Bassols, the secretary of education, including Salvador Novo, Xavier Villaurrutia, Jaime Torres Bodet, and Jorge Cuesta. In one bizarre scene in the novel Bassols sexually harasses Marcela as a way to demonstrate his heterosexuality despite the fact that he is protecting gay men.

By outing these men in her book, Marín adopts an attitude of superiority over them, especially Cuesta. Marín's outing of her husband is in line with the way Foucault has described sexuality in its transition from the nineteenth to the twentieth century: as the truth, a scientific truth that is defined through a myriad of new technologies and sciences, psychoanalysis being the most obvious. In pop culture we come to know a person's character, learning everything about his/her sexuality; and this is even more "true" when the discovery is bisexuality, as in the case of Cuesta (Marlon Brando's role in *The Last Tango in Paris* is discussed later in this chapter).

Marín outs Cuesta gradually to protect herself and slowly gain the sympathy of the reader. Marcela explains that her husband abandoned her because he was "doing something else." In the "traditional" scenario this means the man has a *casa chica* where he keeps his female lover. This is what happened to Marín with Diego Rivera: Frida Kahlo took her place. The estrangement Marín tries to effect in the reader occurs when she starts suspecting that Jorge/Andrés has returned to having homosexual relations. The key here is that he is going back to a previous behavior—this is how readers learn that he has already had homosexual relations. As has been explained, Marcela understands homosexuality as a learned behavior, so she—with her exuberant (hetero)sexuality— is convinced she can "cure" him. She is surprised and angry that despite her efforts her husband has not changed. Marín's heterosexuality fails miserably, like that of the women in Lazo's plays. Her suspicion is confirmed when she finds on her husband's nightstand two key books that flag homosexuality: André Gide's *Counterfeiters* (*Les faux-monnayeurs*; see Pollard 1991: 26–27) and Oscar Wilde's *The Picture of Dorian Gray* (see Nunokawa 1995). They represent the prototypical scenario of the first homosexual/gay/pederast texts of the first generation of gay literature.

A monologue by Andrés explains that he and the rest of the "circle" hate Gonzalo (Diego Rivera) because he accused the Contemporáneos of being homosexuals in a public lecture in which he made homophobic comments. At that point, they decided to take revenge: the poems of *La Diegada* by Chavo (Salvador Novo) represented the first part of the attack. In this monologue Andrés is presented as a weak and despicable person.

After Marcela is divorced, she tells a friend it is better for a woman to have a black or Chinese son (140) than a homosexual one. To have a son of another race is something positive, but having a homosexual son is akin to having a criminal or a prostitute descendant (ibid.). As the character Marcela becomes more and more bitter toward Andrés, her attacks become virulent—for instance, she recounts how Andrés's lover called him "mamacito" (little mama) when they were making love. If we follow Gide's division of homosexuals, Andrés's friend belongs to the worst of the group and the only one that is morally despicable: the invert (I am just trying to contextualize how homosexuals perceived themselves at that time). But this process of moral degeneration also affects Andrés, who was previously a gentleman: "Physically, he is more ugly than ever; he looks old and very thin. One of his friends told me that he stays out late every night; he goes to *cabarets* with his friend, the one they call 'little nard stem' " (203).[16] Once Marín stigmatizes her husband as a homosexual, he is seen in a descending progression until he reaches total degeneration.

Lesbianism

When Marcela goes to Paris she explains to the reader the characteristics that made prewar Paris so fascinating. One of these attributes is lesbianism: "Where women develop sudden passions for other women" (126).[17] In other words, it was common for any woman who visited Paris at that time to be tempted by the possibility of a lesbian relation. If this theoretical possibility does exist, the character Marcela must not fall into temptation, which would mean equating herself with the "despicable" Andrés.

But because this is gossip, there is another subtext: Gonzalo/Diego Rivera abandoned Lupe Marín for another woman, Frida Kahlo, who was a bisexual celebrity. Marjorie Garber has summarized this situation, relying on Hayden Herrera's biography of Kahlo: "[Frida Kahlo] teased and flirted with O'Keeffe at Stieglitz's gallery, as her husband, the muralist Diego Rivera, affectionately reported to a mutual woman friend. 'Frida had many girl friends and lesbian friends,' said a male acquaintance of the period . . . Her husband encouraged her affairs with women . . . because he found the idea of sex between women exciting" (1995: 114). At a party a female painter caresses Marcela and wants to spend the night with her. After the party Marcela tells a male friend from Guatemala about this. She is justifying her coolness:

> In spite of the fact that I had total confidence in myself and that not even for a second did I think it would happen to me, I felt bad. I am not fond of appearing to be scandalized. You saw very well how indifferent I appeared when she was caressing me, so as not to show my thoughts. But I had terrible moments. I confess that I was starting to get a headache. There is no doubt that a woman like her, vicious and beautiful, is dangerous. But how revolting it must be to let yourself be "magically jolted," as the Education Secretary would say. (160–161)[18]

The last reference to lesbianism in the book is in the manifesto that closes *La única*. This is a bizarre (mad) discourse that aspires to represent the true and new left, neither Marxist nor Christian, but more based on what we would today label an ecological manifesto, similar to those of the hygienists from the beginning of the twentieth century. Among the vices of the rich people that are enumerated are the hundreds of pesos they spend watching erotic lesbian shows (247). This is interesting because it tells us about the existence of very expensive lesbian shows for masculine consumption in the Mexico of the late thirties. The attack against lesbianism helps Marín to declare her superiority over Cuesta and Kahlo. Marín perceives male and female homosexuality as vices that belong to the upper class and the intellectuals and artists — if the future of society is in the ordinary people, the *pueblo*, they cannot have these defects.

The Third Sex: Jorge Cuesta

In 1977 Miguel Capistrán published in *Vuelta* a letter from Jorge Cuesta to an exiled Spanish psychiatrist, Dr. Gonzalo R. Lafora. Sylvester reproduces the letter in his book-length study on Cuesta with the following warning: "I am enclosing it in its entirety because it is important not just because of its content, but because it is a crystal-clear example of Cuesta's objectivity and inexorable way of arguing (even if it is a personal matter and under conditions that made the poet feel ridiculed)" (1984: 21).[19] The critic's need to sanitize the poet's life is fascinating. If anything is clear after reading the letter, it is that Cuesta was having very serious problems with his mental health, an issue which does not at all diminish his value as a writer. Sylvester tries to strike a balance between plain literary criticism, a close reading of Cuesta's poems, and the need to protect him from extraliterary attacks like the ones found in *La única*. It can be argued that the critic is trying to avoid an autobiographical reading of Cuesta's poetry. This is like saying that the reader should not psychoanalyze the poet when reading his poems. In the letter Cuesta is upset because his psychiatrist has diagnosed repressed homosexuality as the basis of his mental problems. But according to Cuesta — and this is an astonishing revelation for the reader of the letter — the root of his problems is that he belongs to a third sex. He has started menstruating, and a possible reason for his problem is that he made "scientific" experiments in which he acted as his own guinea pig, ingesting enzymatic compounds. He writes:

I showed you the nature of my hemorrhoids which have afflicted me for the last sixteen years. I was afraid that it was an *anatomic* mutation, with characteristics of androgyny, as these modifications are usually called, or an intersexual state, as they are also called . . . These intersexual states are not a product of my imagination—they are manifested *anatomically.* Nor am I the one who says that the form of this anatomical manifestation in some cases may be a deviation or degeneration of the prostate. (quoted in Sylvester 1984: 22–23) [20]

A few comments are needed. First, nothing of this nature appears in Marín's novel. Somehow she drew a line at what she wanted to say or what she felt she could say. We can speculate that she believed revealing this intimate detail was going too far, especially if we remember that she had always made fun of Diego Rivera's breasts (*chichis*) because they were so big and feminine.[21] There is a more subtle explanation, which involves believing that if you go beyond a certain point the reader's sympathies will change. The truth of the matter is that all the testimonies we have gathered about this book are in favor of Cuesta and against Marín. The French critic Louis Panabière (1983: 81–82) rabidly defends Cuesta—according to him Cuesta never denied his homosexuality—and believes that Cuesta's explanations that his experiments with enzymes could have ended in a sex mutation of some sort are scientifically plausible. The common denominator of both Sylvester's and Panabière's defenses is that Cuesta acts with an impeccable logic in the exposition of his problems. I offer these examples because they can be perfectly contrasted with the "lack of logic" in Marín's novels. Male critics find a perfect masculine logic in a Cuesta who is going mad, and this can be helpful as a litmus test for the mad Lupe Marín.

The Madwoman

Of course, the title of this chapter refers to Gilbert and Gubar's *The Madwoman in the Attic,* which has already been quoted in this chapter. Reading this twenty-year-old book is a gratifying experience; despite a certain candor and optimism which led the writers to stretch certain metaphors more than necessary, it is full of ideas that lead to a better understanding of a novel as unique as *La única.* What most strikes the reader about Marín's novel is how solitary it is, in the middle of nothing, outside of most traditions. This is a common phenomenon in nineteenth-century literature written by women, as demonstrated by Gilbert and Gubar. At that time the United States and Great Britain were more developed in technology and education and had a solid middle class that Mexico lacked. They ended up creating a tradition of feminine literature that culminated in twentieth-century writers like Virginia Woolf and Edith Wharton. Mexico's literary tradition is more limited. This explains why Marín's novel is even lonelier than its counterparts in other countries, because in many respects it is a nineteenth-century novel.

Later in *La única,* when Marcela is still living with Gonzalo (Diego Rivera), there is a scene in which he chases her all over the house intending to beat her up. The chase is interrupted by some visitors who come to see Gonzalo because he is supposedly ill. He rushes into bed and pretends to be very sick, telling the friends that Marcela is the cause of his malady because she is a "witch" (*bruja;* 17). One of the first dichotomies of nineteenth-century literature by women as studied by Gilbert and Gubar is that of the angel/witch, with the story of Snow White being paradigmatic. Marcela is perceived as a monster by others (especially men, although some women, such as her mother-in-law and her best friend, could also be included). Marín develops enormously contradictory feelings about how she should behave with her friends, with her husband's family, and in society. She wants to conform to social norms but at the same time wants to be free and to exert her will. Her body collapses, and she suffers an odd illness which the specialists are not able to diagnose because her symptoms do not point to any known disease. She has anorexia, sleeplessness, agoraphobia, unconsciousness, and other symptoms and illnesses common to the nineteenth-century literature studied by Gilbert and Gubar. They write:

> By projecting their rebellious impulses not into their heroines but into mad or monstrous women (who are suitably punished in the course of the novel or poem), female authors dramatize their own self-division, their desire both to accept the strictures of patriarchal society and to reject them. What this means, however, is that the madwoman in literature by women is not merely, as she might be in male literature, an antagonist or foil to the heroine. Rather, she is usually in some sense the *author's* double, an image of her own anxiety and rage. Indeed, much of the poetry and fiction written by women conjures up this mad creature so that female authors can come to terms with their own uniquely female feeling of fragmentation, their own keen sense of the discrepancies between what they are and what they are supposed to be. (1984: 78)

This observation is astonishing, because it is a perfect summary of *La única,* in which the heroine and the madwoman are the same person and, furthermore, are the author since it is an autobiographical novel. When Marcela becomes sick and is visited by some of the most eminent specialists in Mexico City, the best of them declares her insane (*loca*): her relatives should pay no attention to her (37). During this illness she writes a pamphlet which she wants to read in the market; Andrés, after reading it, also declares that she is *loca* (40). This fascinating discourse is very similar to what one may read in Frida Kahlo's *Diary*. For instance, in Plate 29 there is a self-portrait by Kahlo in which her face is doubled in the face of "Neferúnico. Founder of Lokura" (Neferunico. Founder of Madness; 1995a: 221). Kahlo and Marín share this double identity, with one of the sides being madness. Among other references to madness, Kahlo wrote in Plates 74–76:

> I wish xxxx xxxx xxx xxxxxx = xxxxx — xxxx — I could do whatever
> I liked—behind the curtain of "madness." Then: I'd arrange flowers,
> all day long, I'd paint pain, love and tenderness, I'd laugh as much as I
> feel like at the stupidity of others, and they would all say: poor thing!
> She's crazy. (1995a: 242; parts of the text are unintelligible)

This 1948 text by Kahlo provides a good complement to Marín's novels. Both texts are hallucinatory and were probably written under the influence of strong painkillers.

The beginning of Marín's pamphlet is a mixture of the literary genre of *cuadro de costumbres* and a surrealist manifesto. It starts with the topic of a Mexican cornucopia: cow tripe, bull tongues, maguey worms, prickly pears, *ahuatle* (insect eggs), *pápaloquelite* (butterfly leaves), coriander, oregano, onion, *ahuilote, capulín* (berry), and *camichín*. Another topic with a long literary tradition, especially in medieval and baroque literature, follows: the scorning of the doctor (the favorite topic of Caviedes). The novel continues with a detailed description of Marcela's illness and how the symptoms affect her body. Then a doctor who is acquainted with the latest technologies and research literature cures her. He ends up discovering that the reason is a hormonal dysfunction. This is different from the neurasthenia of the nineteenth-century novel because it is a modern illness, a brand-new advancement in medicine. It implies that many women have been considered mad because physicians lacked the medical knowledge to make the correct diagnosis, as occurred in other centuries when the church considered some sick women to be possessed by evil spirits.

Once Marcela is back to normal she starts caring for her son, who has been living with his paternal grandmother. To her horror, she finds out that the child has a fixation with masturbation and is masturbating compulsively all the time. Marcela believes that his grandmother taught him to do this in order to help him sleep. She beats him mercilessly and tries to bind his hands at night, reasoning "scientifically" that the boy's health will be affected in terrible ways. I wanted to contrast this example with the one about Marcela's madness, because they exemplify the mixture of nineteenth-century science, twentieth-century science, praise of indigenous culture, and scorn of indigenous superstition that existed in early-twentieth-century Mexico. There was a collapse of traditional knowledge, and modern science was beginning to occupy its place; but there were doubts and misinformation as well as significant difficulties about what to do with the indigenous culture. People and society were trying to discern what should be kept and what must be discarded as outdated.

The novel includes a discussion between Marcela/Lupe Marín and Chavo/Salvador Novo in which Marcela expresses a strong feminist opinion concerning a play by August Strindberg that portrays women as inferior. As the reader may infer, the novel is a hodgepodge of themes that bother and worry Marcela. It ends with another aborted manifesto about the workers' need for fitness, directed against the demagoguery of the so-called leaders of the working class. Lola, Marcela's best friend, like her own husband in the previous manifesto, considers her crazy. The last words of the novel are spoken by Lola: "What an animal you are to think of saying this! At least they are going to put you in jail. Now I believe you are crazy! I do not have any doubt that you are crazy!" (251).[22]

Un día patrio *(A Patriotic Day, 1941)*

In Salvador Novo's reading of Marín's book *Un día patrio* (which also has biographical overtones) he says:

> Books "in code" based on contemporary characters have the defect and run the risk that if, as in Lupe's, they lack a strong personality, they will have a limited life span . . . They become hieroglyphs, and as time passes their value as documents diminishes, because their interest is limited to the author's agenda at a given moment. Of course, I was able to recognize my character in *Un día patrio,* but more because Lupe put

in my name with all its letters than because of my portrayal in the book, a portrait that is already outdated. (1965: 228–229) [23]

This novel adds new challenges to those of *La única.* The novel can be divided into two parts. The first is a very strong denunciation of extortion as a form of *mordida* (bribery). A woman is accused of a crime she did not commit after the police falsify the record and the evidence. She is not set free until she pays the bribe. To add insult to injury, the newspapers publish the official police version. The novel denounces "in code," as Novo said, some of the most important journalists of Mexico City. This novel precedes Heinrich Böll's *The Lost Honor of Katharina Blum: How Violence Develops and Where It Can Lead,* which tells the story of a woman whose life is destroyed by yellow journalism.

The second part of the novel, longer than the first, develops the theme of mad love, *amour fou.* Claudio almost dies because his wife does not love him and betrays him. His friend Fernando, a physician, goes to the hacienda where he works and saves him. Later Fernando commits suicide because Claudio does not want to continue being his lover. The very night of the suicide, Claudio is unable to read the desperate signals his friend has been sending him. He decides to go out in search of adventure. It is the day of the *fiestas patrias* (day of independence), and the novel explains that a person of a certain class is not expected to be out having fun with the masses. While Claudio is out on the town, Fernando shoots himself. When Claudio returns home after a one-night stand with an unknown woman, he is imprisoned because the police suspect he has killed his friend, in part because he cannot provide an alibi.

The first story, about Claudio and his wife, is told in a conventional melodramatic tone. The second is more avant-garde and "scientific," full of clinical jargon, as in *La única.* But the most interesting of the three stories is the third. This is the plot line which gives the book its title, because, as in Federico Gamboa's *Santa,* the key scene which eventually leads to the sexual encounter between the lovers happens on the day of independence. The lovers-to-be meet in the Zócalo at the same time that the president is delivering the *grito* (the cry of independence). In *Santa* this device works because it stresses the fact that the character Santa is a metonymy of Mexico. The same cannot be said of Claudio and his unknown lover, unless the idea is that Mexico should be represented by a woman who is in control of her (love) life and who makes her own decisions, instead of the traditional *chingadas* (Paz's terminology,) such as Malinche and Santa.

If the first part of the novel is a precursor of Böll's, the second can be associated with Bernardo Bertolucci's film *Last Tango in Paris* (1972). *Un día patrio* is a novel about the period following the sexual revolution of the twenties, and *Last Tango* is paradigmatic of the sexual revolution of the seventies. The two male characters, Claudio and Paul, are marked by a suicide. Both meet their lovers after the suicides of their previous lovers (Fernando and Paul's wife). One significant difference is that Paul, played by Marlon Brando, is macho and Claudio is bisexual, more oriented toward women but nevertheless a man who had a homosexual interlude with Fernando. Both men are trying to get away from their lives and are full of anger. Then they encounter the ideal male fantasy: sex with a beautiful *unknown* woman. This is the epitome of male fantasy in a patriarchal culture: to have a sex partner available at any moment, free of the concept of guilt. In both the novel and the movie, the fantasy collapses because the two men make the same mistake. There is a moment in which they fall in love and want to bring history, their personal stories, to the anonymous fable they have been representing. Once they are determined to know everything about their female partners and/or fantasies, the women end the relationships. Jeanne in *The Last Tango* kills Paul. In her review in the *New Yorker* Pauline Kael writes: "What they go through together in their pressure cooker is an intensified, speeded-up history of the sex relationships of the dominating men and adoring women who have provided the key sex model of the past few decades—the model that is collapsing" (1973: 11).

This is exactly what Lupe Marín does in her novel, as she speeds up a sex/love story in order to demonstrate the collapse of the traditional patriarchal model. The anonymous woman chooses Claudio, and "she" is the one in charge when they exchange glances: "I caught her staring at me. I was ashamed and nervous" (150).[24] He is very troubled when he realizes that she is the one staring at him, since until that moment he had been confident of being in control of the gaze. The woman separates herself from her companions and gives him a place to meet and a time. After their sexual encounter, which is not described in the novel, Claudio goes to prison due to the timing of his friend's suicide. He becomes so obsessed with this relationship that he eventually loses control of his life: "I needed to see blood or know that horrifying things were happening" (176).[25] When Claudio is released from prison he is very unkempt, and his physical appearance is disgusting. Still, he fantasizes about making love to the unknown woman:

> Instead of considering me repulsive, she would kiss my hands and my face to comfort me. She would take the sleeve of my jacket off and she

would uncover my bare arm and she would kiss it an infinite number of times. She would unbutton my shirt and she would lean her head on my dirty and sweaty chest. She would also put her lips to my neck, my ears, and my hair. I would be so happy if she affirmed her love for me! (177–178) [26]

In *The Last Tango in Paris*, the moment of anagnorisis occurs when Jeanne puts her two fingers in Paul's anus. Norman Mailer (1973) saw the movie as a deviation from the generic expectations of the "fuck movie," as he calls the "traditional" porno movie. Once the genitalia are not present, we are left with the protagonist's physical and symbolic need to release the shit he has in his body and his soul. Given the eschatological references in the movie, it is more precise to use the term "soul" than "psyche." At the very end the movie is no more than an attempt by the male protagonist to release all the evil he has in him, and his sex is reduced—as in the case of Jorge Cuesta—to a prostate the size of an Idaho potato (Mailer's metaphor). Once Paul realizes that Jeanne can save him from all the mistakes in his life and the skeletons in his closet (did he kill his wife?), he falls in love with her and encounters the need for a conventional, middle-class relationship. Is not Jeanne the respectable daughter of a general of the French army?

When Claudio is again able, at last, to see his one-night lover, he is not the neatly dressed and spotlessly clean gentleman he was the first time. This time he is extremely dirty, because his fantasy is that she will cleanse him. She will make a heterosexual of him, a respectable Mexican man, and they will then be able to return to the Creole bedroom where they made love. The room had been perfect, lavishly furnished in imperial style. This is a room in which the protagonists can invest their personalities. Claudio thinks he can bring his filth to this room/womb where he can feel safe and, at last, return to the social class and gender where he belongs. Of course, she rejects him.

6)≡ *Gossip, Power, and the*
Culture of Celebrity

Introduction

In 1994 the cultural historian Neal Gabler published his seminal book *Winchell: Gossip, Power and the Culture of Celebrity*, which was declared the nonfiction book of the year by *Time* magazine. Gabler transcended the biographical genre, using Winchell's life to explain the period of his fame (from the 1920s through the 1940s) and to illustrate how the popular culture trends of his generation, many shaped by Winchell himself, still affect the present. Gabler's hypothesis is that it is impossible to grasp what is happening today in the world of entertainment, information, and mass media without understanding the developments in the period between the world wars.

John Fowles's *The French Lieutenant's Woman* (1969) and similar novels have helped to bridge fiction and history. While the entertainment industry (mainly television) started a process which blurs the distinction between news and entertainment, many of the best fiction writers initiated a parallel process by mixing fiction and history but simultaneously allowing the reader to obtain a rational explanation of historical processes through fiction, keeping them together but discernible. Literature for the most part has succeeded more than radio and later television in creating this cultural hybrid. This procedure had also been widely practiced during the nineteenth century (e.g., Benito Pérez Galdós's *Episodios nacionales*).[1]

Post–World War II experiments with neo-realism and the avant-garde in novels helped develop a new kind of very sophisticated (postmodern) realism, which was extremely engaging because it required the active participation of the reader, who was entertained by the cultural product and at the same time was challenged to understand the historical period developed in the plot. From Alejo Carpentier's *El siglo de las luces* (1952) to Héctor Aguilar Camín's *La guerra de Galio* (1991), Hispanic literature has played an integral part in this literary movement; many texts of the so-called boom and magical realism could be included in this category. A twist to this technique of combining entertainment with analysis of a country's sociopolitical situation has been to use genre novels such as crime stories. James Ellroy in the United States and Manuel Vázquez Montalbán in Spain are two good examples of this process. In spite of their political, social, and historical aspirations, these novels are highly entertaining, and many have been best sellers. Just as Diego Velázquez's paintings such as *Las meninas* are simultaneously high art and entertainment for the aristocracy, these novels try to please the masses, especially the middle class, without compromising their covenant with high art. It is not a surprise, then, that this combination of entertainment and rational analysis appears in other contexts like newspaper op-ed pieces.

Gabler wrote Walter Winchell's biography using techniques similar to those of the new novel, meshing historical content with analysis of the era. In telling Winchell's story, he constructed a theory of popular culture in the twentieth-century United States, while narrating a conventional biography and analyzing the period and country associated with Winchell.

Winchell contributed much to U.S. culture, but his primary influence was his use of language. H. L. Mencken and Ernest Hemingway praised his accomplishments in this field (Gabler 1994: xii). Winchell brought the language of New York streets to the middle and rural classes when this patois represented modernity and the opportunities of a better life that the country was promising to its citizens. New mass media such as radio allowed him to bring the slang and rhythm of life in New York to rural America. He equalized, at least within his limits, the Americas enclosed in the United States. The language of tabloids and radio provided the foundation for this new culture of celebrity.

The second step of this process was gossip, which empowered the people who read and listened to Winchell: knowing their secrets made famous people human (xiii). According to Norman Mailer's interpretation of the movie *The Last Tango in Paris* as gossip (see Chapter 5), what we watch in the film is not a fictive story about an American in Paris but the truth of Marlon Brando's sexuality as it had been promised but not delivered in his movies of the 1950s. We find the same process in Novo's satirical poems like those of *La Diegada;* they are gossip in a classical form, as practiced in previous centuries, especially the seventeenth. As noted in Chapter 5, gossip is ingrained in Lupe Marín's novels. Gabler says:

> Winchell had helped inaugurate a new mass culture of celebrity centered in New York and Hollywood and Washington, fixated on personalities, promulgated by the media, predicated on publicity, dedicated to the ephemeral and grounded on the principle that notoriety confers power. This culture would bind an increasingly diverse, mobile and atomized nation until *it* became, in many respects, America's dominant ethos, celebrity consciousness our common denominator. (1994: xiii)

The process in Mexico paralleled the evolution in the United States. The many Mexicos became unified in a culture of celebrities with the center in Mexico City and to a lesser degree in the tourist resorts like Acapulco and Hispanic communities in the United States. The list of Mexicans who triumphed in Hollywood includes Lupe Vélez, Dolores del Río, the Arozamenas, the Lop-Zar trio, and Lupe Rivas Cacho among others (Merlín 1995: 20). XEW, XEB, XEQ, and other pioneer radio stations played key roles in the development of this culture of celebrities.[2] For the first time in history, millions of Mexicans shared a common knowledge of songs, movies, and artists and also their lives and vicissitudes.

In this context, the so-called golden age of Mexican cinema is the definitive layer which consolidates this culture of celebrity. The television empire of Televisa (the channel of the stars), also owned by the Azcárraga family, represented the final step in the process to articulate the Mexicos through a cluster of popular culture items in the form of commodities. Carlos Monsiváis has summarized the process in explaining the political implications of melodrama:

> In melodrama, suspense equals a promise: Young lady, you will be like your mother, you will learn reality in pregnancy and in material need, and in the incomprehension of that which surrounds you, and in the desire that your prefabricated dreams will balance what you are not going to live. And if you want an identity, look for it in nationalism. If by nation we mean an accumulation of songs, gossip columns, programs and serials, plots where the poor woman gets the love of the rich man without losing her goodness or poverty. (1988a: 146)[3]

This nationalism which developed during the Cárdenas presidency is a paradoxical mixture of the new consumerism coming from the United States and a folklorism like that of the *charros* Jorge Negrete and Tito Guízar. A second paradox of this nationalism is that it is based on popular culture defined in rural terms even though the new culture is essentially urban: radio, cinema, boxing, wrestling, bullfighting, cabaret, *café de chinos, carpa* (tent theater), and the red light district (Merlín 1995: 35). *New Mexican Grandeur* gives a good summary of this process. Melodrama was the genre of choice to express this culture of celebrity; it came via serialized novels of the nineteenth century and serialized radio novels of the twentieth century (which ended up adapting for radio most of the important novels of the previous century).

Language

This entertaining language needed to evoke the brisk rhythm of the streets and be witty. Winchell acquired it from vaudeville; Novo learned it from classical literature (Góngora, Quevedo, and Sor Juana) and the streets and *carpas* of Mexico City, where it was practiced in the neobaroque genre of the *albur*. The *albur* is a pun whose purpose is to insult one's enemy (or the other in general). It may have a homosexual connotation; somehow the speaker tries to sodomize symbolically the person addressed (cf. Mejía Prieto 1990: 9 and 22, 1985: 15). According to Joseph P. Goodwin in *More Man Than You'll Ever Be: Gay Folklore and Acculturation in Middle America* (1989), gay people give mental agility an extraordinary importance (8), and wordplay is very common in conversations (13): "A sharp wit and sharp tongue are prized possessions. Such wordplay requires special linguistic competence, a skill that gays develop probably because of the oral nature of the subculture and because of the pervasiveness of humor in the community" (13). Guillermo Núñez Noriega agrees: "The formula of the so-called homosexual language borrows the artifices of underworld slang, gypsy slang, and cockney, and from everything [needed] to organize your defense against the dominant power" (1994: 14).[4] Daniel Harris adds another twist to this idea:

> Homosexuals were drawn to the image of the bitch in part because of her wicked tongue, her ability to achieve through conversation, through her verbal acuity, her snappy comebacks, the control over others that gay men were often unable to achieve in their own lives. The fantasy of the vicious, back-stabbing *vagina dentata*, always quick on her feet, always ready to demolish her opponents with a stunning

rejoinder, is the fantasy of a powerless minority that asserts itself through language, not physical violence. (1997: 15)

In *El joven* we find words in English — "unless you know how to pronounce it who would dare to have a *marshmallow puff?*" (1933: 15) — and especially the perky rhythm of the city. Novo's *novocablos* (words invented by him) are everywhere in his writing, including his newspaper articles such as those compiled in *Avila Camacho* (1965): *prostiputa* (86), *izquierdoloso* (132), *mozartimaña* (198), *acolítico* (follower with colitis; 384), *pitoperezoso* (386), *proustatitis* (403), *XEQtivos* (529), *compoeta* (561), *candidito* (candid candidate such as Padilla, who ran and lost against Alemán Valdés; 628), and *chopinche* (a "pinche" or bad rendition of Chopin; 728). In his satirical poetry we find the following (about Diego Rivera and Guadalupe Marín):

> Aprende en la estepa las cosas que sepa:
> De quien las trabaje son tierra y mujer.
> ¡Que cuanto le quepa se meta en la pepa,
> pues él no la puede por cable joder!   (1978 [1970]: 14)

[He is learning in the steppe everything he knows / the land and the woman belong to those who work them. / She'd better put everything she can in her cunt / because he cannot fuck her by cable!]

That poem makes fun of Diego Rivera's Communist ideology. The next one refers to Nobel Prize–winning Chilean poet Gabriela Mistral. This poem defies the idea of Mistral's life as hagiography — schoolteacher of the Americas, a motherly figure. Novo outs her and depicts her as a lesbian having oral sex with another writer:

> Tu juventud pasó como la brisa
> Que el radio lleva en onda estrafalaria.
> Entre tus piernas queda una poetisa:
> Es fulana de tal que gargariza.

[Your youth passed like the breeze / transported by the odd wave of the radio. / You have a poetess between your legs: / It's "what's-her-name" gargling.]   (1978 [1970]: 57)

Witticism is the most important characteristic of this language. As suggested in the section on *Nueva grandeza mexicana* in Chapter 1, the *teatro de revista* (vaudeville in the United States) was a necessary transition between a rural and urban country and made extensive use of the pun, especially paronomasia and calambur. Gabler says Winchell comes from vaudeville, which "anticipated the values of mass culture" (1994: 44) and was the genre that accompanied the United States in the transition from an agrarian society to an industrialized nation. The process in Mexico, although different from that of the United States, is similar in two ways: the continuous growth of urban settlements in the twentieth century, with strong industrial components which accentuated the divorce between rural areas living in past centuries (Lazo's *La huella* and Marín's *Un día patrio*) and the modern city. Even within the city the difference between *colonias* was not just one of kilometers but also of centuries. There were parts of the city that embraced the new era and new technologies with abandon, and other sectors where secular traditions and poverty persisted (García Canclini 1995). Mexico City surpassed one million inhabitants in 1925.

Vaudeville in the United States and the *carpa* and *teatro de revista* in Mexico were experiments with the new culture that abandoned the constraints of the nineteenth century, the Victorian period or the Porfiriato in Mexico's case. Gabler says:

> Vaudeville was incautious, unselfconscious and liberated; it valued idiosyncrasy and novelty in its performers and exposed audiences to different cultures, new values and a fresh, exuberant, often irreverent style. (1994: 44–45)

What Novo learned from theater—be it classical (i.e., baroque), contemporary, or "*naco* [low-class] trash"[5]—was the theatricality of life, life as a dream, life as representation. The city is the new theater where people represent different roles: *pachuco* clothes or tuxedoes are no more than costumes.

A new and old culture of celebrity is promoted—"old" because this is not a new phenomenon. Maravall had already theorized usurpation in the picaresque novel (1986: 525–590). According to Maravall, the *pícaro* systematically usurps symbols of the upper classes. In Mexico during the Porfiriato, even if it was a liberal political modus operandi within the parameters of the nineteenth century, the regime retained a symbolic system replete with elements of the *ancien régime*. A close reading of the *Manual de urbanidad y buenas maneras* (Manual of Good Manners) by Manuel Antonio Carreño (d. 1874) provides endless examples of this phenomenon. This book of manners (which is still in print!) is a brutal choreography that rules every single movement (or lack thereof) that a person must execute twenty-four hours a day to demonstrate to the rest of the society that he or she is a gentleman or a lady. It contains

rules about how to interact with God and relatives, hygiene, how to un-
dress, how to sleep (decent people are not supposed to move while in
bed), how to get dressed (you are not supposed to see your naked
body), what to wear at home, how to walk, how to behave in different
buildings and institutions, what to talk about and how to talk; rules
about banquets, dances, funerals, servants, foreign people; and so forth.
There are more than 400 pages of regulations that young men and
women of the upper classes had to memorize and follow as if they were
the movie scripts of their lives. But after the Revolution, with the rise of
the new middle class and urban developments, everything changed.
Once this closed structure of symbols and rules was usurped and its values were distorted, a new system had to be put in place.

The old regime had established as one of the principal markers of nobility the access to leisure time; in the new regime, after the Revolution,
this process evolved to a democratization of entertainment. Those with
access to the most expensive forms of entertainment and those in charge
of entertaining the masses (and making obscene amounts of money
thanks to new technologies of reproduction) became the new "aristocracy" of this celebrity culture. At the same time, this process of democratization, as Gabler reminds us, ushered in a taste for lowbrow and
trash culture (as in the baroque and romantic periods). Let us not forget the example of Valle-Inclán writing the highbrow play *Luces de bohemia* by stringing together quotations from *revistas,* operettas, and
zarzuelas (see Chapter 1). The democratization process is also already
present in Góngora when he employs the slang of delinquents and black
slaves, which he alternates with the re-aristocratization of poetry in
other contexts (Navarrete 1995).

The Method

The life of a celebrity is an everyday spectacle where the personality is
always in character, ready to represent the play of his or her life. In
newspaper columns and on radio and television programs Novo displayed his life, his excessive elegance, his physical presence, his beautiful, strong, convincing voice, his plucked eyebrows, his makeup, his
hairpiece, his dandyism (Ross 1989), his display of controlled homosexuality, and overall his everyday life as a spectacle, always sur-
rounded by friends and celebrities presented as supporting characters
of the ongoing show. Gabler directs our attention to two aspects of popular culture that have changed our way of perceiving reality. One has

to do with the tabloids: "Tabloids told stories. Day after day they presented their readers with serials—real-life soap operas complete with stars, melodrama, lurid details and cliffhangers" (1994: 75). This is an important lesson that Novo learned. He started to serialize his articles, repeatedly using the same characters, who were recognized by the readers; some of the characters were already famous, and others were made famous by Novo.

At the core of this narrative was gossip. Gabler explains the relationship between Winchell and gossip as follows:

> In gossip one could create a national "backyard fence" over which all Americans could chat. Like slang, gossip also made one feel knowing, ahead of the curve. And like the tabloids in which it first appeared, it could be a means of wreaking vengeance in a country that prided itself on its social mobility and provided very few outlets for class antagonism. (1994: 81)

Gabler's lengthy explanation of the new phenomenon helps to explain the change Novo made in his newspaper columns after Cárdenas's presidency and during the Avila Camacho period:

> In a very real sense, then, social authority in the early thirties had been turned on its head; it now derived from the media, or as Walter put it, "Social position is now more a matter of press than prestige." And since the king of the media in the thirties was Walter Winchell, café society was in many ways a function of him. A mention in his column or in his broadcast meant that one was among the exalted. It meant that one's name was part of the general fund of knowledge. It meant that one's exploits, even if they were only the exploits of dining, rated acknowledgment. It meant that fame rather than accomplishment validated one's life.
>
> On its face it seemed absurd that a nation racked by unemployment should care about a band of swells whose deepest concern was whether they rated a column mention . . . Yet people did care, and they read about café society as if it were an exciting new social drama . . . café society was an imaginative world shimmering with glamour, just as so many Depression movies did. For most Americans, "café society" immediately triggered images of women in smart gowns and men in satin-colored tuxedos, of tiered nightclubs undulating in the music of swell bands, of cocktails and cigarettes, of cool talk and enervated elegance, all of which made café society one of those repositories of dreams at a time when reality seemed treacherous. (1994: 185)

In 1965 Salvador Novo's personal secretary, José Emilio Pacheco, compiled 800 pages of materials from newspaper articles written by Novo during the six-year term of Manuel Avila Camacho. In the prologue Novo explained the changes he made for the period 1940–1946. During the Cárdenas presidency, he had served as a political analyst, presenting a moderate-conservative view of the Marxist president. When the new magazine for the middle class *Mañana* requested Novo's collaboration, he decided to accept, with specific conditions:

> My condition to write in their new magazine was that the weekly section of my commentaries should be about events that touched me in the most direct and personal way: a true diary in which to tell my impressions of the small world surrounding me — like taking notes or shooting pictures with my camera to fix moments, places, and faces in my everyday path. The editors accepted, and this was the start of the weekly publication of "El Diario de Salvador Novo." (1965: 7)[6]

The column Novo ran during the Cárdenas presidency was titled "La semana pasada" (Last Week). It remained anonymous because it was similar to an editorial commentary. Novo had a small group of people who helped him gather materials and at times ghostwrote articles. Novo described "La semana pasada" as "una novela en borrosa marcha" (a novel on a blurred path; 8); in fact it was the necessary seed for new articles he would later write. According to Novo, the new column, "El diario," was as successful as the old one but addressed a different public. He defines the "Diario" as a mixture of two ingredients: social notes (especially parties and trivial gossip about celebrities), written using the technique of the serial or melodrama, and the personal confession. Novo makes a pun when noting that these articles were a "brief search for lost time" (1965: 10), explaining that Proust provided the subtext for his journalistic writing.

Several other ideas from Gabler's book about Winchell deserve comment because they further illuminate an understanding of Novo. The first concerns radio. When Novo was composing for the written press, he was also a radio personality. Among other things he had a fifteen-minute commentary in the BBC edition for Latin America, a very prestigious job. His recordings reveal a magnificent voice, soft and articulated but virile and energetic at the same time.

According to Gabler: "Radio, newer and without any tradition of its own, made no such distinction between entertainment and news" (1994: 214). This is a very interesting social comment because it helps to explain the new journalistic genre Novo was developing, where he could interweave hard news with comments and soft news.[7] In its early years radio was purely an entertainment medium—newspapers held a monopoly on news, and news broadcasts did not exist on radio.[8]

There is a final comment from Gabler's book about Winchell that can be applied to Novo:

> By the late thirties there were many more of them [columnists] clawing, nearly all of them marginalized Americans—Jews, Catholics, women, homosexuals—venting national frustrations through their own. (1994: 249)

Novo's homosexuality was a subtext of his articles which allowed him (and his readers) to play two roles: as a person at the center of the cultural, financial, and entertainment life of Mexico City and, at times, as someone marginal, a social climber (like the *advenedizo* of *La mulata de Córdoba* or like Lupe Marín) who has made it, placing himself in the group of *apretados* (the tight ones, a perfect name if one considers how difficult is to become one of them).

Gabler's *Life the Movie: How Entertainment Conquered Reality* (1998) is useful in explaining the procedure that Novo used to narrate his life as spectacle. Gabler's analysis is based on Daniel J. Boorstin's seminal study *The Image; or, What Happened to the American Dream* (1961), also known in later reprints as *The Image: A Guide to Pseudo-Events in America.* Boorstin described the celebrity thus:

> He is neither good nor bad, great nor petty. He is the human pseudo-event. He has been fabricated on purpose to satisfy our exaggerated expectation of human greatness. He is morally neutral. The product of no conspiracy, of no group promoting vice or emptiness, he is made by honest, industrious men of high professional ethics doing their job, "informing" and educating us. He is made by all of us who willingly read about him, who like to see him on television, who buy recordings of his voice, and talk about him to our friends. His relation to morality and even to reality is highly ambiguous. (1961: 58)

Boorstin defines the pseudo-event as "an ambiguous truth" (34) and also affirms that "the celebrity is a tautology" (74). This explanation of celebrity defines what Novo does with his own persona in his articles. But in Novo's case he supervised making himself a celebrity.

In the prologue to his edition of *Avila Camacho,* José Emilio Pacheco describes the genre Novo created. In order to do so, Pacheco must contextualize the period. No translation is necessary because most of the words either are English or are cognates; this exemplifies what Pacheco is trying to tell us — that U.S. popular culture and consumerism had a deep impact in Mexico at the beginning of the forties:

> Es ya el primer triunfo del american way of life. Ladies Bar, cocktail parties, cabarets, secciones de sociales, drive in, colgate, palmolive, cocacola, pepsicola, sevenup . . . triunfan los sándwiches y el lunch comercial; los industriales, banqueros, nuevas "columnas de la sociedad," almuerzan y beben jaiboles [highballs] en sus clubes. (1965: 16)

One more of Pacheco's ideas, almost lost in the farrago of American bits of the 1940s, is basic to understand the culture of the period. According to him one of the most important changes was the liberation of many women, despite the attempts by Mexican society to stifle any possible movement in this direction. Pacheco refers to "un machismo que muere en la idolatría a Jorge Negrete" (a machismo dying in idolatry of Jorge Negrete; 1965: 16). Negrete is the epitome of Mexican machismo at its peak, but after him the decline was constant. Pacheco tries to explain Novo's diary: it is unlike those of François Mauriac, the Goncourt brothers, or Federico Gamboa — it is more frivolous, open, and intimate; but because it is a diary that is going to be printed, the author is excessively conscious of the process. Eventually it becomes a matter of image, a hybrid between the real image of the author and the one he wants to project: "This genre of memoirs belongs unconsciously to fiction" (17).[9] Pacheco says that the rhetorical figure dominant in this diary is the pleonasm, because there is no such thing as a life which is not daily. Twisting Novo's wordplay with Proust, Pacheco observes that the pilgrim/author in Novo's diary "is wasting time while looking" (19). Therefore this Proustian protagonist is no more than the young wanderer of the *Soledades* and *El joven;* the only difference is that the young man now is thirty-six years old, belongs to the middle-upper class, and has learned how to make a decent living without having to sacrifice his wandering.

Salvador Novo's Lifie

Gabler defines "lifies" as "movies written in the medium of life," which have been possible since the techniques of theater were applied to "politics, religion, education, literature, commerce, warfare, crime" (Gabler 1998: 5). What Gabler (and Boorstin) have forgotten is that this phenomenon is not new; one of the main characteristics of the baroque was the application of theatrics to life, especially in the court.

Novo read the cultural parameters of his age and was conscious of the power of his writing, his image, and his voice. Thus he was able to configure himself as a celebrity — a commodity — and make a living selling himself. In numerous occasions in his articles he refers to himself as a prostitute when describing his journalistic work; the second part of the veritable allegory he presents is that when he wrote serious literature, for which he made no money, he became either the giving mother or the lover. But, as Gabler says, it is not just about money:

> [Intellectuals] knew that in the end, after all the imprecations had rung down around it, entertainment was less about morality or even aesthetics than about power — the power to replace the old cultural order with a new one, the power to replace the sublime with fun. (1998: 21)

Gabler's comment is pessimistic, but there is some truth to which we can relate. Margo Glantz reminds us (see Chapter 1) of the Mexican political system's tendency to absorb its intellectuals and make them part of the system. Novo's access to celebrity status allowed him to be part of the system, but he could impose conditions because he was not economically dependent on it. Novo understood perfectly this Foucaltian premise that power was at the core of the new mass entertainment industry. For instance, in the Avila Camacho period, he was allied with Alemán Valdés and attacked Padilla on several occasions.

Celebrities

By far the most often named celebrity in the "Diario" is Dolores del Río. She is presented as a diva, a Hollywood star who has returned to Mexico to continue her career. At the beginning of the 1940s the two most important actresses in Mexico were Dolores del Río and María Félix. The change in the nature of Novo's articles can be seen by comparing the "Diario" to *Lázaro Cárdenas*: in the 700 pages of *Lázaro Cárdenas* there is not a single mention of Dolores del Río, while there are almost 40 references to her in the "Diario." She was Novo's neighbor in Coyoacán; therefore, it is logical that the first mention is about her moving to the neighborhood (September 14, 1943). He also says that she had a cold and had to interrupt filming of *María Candelaria*, which was being directed by Indio Fernández. The truth is that there were many problems during filming: Fernández had assaulted Dolores del Río and her mother (Ramón 1997: 20), and the star threatened to stop the production of the movie. Novo also informs readers of some problems with a hydraulic pump at her house. This is trivial information; but the public was eager to read this material, even the sanitized version. Gabler says:

> Where movies and television provided a sense of community forged from the shared symbols of popular culture, lifies now provided community as well from shared gossip and trivia about celebrities. And where popular culture empowered the audience by sticking a thumb in the eye of high culture, celebrity lifies empowered the audience by investing it with a degree of collective control over the stars of the lifies. As Elizabeth Taylor wrote, "The public seems to revel in the imperfections of the famous, the heroes, and to want to be in a position of attacking—which I guess makes them feel a little bit superior." (1998: 168)

I started this chapter by noting how some significant postmodern novels since War World II portrayed history through fiction and how radio and television blurred the distinction between them. According to Pacheco, the "Diario" is fiction, and Novo considered these articles a sort of novel. It is understandable, then, that Dolores del Río is presented in this collection more as a fictional character than as a real person. She is performing her life in several media, and Novo is just one more of the array of reporters, cinematographers, script writers, movie directors, paparazzi, agents, husbands, and lovers in charge of helping her to represent her lifie. Dolores as a character is a movie star and behaves within the parameters established in the collective unconscious for that role.

The diary of January 24, 1944, begins with a telephone call to Novo from Agustín J. Fink, producer of Mundiales Films, to invite him to the premiere of *María Candelaria* as the star's companion. Novo declined the invitation only in part and went to the theater by himself. Once the program before the movie was over, he went to greet Dolores del Río and Fink and to sit with her. She says: "Angel (ényel) — me dijo—; no te perdonaría que no estuvieras junto a mí hoy" (Angel, I would not have forgiven you for not being close to me today; 1965: 95). The first word she utters is in English in the original, and the syntactical construction is anglicized. This is the only direct quotation in the "Diario" and serves to remind the public that they are dealing not just with a movie star but with a Hollywood movie star who also happens to be Mexican.

Novo recreates the melodrama of the movie and develops a tension to revive the stress of the premiere, the fact that the actress was nervous, "as if it were her first movie" (ibid.). The previewing circumstances were quite unfavorable; the large, standing-room-only crowd had to endure two newsreels, one trailer, one cartoon, and one episode of *Calaveras del terror* (Skulls of Terror). Novo labels the newsreels idiotic and the episode embarrassing. The audience members were already tired when the movie started. Now Novo gives us exclusive information: Dolores del Río's hand was "helada y crispada" (cold and tense; 96). He was holding her hand! The beginning of the movie was slow; the producers had decided to leave some key scenes without music to stress Dolores del Río's performance. But when the public saw the climactic scene in which she accepted the help of the painter, they roared with applause. The movie was a success. Del Río was radiant, happy. The real-life melodrama paralleled the melodrama in the movie; the public had an appetite for both the story told in the movie plot and the movie of the life of the protagonist.

As noted, the "Diario" was written against the background of the folkloric *charro* nationalism of Jorge Negrete, among others. Thus it is very interesting to note Novo's confession that he found Indio Fernández unpleasant because he was always in character, dressed in black as a *charro*. After talking with him several times, Novo changed his mind. This is one more example of a lifie; it is not just that some stars represented *charros* in the movies: they became *charros* in real life. Gabler tells the story of Buffalo Bill, the famous Indian scout whose life was popularized in dime novels. He decided to cash in on his popularity by moving to the East, where he put together a show like his fictionalized life; afterward he returned to the West, now dressed not in ordinary clothes for his job but in the costume popularized in the novels and shows.

The end of the entry shows Novo at his best; he says that all the celebrities are going to a party at a fashionable restaurant. He promises to go after he picks up his car, and then he goes home. This perfectly represents the Novo he wants to portray, someone who is invited to the best places, who holds the hand of the star during the premiere, but at the same time is marginal; when not in costume, he is just the gay Novo. Behind the mask of the celebrity in the theater is the mask of the character Novo, and behind that mask there is a writer who happens to be the "real" Novo.

An entry related to Dolores del Río on October 15, 1945, is also interesting (1965: 503–507). The first paragraph is perfect, and Novo confesses that he has been preparing himself to start a new major literary work. He jokes that he now has the three units (*unidades*) of the writer: time, adequate space, and the will to act. Novo vacillates between writing a novel about his life and writing his memoirs. If he chooses the novel, it will be strongly edited and very detailed; if he opts for the memoirs, it will be with "the help of my excellent memory and the severity of my bare objectivity, which I even use on myself, or above all in its entirety against myself" (503).[10] Novo explains that the subtext will again be Proust. He ends up choosing the memoirs; while he is writing, Dolores del Río calls because she needs his help in buying a lamp. As they talk about the two possible projects, she indicates that she is against the memoirs for two reasons: first, because she is not in favor of looking back; and second, because Novo is still young. Her comment inspired the book's title, *La estatua de sal* (The Pillar of Salt).[11] Novo tells his readers how beautiful the lamps by Garagarza are and narrates how they go to SyR to pick up a fur coat. Here Novo plays perfectly the role of "husband," lost among women's stuff and slightly scandalized by the astonishing prices of the store. He does so well that Dolores del Río and her friend Carmen López Figueroa buy him four ties.

Another typical entry of the diary is dated December 23, 1945. Novo and "casi todos" (almost all of us) have been invited to the *posada* at Dolores del Río's house, La Escondida. They form an "us," a homogeneous group: the beautiful people of Mexico in 1945. They meet at Salvador's to go together. "Eduardo" proposes dressing as "typical" Mexicans as seen in U.S. movies, so they have to wear straw hats and serapes. Eduardo does not have a last name in the entry because readers knew he was Eduardo Villaseñor, director-general of the Bank of Mexico from 1940 to 1946 (Camp 1982: 316) and author of the novel *Extasis, novela de aventuras* (Madrid, 1928). The second member of the community is Carlos Chávez, composer and director of the National Symphony of Mexico (and future director-general of Bellas Artes). Incidentally, Chávez felt the cold so much that he was very happy wrapping himself in the serape. The third member is Cantinflas; Novo notices that he is now smoking Philip Morris cigarettes instead of Delicados. Others present are the bullfighter Cagancho; the Spanish actor Armando Calvo; Pedro Vargas, wearing a serape/Spanish cape in white and looking "like the ambassador of Ethiopia" (1965: 560); and Orson Welles, who did not want to get burned by the firecrackers. Cantinflas made everybody laugh by chasing the guests with a stick, pretending he did not know where the piñata was. This was the wonderful Mexico close to the end of War World II. It is not difficult to imagine why middle-class magazine readers were fascinated by the character Novo, who was living in this Churubusquesque world of beautiful women, movie stars, bankers, bullfighters, musicians, and aristocrats.

The entry of March 5, 1945, is also worthy of comment. In the previous item of the "diary," Novo had promised to stop smoking; he begins the day by breaking his promise and regretting his decision. Novo is at home because Orson Welles and Rita Hayworth are coming to have breakfast in his garden: eggs and coffee for Welles and ham, fruit, and tea for Novo. They compliment each other on their work as newspaper columnists and acknowledge that they read each other as much as they can. Then Novo explains to his readers the vicissitudes that *Citizen Kane* endured and how Welles became interested in Mexico in 1940 when he was Dolores del Río's companion and wanted to do a Conquest movie with himself as Cortés and Dolores as Malinche. Instead, he began a project about a bull named "Bonito" and a kid from Aguascalientes; but he did not finish it. Welles says he has seen and enjoyed *Flor Silvestre* and *María Candelaria* and that he would like to visit Dolores. Then they talk about the recent death of Maximino Avila Camacho (d. February 15, 1945).[12] Welles tells Novo that there are similar characters in Brazil and China and that he had an interview with Don Maximino and was unimpressed, but Rita Hayworth (who did not know him before the meeting) perceived perfectly what kind of man he was. Of course, Novo does not say what kind of man General Maximino was, but the readers knew—the ellipsis has a strong impact because his violations of human rights were legendary.

Welles was in Mexico covering a meeting of American foreign ministers, and Novo tells a funny anecdote. Welles tried an experiment: he eulogized the Mexican secretary of foreign affairs, Luis Padilla, so much that at a given moment he should have realized that Welles was pulling his leg. But Padilla did not; he absorbed the praises without any problem. The last part of the article includes the arrival of Rita Hayworth, the description of her beauty, and the image of Welles and Novo walking in the garden and Rita, engrossed in her own thoughts, nibbling a pear. The article is a mixture of serious and frivolous topics, with a perfect cinematographic set (Novo's garden), perfect actors representing the roles of intellectuals and gentlemen, and the astonishing beauty of one of the most important stars of Hollywood. Rita Hayworth was at the peak of her career, and this scene happened just a few months before the filming of *Gilda*. Novo does not indicate what language they used (maybe English) and makes no reference to the fact she was Hispanic; her real name was Margarita Carmen Cansino.

The cast of Novo's lifie contains many celebrities who are still famous: for example, Joan Fontaine, Tennessee Williams, María Félix, Bette Davis, Frida Kahlo, Pedro Infante, Pedro Vargas, Miguel de Molina, Aldous and Thomas Huxley, Agustín Lara, Indio Fernández, King Carol of Romania, and a whole array of writers, bankers, and beautiful people.

Novo represented in his diary a virtual reality of celebrities where readers could project their fantasies, frustrations, and desires. This was a theme park of beautiful people always dressed in their tuxedos and evening gowns, always ready to visit Acapulco or New York and stand as true representatives of the Mexican miracle that was going to bring prosperity to all Mexicans as well as the always elusive modernity.

Politics

In the November 16, 1944, entry (1965: 271–275) Novo compared the Porfiriato to Avila Camacho's revolutionary Mexico in little more than 1,500 words. The pretext was that he was watching an operetta in a half-empty theater. He asserts that the only solution for these kinds of shows is to have them performed in their former splendor: with a magnificent orchestra, costumes, and performers. But this is not possible because times have changed: 1944 is dominated by movies; people prefer to pay to see María Félix instead of María Conesa. At the core of his comments, there is a statement that deserves explanation: "That society [the Porfiriato] had its hierarchies established by individualism" (271).[13] The initial reaction is to say that Novo was wrong, because the first effect of individualism was to break the hierarchical society.

According to Maravall, *individualismo* is the philosophical current produced by the social crises of the first modern centuries (1986: 294). This is "the ideology of a deep crisis of inconsistency of status" (ibid.).[14] The history of nineteenth-century Mexico admits an interpretation within these parameters: independence, the two empires, the Reforma, and the Porfiriato could be understood as different attempts to stabilize status, first to restore the hierarchical society of the colony and later to reform the following disorders. The country had to reinvent itself several times, which demonstrates how inconsistent status was — especially when three systems of class, caste, and race were at stake. Maravall says:

This individualism (which was very far from having broken all its ties to the order of the hierarchical world, although it was considered the first fearsome and threatening blow against it) starts by asserting the value of the individual, of all individuals. (1986: 293–294) [15]

Maravall, following W. W. Rostow, asserts that the crisis which led to individualism reached as far as the nineteenth century (1986: 296). According to Maravall, during this century individualism was widely attacked by Catholics, Protestants, and socialists because they felt it threatened their systems of values.

Novo apparently has a nostalgia for the oxymoronic liberal aristocracy of the Porfiriato, but his intellectual sophistication makes us wary of this explanation. The label "reactionary" has been applied indiscriminately to those Mexican writers, especially Marxist intellectuals, who were circumspect with regard to the Revolution. In his "Diary" Novo compares the theater of the Porfiriato with the contemporary movie theater. He prefers the former, because it was divided by social classes and people knew where they belonged: there was a sense of order. This is the hierarchy and order that Novo wants for society, but it is only the first part of the equation. Where is the role of the individual? The individuality is that of the artist on stage. According to Novo, the Porfiriato was the period when the real star system existed—what truly mattered was the talent of the single artist, with very little help from machines and devices. The 1944 movie star system is falsely individual because it is industrial; it is the product of teams of workers and the cluster of different talents. Nineteenth-century theater was handcrafted, the product of artists/artisans who were allowed to display their ability individually.

When Novo makes a reference to "masses," he uses quotation marks to make the reader understand that he is referring to Ortega y Gasset's classic study *The Revolt of the Masses.* Novo attacks Marxists, asserting that they unjustly label as reactionaries those who do not share their political position. He says that the real romantics are the Marxists and the "reactionary" romantics are the true realists. According to Novo, authentic classicism resides in nature, where there is a hierarchy harmonized by individualism. The attempt to destroy hierarchies, especially with the help of industrialization, is no more than an inane romantic effort.

Novo agrees with Ortega and other contemporary thinkers in believing that "modernity has failed to establish a legitimate social order" (Cascardi 1989: 340). He also agrees with the following:

Ortega argues that what follows from the revolt of the masses is a loss of social pressure and a slackening of the authority of social norms that amount to the suppression of social energy itself. (Cascardi 1989: 344)

This is why Novo stresses the importance of the individual, especially the artist, who is the only one able to transcend the slackening of modern society. Like Ortega, Novo does not fall into an easy nostalgia for previous times; both know the historical process is irreversible. What Ortega said (which was misunderstood and misquoted) is that the nobility of old times conquered a system of privileges and fought to keep that system of privilege. In a democratic society rights are given, and the people do not fight to preserve them; they are taken for granted, but people should realize they must be defended. Novo's easy metaphor about nature fails; he should have read Ortega more carefully and agreed that there is nothing natural about society because it has been constructed by humans. Novo does not say that a natural society ever existed, but he aims at a more harmonious society. He is right when he realizes that the modern industrial society is not a panacea and that a new set of moral problems is created with the entry of the masses into politics.

Hypochondria

Guadalupe Marín adapted the topic of the ill woman common in nineteenth-century literature to her own circumstances (see Chapter 5); she understood that illnesses were ideologemes with a double valence, one of oppression and another of liberation, because they allowed women to move to (real and metaphorical) rooms of their own, as in Virginia Woolf. Marín also knew that the muralists had portrayed a new naked Mexican woman in the light of the sexual revolution of the 1920s and wanted to have some control over how her own body, as synecdoche of the new (and traditional) Mexican woman, was depicted.

The technology of illness (in Foucaltian terms) was an invaluable tool for the patriarchal Victorian culture in its fight against the first protofeminist movements. A similar phenomenon had also occurred during the baroque period with mystic nuns (Franco 1989), when they were allowed to give voice to their bodies and to verbalize their stigmata as long as male confessors and church authorities had the last word and, if needed, could silence them.

Juan Goytisolo and Malcolm Read have been quoted explaining Quevedo's purpose when he put the human body in many of his writings as an attempt to balance the double process that modern society was developing to control the shaping of modern subjectivity—one of abstraction (angels) and another of reification (machines)—to control the body. Quevedo wanted to remind us of our animality and its importance at a time when modern subjectivity was being negotiated and defined.

The presence of Novo's body is at the core of his literature. He is comprised of his intelligence, culture, wit, and wisdom, but he is also his body, with plucked eyebrows, makeup, wigs, toilette, perfumes (he always wanted a discount), mouth, penis, testicles, anus, hands. By introducing his body, his gay body, into his diary, he could add another twist to his lifie. This sort of striptease with its play of concealing and revealing helps readers keep their attention on the commodity and object of desire, Salvador Novo, and adds value to the product. As noted, he repeats several times that his newspaper and magazine articles equal prostitution when compared to the "real love" of literary texts, where the writer does not make money.

With his hypochondria as an alibi, Novo can display parts of his body and his intimate thoughts and fears. He becomes the object of the gaze but is in control of what is shown; we can only read about what he reveals—and, of course, it is part of our duty as readers to fill in the gaps of what is not said.

On January 11, 1944, Novo unabashedly tells us that while he was dreaming he wet his bed. On January 13 the topic is colitis; he has had a conversation with Dr. Zoraya, the Secretariat of Health Administration's officer in charge of distributing penicillin, a rare commodity during War World II. Because Dr. Zoraya finds Novo thin, he learns that Novo has had colitis. According to the physician, new research indicates that colitis is an imaginary illness; Novo is not convinced and wishes he could have penicillin. On June 13, 1944, Novo declares he is not going to work hard while ill. He has to remember all the Antonios he knows because it is their saint's day. On July 13, 1944, he confesses that he took Benzedrine (an amphetamine) before performing in a charity play. The result was that he remained very calm during the play; but the pills produced insomnia afterward, and he spent the whole night unable to sleep, repeating again and again the lines of his character.

On December 25, 1944, Novo writes one of the longest entries of the diary. He does not mention the Christian holiday, which intrigues the reader (who expects to read something trivial related to the spirit of Christmas, some folkloric insights, a reference to the blues of those without their loved ones, or any of the usual topics). Instead of reading something related to the festivities, the reader finds an extensive reflection on the health and psyche of Novo's favorite topic: himself: "One of my frustrated ambitions (maybe the highest, most recurring, and most neurotic) has always been to be an ordinary person, humble, anonymous, and common" (281).[16]

Of course, Novo is not an ordinary person; he never rests like other workers, because he has decided to work different jobs. His body's response to complaints about the excess of work has been to create an allergic and seasonal colitis, which makes him take to his bed at the beginning of every winter. He is sent to two labs; in the first one, he reads the diplomas on the wall and speculates that the deans and university presidents who presented all those awards and degrees are either deceased or retired. Then he explains how they extracted blood from his ear to count his leukocytes to check for infection and how he also had to send something to the lab which would be considered the worst and grossest act if it were not done for medical purposes. The results indicate that he suffers from lymphocytosis and eosinophilia. He does not like the idea that he learns from the specimen that he has neither amoebas nor aertricks but instead has *Bacillus coli* and *Enterococcus*. Novo takes the test results to Dr. Manuel Alamillo Torres, who, after an examination, tells him that part of his lungs lies dormant and that he has the body of an athlete but does not use it to its full potential. Then Novo starts the auto-analysis of his situation: because he was pampered in excess by his mother, his natural laziness toward physical exercise was aggravated; being very young, he developed neurasthenia and an inferiority complex in everything related to gyms and sports.

Dr. Alamillo requests more tests, a hemogram, the Rose of Bengal test, and one to measure his icteric index. He shows the results to four doctors, but the diagnosis is pure Novo:

> On Sunday, the eve of my trip to Acapulco, I visited my uncle Manuel and showed him the results of the tests. He prescribed a quick treatment of sulfas, Redoxon, liver, and vaccines of coli bacilli, which I bought on my way home. I added these to the medicines that I had prescribed for myself and that I had been ingesting for a few days without telling these eminent physicians.[17]

He knows that his doctors are going to read his article and that his readers know that his doctors are also readers. Novo displays this piece of mischief because he cannot avoid the temptation of trying all types of medicines. He wants to share with his public the surprise and anger of his doctors when they learn he has been taking all kinds of medicines at the same time and jeopardizing his health.

On March 4, 1945, Novo recounts the frustration and nervousness of trying to quit smoking and how he does not succeed. On April 26, 1945, there is a small masterpiece of literature which describes a tooth extraction. He tells about the pain, a panic attack, his tears, the frustrated attempt to do the extraction with Metaphen and cocaine, and at the very end the rush to transport him to another doctor so that he can do the extraction with gas. Novo is very happy because he got what he wanted and did not suffer with the gas. On January 11, 1946, he explains an X-ray in detail, in surprisingly entertaining fashion.

The entry of March 30, 1946, recounts a strange episode, something between a prank and a medical emergency. The composer Carlos Chávez and Novo are not feeling well, and the doctors suspect appendicitis in both cases. Chávez is rushed to the clinic and requests that Novo be brought to the hospital, using the pretext that he needs more tests. Novo gets the "prescribed" tests and is operated on before Chávez.

These examples are childish, but they add to the exposure of his life, illustrating how he can put together this cluster of anecdotes, bits of life, culture, gossip, etc., and make something out of it. He keeps the reader's attention as well as a novel would—and a very interesting novel at that.

Coda

The writers of satiric poetry during the Golden Age knew that literature could mean power and the possibility to ascend in the social scale. Margo Glantz reminds us that the Mexican political system had a tendency to bring important writers of the country into the system and that they ended up being part of the machinery. Novo certainly believed in literature as a means of social mobility and that it was legitimate to use his talent at the service of his personal cause. He also mediated between the "traditional" Mexico of the Porfiriato and the new Mexico City of immigrants; and when it was needed he provided reassurance against the anxieties of the period. At the same time, and this is only a partial contradiction, he believed that conflict could make superior literature; therefore, when necessary, he used abrasiveness. In his work as mediator between classes he wanted to teach the upper class of the Porfiriato that there was something to be learned in the trenches. He belonged to the "in" group but also had to work every day and never forgot where the masses were.

The last and most important point is that Novo knew you are not supposed to "ruffle the *buga*." The heterosexual country and/or the establishment could accept him because of his many talents as a writer and could even accept that he introduced homosexual particles here and there; but literature was a means to avoid being condemned as a homosexual rather than to celebrate being gay.

Notes

Chapter 1. Neo-Baroque

1. "La 'anomia' . . . no es, sin embargo, una mera negación de un régimen normativo socializado y nada más. Conlleva la no aceptación de las pautas en cuanto éstas regulan el acceso a determinados objetivos y lo dificultan, provocando la ruptura de aquellos que se proponen alcanzar como sea tales objetivos. A tal objeto se tendrá que seguir otras vías, las cuales se consideran ilícitas ante el régimen de la sociedad establecida en la que se vive. Esto es así, ya que las permitidas para el marginado resultan o impracticables o ineficaces" (1986: 416).

2. José Agustín's *Tragicomedia mexicana* (1990) offers a postmodern analysis of the history of contemporary Mexican culture from Lázaro Cárdenas to Miguel de la Madrid Hurtado, putting together both (high and low) culture and politics.

3. There is an interesting parallelism between Balbuena's book and Novo's account of his trip to Spain in *La vida en México en el período presidencial de Miguel Alemán* (Life in Mexico during the Presidency of Miguel Alemán). Balbuena does not compare Mexico City to any city in Spain, a very interesting ellipsis that has been interpreted in different ways — mainly either as respect for Spain or as an indication of the superiority of Mexico (Sabat de Rivers 1996). *Miguel Alemán* is essentially two different books, the first part being one of the few Latin American accounts of the aftermath of World War II in Europe (a wonderful book that should be published independently) and the second part a testimony of Novo's function as director of the theater program at Bellas Artes. On his trip Novo visited Francisco Franco's Spain; but instead of being opinionated as he was in France, Great Britain, and Italy, where he criticized everything, he was very frugal in his account of Spain: "Madrid había sido, si no una decepción sí una indiferencia, de la que sin duda tenía mucha culpa la ineptitud de mi personal administración como viajero. En tan corto, turístico tiempo, ¿qué podía conocer de España, de Madrid mismo? Deliberadamente había cerrado los oídos de mi atención a todo juicio político sobre el régimen" (Madrid had been, if not a disappointment, an indifference; no doubt my ineptitude in managing my time as a traveler was to blame. In this brief, touristic time, what could

I know of Spain, of Madrid? I had deliberately closed my ears to any political judgment regarding Franco's regime; 95).

4. "De cuyo noble parto sin segundo / nació esta gran ciudad como de nuevo / en ascendiente próspero y fecundo" (15).

5. One of the principal mistakes of the theorization of the Barroco de Indias is to attempt politically correct readings of the Spanish or Creole writers writing in America. They responded to the political values of the period in which they lived and had the prejudices of the time.

6. "Y admírese el teatro de fortuna, / pues no ha cien años que miraba en esto / chozas humildes, lamas y laguna; / y sin quedar terrón antiguo enhiesto, / de su primer cimiento renovada / esta grandeza y maravilla ha puesto" (82).

7. Let us remember that baroque discourse is essentially oral: the sermon in the Barroco de Indias and the official discourse in the presidentialist regime. In another work (Oropesa 1996b) I have explained the role of the Mexican president as the official liar of the nation. Instead of being the Orwellian Big Brother, the Mexican president is the Big Liar.

8. "En México se ha exacerbado un fenómeno que ya había empezado a surgir hace varias décadas, que es la institucionalización absoluta de la cultura. Todo pasa por el sistema, y ser escritor significa de alguna manera estar mediatizado por el poder, y al mismo tiempo tener los beneficios del poder. Uno puede gozar de muchos privilegios gracias a la escritura. Uno puede estar en lugares claves en México por el puro hecho de escribir y escribir con cierta repercusión. Un escritor que dice cosas en el periódico que pueden ser temibles, es inmediatamente captado por el estado y pasa a ser parte de él. Sus libros se publican en ediciones muy importantes, se difunde, se lo toma en cuenta en la televisión, se le hacen entrevistas. Por otro lado, hay una especie de polarización entre la gerontocracia y la efebocracia; los viejos definen quiénes son los escritores jóvenes realmente importantes y los castran, los hacen fundamentales, los inflan tanto que los destruyen" (108).

9. The camp sensibility displayed by Novo in his satiric poetry is discussed in Chapter 3.

10. "Y quizá yo hubiera extremado mi indiscreción hasta informar a mi deslumbrado amigo de que allí, en el callejón de la Condesa, cabe el cual se yergue orgulloso y opulento el edificio que corona el Club de Banqueros, hubo hace cosa de un siglo una sucia tortillería, y corría un caño, y pululaban los perros, y se crió, recogido por una anciana pobre y caritativa, el héroe romántico de Payno. Y le habría dicho que ese 'Sanborn's' *frontero*, en que podíamos haber comido, o comprado un dentífrico, o un traje, o plata, o baratijas, o pinturas, o dulces, o *purgantes*, o admirado un fresco de Orozco, es el Palacio de los Azulejos, cuya historia puntual escribió el señor marqués de San Francisco, y antes de ser lo que es, alojó a un Jockey Club de los *'apretados'* científicos que era el punto final del *'flaneo'*" (1992: 30–31).

11. "Allí habríamos compartido con éstos el neurótico privilegio de sentirnos, desde la terraza que mira a la Alameda, los amos de México y los autores de su desarrollo, después de haber sorbido high-balls frente a las pinturas de Angel Zárraga" (29).

12. "Si ahora se mostraban ruidosamente alegres; si empezaban a tambalearse un poco, nadie podría adivinarlo cuando mañana sus columnas tronaran, modelos

de austeridad, contra la corrupción administrativa y contra la miseria en que la ineptitud de las autoridades revolucionarias tiene sumido a un pueblo que no come porque todo cuesta un sentido, y ha habido que importar maíz, y el comunismo, por otra parte, nos amenaza" (35).

13. "Acababa de triunfar la Revolución — una revolución campesina — y el teatro de revista se solazaba en ridiculizar al payo, al ranchero ventrudo y ladino, o tonto, que el 'cuatezón' Beristáin personificaba en la escena. Funcionaba en ella un humorismo elemental de retruécanos, a costa de la gruesa tontería (trasunto del 'bobo,' del 'simple,' del primitivo teatro español) del ranchero considerado como el prototipo popular de la época zapatista. Así, Beristáin era, todavía, 'he who gets slapped' — el que recibe las bofetadas de sus tanteadores, y suele devolverlas, para que el público ría, satisfecho de su personal, evidente superioridad. Roberto Soto, que más tarde polizaría en su barriga toda una época de la Revolución, de la capital, y del humorismo correspondiente a ambas . . . Cuando el callismo entronizó a un Morones obeso como Soto, y Soto dio con el próspero modo de ofrecer en su Lírico a la represión ciudadana la válvula tumultuosa de escape de ridiculizar a los líderes gordos y a los diputados con pistola" (41).

14. "Amaneció una nueva época verbalista, confusa, oratoria, prometedora sin compromiso, que los periódicos sesudos llamarían 'demagógica.' La antena sensible que recogió la nueva vibración; que dió en el clavo del humorismo que en la nueva época descargara sus represiones, se llamaría Cantinflas, y sería, una vez más, el fruto oportuno y maduro de esta ciudad. Si fuera de ella, y hasta medidas universales gracias al cine, la dislogia y la dislalia en que por la boca de Cantinflas disparata nuestra época, ha alcanzado éxitos y consagración, es porque ocurre y da la casualidad de que también fuera de México los hombres respiren desde hace algunos años el clima asfixiante de la verborrea, el confusionismo, las promesas sin compromiso, la oratoria, la palabrería ininteligible, malabarística y vana. ¿No han dicho campanudos discursos a su turno Hitler, Churchill, Molotov, Eden, Goebbels, Roosevelt, Staling [*sic*], De Gaulle, Franco, Perón, Lombardo Toledano?" (41–42).

15. "Desde las Lomas, la ciudad se veía flotar en un halo tenue que recortaba sus perfiles: volcada sobre el valle, tendida entre los siglos, viva y eterna. Ya recogía, como una madre gigantesca y celosa, el retorno fatigado de sus hijos. Bajo los techos de aquella ciudad: en el llanto del recién nacido, en el beso del joven, en el sueño del hombre, en el vientre de la mujer, en la ambición del comerciante, en la gratitud del exiliado; en el lujo y en la miseria; en la jactancia del banquero, en el músculo del trabajador; en las piedras que labraron los aztecas; en las iglesias que elevaron los conquistadores; en los palacios ingenuos de nuestro siglo XIX; en las escuelas, los hospitales y los parques de la revolución, dormía ahora, se perpetuaba, se gestaba, sobrevivía, la grandeza de México" (104–105).

Chapter 2. Gay and Baroque Literatures

1. "Allí sale un mancebo, la principal figura que Vmd. nos representa, y no le da nombre. Este fue al mar y vino del mar, sin que sepáis cómo, ni para qué; él no sirve sino de mirón; no dice cosa buena, ni mala, ni despega su boca; sólo hace una descortesía muy tacaña y un despropósito: que se olvida de su dama ausente, que tan-

tas querellas le costó al salir del mar, y se enamora de estotra labradora desposada en casa de su mismo padre, donde le hospedaron cortesmente, sin que sirva aquello de nada al cuento, sino para echarlo a perder y rematarlo sin artificio ni contento alguno."

2. "Pero para seguir este intento es fuerça ver primero, qué género de Poema es este de las *Soledades,* de que resultará conocer, si es capaz de grandeza, veráse si la tiene y si es razón que la tenga. Dexando pues varios pareceres, supuesto que no es dramático, tampoco puede ser épico, ni la fábula o acción es de Héroe, o persona ilustre, ni acomodado el verso; menos es romançe por más que tenga dél mixto, porque demás de no aiudarlo el verso, ni introduce Príncipes por sujeto del Poema, ni Cortes, ni guerras, ni aventuras, como el Ariosto, el Tasso Padre y el Alamani; Bucólico no es aunque en él entren Pastores, ni Haliéutico, aunque pescadores, ni Cinegético aunque caçadores; porque ninguno destos es sujeto adecuado y trata o a de tratar juntamente de otros; pero porque introduce a todos los referidos es necesario confesar que es Poema, que los admite y abraza a todos: qual sea este, es sin duda el Mélico, o Lyrico llamado así por ser canto, que esto es Melos, al son de la Lyra" (425).

3. "Solo podrá escrupulizar el ser más largo este Poema, que los que en género de lyrica dexaron los antiguos y no ser de una sola acción sino de muchas. Pero en lo que toca a dilatarse, bien sabe Vm. que importa poco, pues más o menos no varían la especie. En quanto a la acción o fábula, bien se pudiera sustentar por una, siendo un viaje de un mancebo náufrago, pero antes queremos que sean muchas y diversas: porque de la diversidad de las actiones naçe sin duda el deleyte antes que de la unidad" (426).

4. "Y que sea esta poesía inútil pruébolo. Ella no es buena para poema heroico, ni lírico, ni trágico, ni cómico . . . ¡Gracioso trabajo sería la *Ulisea* o *Eneida* escrita en aquel enigmático lenguaje! . . . ¡Oh diabólico poema! Pues ¿qué ha pretendido nuestro poeta? Yo lo diré; destruir la poesía . . . ¿En qué manera? Volviendo a su primero caos las cosas; haciendo que ni los pensamientos se entienden, ni las palabras se conozcan con la confusión y el desorden" (10).

5. "¡Con qué juicioso tacto está armonizado el Océano, ese dragón de oro del Sol embistiendo con tibia lengua, y ese traje mojado del joven, donde la ciega cabeza del astro 'la menor onda chupa al menor hilo'! En estos ocho versos hay más matices que en cincuenta octavas de la *Gerusalemme liberata,* del Tasso. Porque están todos los detalles estudiados y sentidos como en una joya de orfebrería. No hay nada que dé la sensación del Sol que cae, pero no pesa, como esos versos: 'que lamiéndole apenas . . . lento lo embiste . . .' Como lleva la imaginación atada, la detiene cuando quiere y no se deja arrastrar por las oscuras fuerzas naturales de la ley de inercia ni por los fugaces espejismos donde mueren los poetas incautos como mariposas en el farol. Hay momentos en las *Soledades* que resultan increíbles" (231–232).

6. "Proceder por alusiones. Pone a los mitos de perfil, y a veces sólo da un rasgo oculto entre otras imágenes distintas. Baco sufre en la mitología tres pasiones y muertes. Es primero macho cabrío de retorcidos cuernos. Por amor a su bailarín Ciso, que muere y se convierte en hiedra, Baco, para poder continuar la danza, se convierte en vid. Por último, muere para convertirse en higuera. Así es que Baco nace tres veces. Góngora alude a estas transformaciones en una *Soledad* de una man-

era delicada y profunda, pero solamente comprensible a los que están en el secreto de la historia:

Seis chopos de seis yedras abrazados
tirsos eran del griego dios, nacido
segunda vez, que en pámpanos desmiente
      los cuernos de su frente.

"El Baco de la bacanal, cerca de su amor estilizado en hiedra abrazadora, *desmiente*, coronado de pámpanos, sus antiguos cuernos lúbricos" (241).

7. "En *El joven* se trata el tema homosexual de tres maneras: primero, al mencionar los espacios citadinos en donde se producen los encuentros homosexuales, segundo, por las citas de textos y autores que se han relacionado con dicho tema y, tercero al hablar del descubrimiento de su propia orientación homosexual" (166).

8. "Federico García Lorca es ahora el ídolo de Buenos Aires . . . Me invita Pedro [Henríquez Ureña] a esta función [*La zapatera prodigiosa*]; quizá ahí me pueda presentar a Federico. Ha dado conferencias, ha tocado y cantado, lo adora todo el mundo y los diarios se llenan con sus retratos. Ante tamaña popularidad yo vacilo en mi deseo de conocerlo. Lo admiro mucho, pero no querría ser simplemente un admirador suyo más, y quizá no habrá medio de ser su amigo" (188).

9. "Federico estaba en el lecho. Recuerdo su pijama a rayas blancas y negras . . . Federico imponía su voz un tanto ronca, nerviosa, viva, y se ayudaba para explicar de los brazos que agitaba, de los ojos negros que fulguraban o reían. Cuando se levantó, mientras tomaba su baño, se volvía a cada instante a decir algo, porque se había llevado consigo la conversación, me senté en la cama . . . Federico entraba y salía, me miraba de reojo, contaba anécdotas, y poco a poco sentí que hablaba directamente para mí; que todos aquellos ilustres admiradores suyos le embromaban tanto como me cohibían y que yo debía aguardar hasta que se marchasen para que él y yo nos diéramos un verdadero abrazo. Por ahora, tenía que ir a ensayar *La zapatera*, que se estrenaba esa noche misma. Allá nos veríamos para conversar después de la función, si era posible, y si no, al día siguiente yo vendría por él para almorzar juntos, solos" (198–199).

10. "Yo llevaba fresco el recuerdo de su *Oda a Walt Whitman*, viril, valiente, preciosa, que en limitada edición acababan de imprimir en México los muchachos de Alcancía y que Federico no había visto" (201).

11. "Comencé a leer a Gide en 1920, y desde entonces no hubo una sola obra suya que me escapase . . . Gide se puso muy de moda entre los jóvenes de entonces, cosa que no dejaban de tomarnos a mal y de criticarnos" (586).

12. "En cierto modo, *Si le grain ne meurt* suscitó más escándalo que el *Corydon*. Este era un tratado dialogado, una reexposición de conclusiones sexuales ya conocidas pero abstractas, en tanto que en *Si le grain*, Gide confesaba practicar lo que predicaba, decía cuándo y cómo empezó la cosa, y describía con bastante delectación morosa y evocadora su primer satisfactorio sofocón beduino en la cálida arena del desierto" (587).

13. "Pero en ese cuarto de siglo, dos circunstancias de la inteligencia, aparte todas las de la sociedad, habían contribuido a desvanecer suficientemente la hipocresía: la una en la ciencia, la otra en la literatura: Freud en la una, Proust en la otra"

(587). "El tema, en efecto, de 'l'amour qui n'ose pas dire son nom,' había sido, si rarísimas veces tocado por los novelistas del XIX" (588–589).

14. "[*Conducta*] ha venido a impartir autoridad científica escueta (privándolo en consecuencia de toda singularidad artística, de todo carácter esotérico) al hecho simplemente zoológico de que es artificial y por tanto endeble, discutible e inválido, todo encasillamiento convencional de aquel orgasmo que en resumidas cuentas es todo lo que el hombre procura y se busca, y se encuentra, en cualquiera de las formas, ocasiones o modalidades que la oportunidad del momento le ofrezca.

"Adiós, claro, toda reverencia por los sagrados y ficticios papeles de la paternidad, de la maternidad, resultados imprevisibles y laterales de un simple orgasmo. Pero adiós también al tabú de su búsqueda y de su consecución en terrenos o en formas vedados, no por la naturaleza; sino por las buenas costumbres. Ni el cien por ciento A químicamente puro; ni el cien por ciento B químicamente impuro, se dan entre los hombres. Cual más, cual menos; unos una vez, otros antes, otros después, otros todavía, aparecen tabulados por el *Kinsey Report*, comprendidos, a elección, en alguno de los porcentajes de las columnas, ninguna totalmente negra, ninguna totalmente blanca.

"La vida, pues, de Gide, tuvo la fortuna de alcanzar una época en que la ciencia y su influjo sobre la moral desvanecerían el escándalo en que, por lo demás, no incurrió nunca. Una fortuna que favorece así la pureza de la luz a la cual, descartado el estúpido tabú que en otra época le habría acaso aniquilado, puede admirarse su obra" (588–589).

15. "Es, pues, un poeta de la inteligencia, un poeta del concepto, una poetisa de la razón. Si examinan por ejemplo la serie de sus sonetos sobre el amor, encontrarán una clave sobre este tema. Estos sonetos pueden parecer fríos, si es que la inteligencia, *que a mí no me parece*, admite este término. Pero Sor Juana no es sólo una poetisa de la razón; es también un poeta del sentimiento. Puede en ella predominar lo que llamaba yo en la conferencia pasada el poder lógico de la palabra" (779).

Chapter 3. Satiric Poetry

1. "La ideología republicana y democrática liberal fue una superposición histórica. No cambió a nuestras sociedades pero sí deformó las conciencias: introdujo la mala fe y la mentira en la vida política" (1982: 30).

2. "Por doble contagio de la estética neoclásica y de la romántica, una enamorada de la corrección y la otra de la espontaneidad, es costumbre desdeñar a estos juegos [ecos, acrósticos, aliteraciones, poesía retrógrada, centón, paronomasias y otras lindezas]. Crítica injusta: son recursos legítimos de la poesía" (1982: 83).

3. "Apareció Salvador Novo, un maestro del género. Tuvo mucho talento y mucho veneno, pocas ideas y ninguna moral. Cargado de adjetivos mortíferos y ligero de escrúpulos atacó a los débiles y aduló a los poderosos: no sirvió a idea o creencia alguna sino a sus pasiones y a sus intereses; no escribió con sangre sino con caca. Sus mejores epigramas son los que en un momento de cinismo desgarrado y de lucidez, escribió contra sí mismo. Esto lo salva" (524).

4. "Mientras Novo hacía una suerte de ostentación de sus inclinaciones sexuales, Xavier defendía su vida privada. No creo que fuese hipocresía. No se ocultaba

y era capaz de hacer frente a la condenación pública. Era discreto lo mismo en la vida real que en la literatura" (16).

Chapter 4. Agustín Lazo (1896–1971): Xavier Villaurrutia's Shadow

1. "Colaboró como escenógrafo y dibujante de trajes para el grupo 'Orientación,' bajo la dirección de José Gorostiza, en obras como *Antígona, Macbeth, Una petición de mano,* en el entremés del *Viejo celoso, El matrimonio* de Gogol, *Lillom* de Molnar, y en otras obras de autores mexicanos como *Ifigenia cruel* de Alfonso Reyes, *Parece mentira y En qué piensas,* de Villaurrutia, o *La escuela del amor y Ser o no ser,* de Gorostiza. Hizo también traducciones — casi siempre en unión de Villaurrutia — y adaptaciones de las siguientes obras; *El secreto,* de Henry Bernstein, *La hija de Lorio,* de D'Annunzio, *La verdad de cada quien* de Luigi Pirandello, *No habrá guerra de Troya,* de Giradoux, *Nuestra diosa* de M. Bontempelli, *Minnie la cándida,* del mismo autor y *La nueva Eloísa* de Alfred Savoir."

2. "Hizo la escenografía y el vestuario de *Asia* de la pluma de H. R. Lenormand y de *La hiedra,* de Villaurrutia . . . Como escenógrafo, los críticos de la época mencionan como aportación de Lazo una buena 'estilización' lograda a través de la economía de elementos y la simplificación de la escena en sus más exactos valores, usando sólo los objetos indispensables" (13).

3. "El grupo de los amigos del teatro, que dirige Cipriano Rivas Chérif, puso en escena la semana pasada el *Don Juan Manuel* de Agustín Lazo en la Posada del Sol. A sus anteriores presentaciones no me habían invitado, y a ésta no pude concurrir. Al parecer, es una agrupación de ricos, en que para ser miembro se necesita hacer una aportación de cinco mil pesos, y es una empresa no lucrativa. La concurrencia tiene que ir vestida de smoking a las únicas funciones que van.

"En el *Don Juan Manuel* trabajan tres muchachos de la escuela [de teatro del INBA]: Beatriz Aguirre, Agustín Sauret y Mario Muratalla. Agustín vino a verme hoy para explorar la posibilidad de que su obra sea repetida en un teatro en que pueda verla más gente: esto es, en Bellas Artes" (260–261).

4. "Sucumbió lentamente veinte años más tarde — abrumado por las riquezas que sus parientes iban legando sobre este descendiente último de una ilustre y rancia familia mexicana" (8).

5. "Lazo es probablemente el introductor más directo del surrealismo en México" (129).

6. "Nuestra vida conyugal no existió nunca . . . No somos marido y mujer. La noche de nuestra boda saliste de la alcoba intempestivamente, sin decirme nada. No pretendí, ni pretendo saber lo que pasó en tu alma. Es un misterio . . . Vivimos detrás de una fachada, podríamos decir . . . como dos amigos, porque después de aquella primera noche inexplicable tú no volviste a mis habitaciones" (17).

7. "El tema de la obra [cualquier obra teatral] es la *tensión* en torno a un enfrentamiento, no la historia de ese enfrentamiento" (177).

8. "El amor — el verdadero amor — me alejó de sus placeres, pero no sin dejarme convencido de que no había en mi persona ningún error de la Naturaleza" (96).

9. "Llore usted . . . a partir de este instante, sus lágrimas correrán libremente; no volverán a estancarse sobre los sentimientos . . . Y considere, para su consuelo, que

esas ofuscaciones de los sentimientos eran realmente funestas en épocas lejanas. Recuerde los ejemplos que, de ellas, hicieron los poetas de la antigüedad . . ." (105).

10. "Ahora te necesito para que guardes el secreto que, los tres, establecimos antes. Para todos, ya lo oiste, no emprendo sino un viaje: en cambio, tú sabes que no regresaré jamás" (155).

11. "Llegué al teatro a las ocho y media, en la creencia de que enseguida comenzaría la representación del *Don Juan Manuel* de Agustín Lazo. Pero en su decorado, lo que estaba ocurriendo eran los exámenes de la escuela de Opera. Señoritas de traje largo y señores de tuxedo emitían górgoros melodiosos ante una concurrencia plausible y frente a la orquesta que Lalo Hernández Moncada dirigía. El examen había empezado una hora tarde, y la función se retrasaría en consecuencia . . . *El caso de don Juan Manuel* que ha tratado con Freud de la mano para psicoanalizarlo y descubrir, en la neurosis que le induce a matar transeúntes a hora fija y preguntada, el fondo tenebroso de un complejo de Edipo que es lo que le aleja de su mujer, en quien vuelve a ver a su Yocasta cada vez que intenta perpetuar el apellido de los Solórzano. El análisis se lo hace un franciscano, que es lo que realmente ha sucedido entre nosotros los católicos con la confesión, desde mucho antes que se inventara el análisis médico. Ningún símbolo freudiano ha escapado a la consideración del autor; ni el pañuelo ensangrentado, fetiche que guardaba don Juan Manuel en una cajita después de cada fechoría, y que simbolizaba la intención malsana, verdaderamente enfermiza, de las nupcias no cumplidas con su señora" (1967: 276).

12. In his history of the Mexican theater between 1920 and 1950, John B. Nomland (1967) gives an analysis of *El caso* without imaging the homosexual overtones. He offers this surprising possiblity: "el sacerdote le dice que debe orar, y se adivina que el futuro de don Juan Manuel está en la iglesia, ya que el cura y el sobrino deciden no decir nada" (The priest tells don Juan Manuel that he must pray, and we guess that don Juan Manuel's future is in the church, because the priest and the nephew decide not to tell anything to anybody; 229).

13. "La 'Niña Sara' la llaman, temblando, sus criados. Es rica y huérfana de padre. Por lo que se refiere a su madre, a quien, al menos en su casa, nadie nombra, se sabe que fue una negra. Su padre fue un 'San Juan,' hermano de don Carlos, rico como nadie en Rincón brujo, dueño de los trapiches e ingenios que más tarde compró don Juan Reyes. El padre de Sara murió hace años. Sara es el fruto de la sensualidad de Luis San Juan que, en una noche de embriaguez, hizo traer una negra a su casa, una negra sensual, para tener un hijo de ella. Ese hijo fue una hija: Sara. Nadie en Rincón Brujo la quiere; nadie la recibe. Sara, orgullosa, desafía esta situación. Si en el fondo tiene, ella que está hecha de miel y alcohol de caña, una amargura se sobrepone al destino y se ha jurado a sí misma vengarse de los 'San Juan' que no le reconocen parentesco, y aún de los habitantes de Rincón Brujo que la desdeñan . . . Los antecedentes de este *drama de amor y de misterio* datan de muchos años. Ahora, en 1910 van a cristalizar de este modo" (192; emphasis added).

14. "En el patio el 'Cuadrado,' administrador de la casa, fuerte y groseramente sensual, da órdenes en nombre del amo" (198).

15. "EL CUADRADO.—No, no te dejaré entrar. El amo nunca me lo perdonaría. (Una ola de sensualidad grosera le sube a la cabeza, como el alcohol que ha bebido) . . . No, Sara. No entrarás. (Luego, acercándosele, confidencialmente.) Ven mejor con nosotros, conmigo, allá afuera, bajo los árboles . . ." (201).

16. "EL CUADRADO.—Pero lo que no saben es que, esa misma noche [la de bodas], Pedro la pasó emborrachándose con nosotros, conmigo. Sin entrar a ver a Emilia. Y así todos los días, por una razón o por otra . . ." (208).

17. In 1964 Francisco de Monterde published his article "Juárez, Maximiliano y Carlota, en la obra de los dramaturgos mexicanos," where he essentially studies *Corona de sombra* by Usigli and *Segundo imperio* and states correctly that the historical basis of the two plays is *Juárez y Maximiliano* by Franz Werfel, translated by Enrique Jiménez D. and with a study by J. M. Puig Casauranc, one of the sponsors of the Contemporáneos group. *Juárez* was published in Mexico in 1931. Monterde makes only brief mention of *Segundo imperio*, saying that he thinks the play was never represented and that Usigli thought the end of the play was weak and ambiguous.

18. In the introduction to the play *La huella* there is a portrait of Lazo and a brief bio-bibliography that says: "Su primera Pieza [*sic*] original, *Segundo Imperio*, la escribió a fines de 1945" (His first original play, *Segundo imperio*, was written at the end of 1945).

19. "RAMIREZ.—La llegada de esos generales avivaría la enemistad entre el sector a que se refiere el Ministro Lares y la clase media; esa raza mestiza que Sus Majestades tienen especial empeño en atraer" (66).

20. "Según la investigación de V. González Loscertales (1976), entre 1882 y 1911, por lo que respecta a la agricultura, los españoles, repartidos por todo el país, llegaron a poseer el 27 por ciento de la superficie total de la tierra cultivable, mientras que prácticamente monopolizaban determinados ramos de la industria (textil, alimentaria . . .), predominaban en el comercio y controlaban mucho de los principales bancos. En conjunto, en este período constituían el grupo extranjero más influyente del país . . . Los españoles, tanto en el Distrito Federal como en ciudades de otros estados, monopolizaban prácticamente el comercio de *abarrotes* (ultramarinos), favorecidos por el hecho de que el tipo de productos que en ellos se expendían (aceites, enlatados, vinos, etc.) derivaban precisamente del comercio exterior sostenido con España. El comercio de *abarrote* era también en ocasiones casas de empeño y resultaba frecuente que el comerciante cuya amplia gama, como advierte acertadamente M. T. Jarquín . . . abarca desde el 'modesto abarrotero al hombre de negocios a gran escala,' lo utilizase como medio de especulación que le permitía realizar inversiones en otros sectores económicos. Algunos españoles representan magníficos ejemplos de esta movilidad, alimentada en buena medida por las relaciones de paisanaje que convierten a los comerciantes españoles en un grupo cerrado, que les permitió adquirir experiencia y capital" (Cagiao 1992: 307).

21. REMEDIOS.—Mi hermana declaró que no se casaría, porque se había equivocado.

LA SRA. LAURA.—¡Palabras absurdas! . . . Nos consta que Guadalupe quería a Ernesto. Nadie influyó en su ánimo para que correspondiera a las prolongadas asiduidades de él.

REMEDIOS.—No, en eso estamos de acuerdo, hasta el día del cambio inesperado, mi hermana daba muestras de estar enamorada. Y no podía decirse que en sus sentimientos influyera otro factor porque, desde el punto de vista social, su matrimonio no era brillante: Ernesto no era, aún, el hombre próspero que llegó a ser más tarde.

LA SRA. LAURA.—El no era sino uno de tantos extranjeros emprendedores, recién llegado al país; y del que, ni el nombre ni la posición . . .
REMEDIOS.—¿Correspondían a nuestro nombre y a nuestra posición? . . . No, claro está, pero Guadalupe afirmaba cuando se decidió a aceptarlo, que él era un hombre decente . . . (7)

22. "GUADALUPE.—Has comprado tierras, muchas tierras: las tierras disponibles y—sobre todo—las no disponibles. Tu páramo ha crecido, sigue creciendo como una gran mancha de aceite en el tepetate. Tus caminos se tienden hacia los linderos del yermo, en espera de prolongar sus tentáculos por las Haciendas, por las rancherías, por los ejidos vecinos; por todos los lugares donde aún queda una poca de tierra que arrebatar—perdona: que comprar—. Y mientras más crece tu yermo—yermo y páramo no dejará de serlo nunca—más se concentra el rencor, si no es que el odio, de todos los que despojas, de todos los que oprimes, de todos los que explotas; porque ¡claro está, cómo ibas a anexarte la tierra sin su gente! . . . El rencor se concentra pero también se extiende en torno a tu páramo dorado y amenaza con envolvernos, con sumergirnos a todos; porque el odio que se despierta, que se incuba día a día con pequeñas trampas, con pequeñas usuras, con pequeñas rapiñas—¡imagen de la grande, de la enorme rapiña!—el odio anónimo, el odio emboscado no distingue culpables de inocentes" (53).

23. "Amparito, dígase claro, no tenía ambición de lujo sino de decencia; aspiraba a una vida ordenada, cómoda y sin aparato" (130). "Por esto [Amparito] aspiraba a la familia, al matrimonio, y quería que fuese su casa firmísimo asiento de las leyes morales. La religión, como elemento de orden, también la seducía" (131).

24. "Luis es un joven mestizo, de tez bronceada, de cabellos muy negros y lacios. Viste pantalón ajustado de paño negro, sin botonadura; chaqueta de gamuza, y sombrero ancho de fieltro gris que lleva, ahora, en la mano" (15).

25. "LUIS.—Es realidad, debe ser realidad. Nos mirábamos sin conocernos, entre las cosas mudas; nos mirábamos hasta el día en que, sin saber cómo, . . . descubrimos en nosotros un mismo sentimiento de la vida. Yo estaba solo; ¿quién era? ¿a dónde iba? ¿qué buscaba? . . . Mi vida a través de los carriles, sobre el tepetate, entre los magueyes, entre la gente de mi propia raza, era una soledad enorme, insospechada. La gente, el sol, la tierra; lo que creía amar y comprender, no era sino una ilusión, formada por mi misma soledad para ayudarme a vivir. La realidad es ésta: es este amor que mitiga, que sacia, la soledad en que vivía" (31).

26. "GUADALUPE.—La noche en que viste mis manos asidas a su espalda— no implorando—la noche en que contuve la sangre de su frente con mi velo blanco; aquella misma noche fui suya, enteramente suya. Nuestra unión, por ser sin esperanza, fue completa" (61).

Chapter 5. Guadalupe Marín: The Madwoman in the Murals

1. "Jorge Cuesta murió en 1942, y su fallecimiento terrible aún eriza los pelos: el maestro se emasculó después de un asedio frustrado a su propia hermana (versión Elías Nandino)" (28).

2. Carlos Monsiváis can be added to this list: "Lupe, resentful, writes *La única*, a more than transparent novel-in-code, where with a vengeance she presents Cuesta and his family as evil and decadent characters" ("Lupe, resentida, escribe *La única*,

novela-en-clave más que transparente, vindicativamente presenta a Cuesta y a su familia como personajes malvados y decadentes"; 1985: 13).

3. "Lupe cantó corridos y coplas. A Diego lo embelesaban sus *Borrachita me voy, El quelite* y *La barca de oro*. Concha Michel hizo segunda. Tina también. Hasta Antonieta Rivas Mercado, con su sombrero de campana metido hasta las cejas según la última moda de París entreabrió sus labios delgados para seguirlas. De todas, la más deslumbrante era la pantera. Con su pelo negro recogido en vano escapándose crespo y fuerte, crin de caballo a los cuatro vientos, Lupe era una figura formidable. Sus larguísimas piernas cruzadas se extendían frente a ella y al subir la falda mostraba unos muslos alargados y nobles, sus manzas de uñas pintadas de rojo deteniendo sus rodillas, su cabeza echada para atrás, su pecho ahuecado siempre con algún collar de cuentas de jade y plata, alguna sonaja precolombina, toda la miraba Diego los ojos prendidos a la boca llena, los labios gruesos y movedizos y los grandes dientes blancos de su niña, bárbaramente espléndida en rojo y oro, con pesados festones de tira dorada y aretes largos que tintineaban" (155). "[Tina Modotti] recordó la definición del Dr. Atl: 'Lupe es una furia que nació antes del diluvio universal' " (174).

4. "En su libro *La única*, autobiografía apenas disfrazada y lastimosa por su odio y maldad, atribuye a Cuesta un papel particularmente repugnante . . . Si Jorge era un intelectual refinado, encerrado en sí mismo, Lupe era apasionada, exuberante . . . Cuesta quedó fascinado con esta mujer sensual, frívola, viva, totalmente incomprensible para un personaje como él. Pero más que pasión fue curiosidad lo que ella le inspiró . . . Lupe abandonaría a su hijo prácticamente de inmediato y exigiría el divorcio" (51–52).

5. "En la capilla de Chapingo, Diego había terminado de trazar la figura principal, una Lupe de vientre abultado, pechos agrandados por la maternidad y una frondosa cabellera. 'Lo que más me gusta son mis chichis,' había comentado Lupe. 'Pero yo allí toda encuerada, en una capilla, ¿qué van a decir en Guadalajara, gordito? Lo que sea de cada quién, son mejores mis chichis que el chile de Diego' " (193).

6. "En el muro del fondo la tierra fecundada. Tras ella el viento que se convierte en fuerza matriz, como agua y el fuego, para producir la energía, es decir: la electricidad todopoderosa, al servicio de la familia humana" (237).

7. "*La Diegada*, serie festiva y maledicente de cuartetas y sonetos que, entre otras substancias corrosivas, celebran los amores de Lupe y Jorge Cuesta, tuvieron un final trágicamente truculento. Rivera tomó y cobró venganza en la portada de *La única*—especie de novela autobiográfica escrita por la señora Marín, que, con seráfica inocencia ilustró Diego—; allí, de un torso de hermafrodita surgen dos cabezas: la del lado izquierdo corresponde a un adolescente y por lo mismo es ambiguo, con un pezón pequeño y obvias coincidencias con Jorge Cuesta; la del lado derecho es Lupe Marín, adornada con enormes aretes y pezón descomunal, con evidente substituto fálico. Las manos, colocadas a la altura de la cintura, sostienen una bandeja y sobre ésta reposa la cabeza—a semejante de Salomé y San Juan Bautista—, decapitada del poeta importante del grupo de los Contemporáneos. Para mayor ferocidad y cauterio, las letras del título salen y cierran una especie de sistema circulatorio o comunicantes vasos" (42).

8. "Entre el grupo 'jotista' [Los Contemporáneos] y las mujeres existe, en verdad, poca diferencia. ¡Sin embargo, las mujeres en toda época y en toda circun-

stancia siempre son más agradables! . . . Toda mujer de talento por lo general es fea . . . Las mujeres mexicanas que escriben son agradables . . . No me explico que estas damas teniendo encantos tan apreciables se den a la pesada tarea de escribir y deleitar a los burgueses" (127).

9. "Es la historia de una desequilibrada mental que analiza su disparatada vida. Libro absurdo y latoso con pretensiones de erudición, en paradójica contradicción al ver que una loca razona. Marcela es una mujer defraudada en el amor, en sus dos matrimonios, en sus sentimientos de maternidad. El romanticismo se desborda en su corriente pesimista e inadaptación. A veces el lenguaje se orla de un naturalismo nauseabundo" (75).

10. "Nadie trabaja por ocuparse de política. Es la única manera de llegar a tener automóvil. Por eso, en política, es donde realmente sí ha habido movimiento. Aunque los cambios sin trascendencia, como siempre. Ya sabes, todo queda en familia. Sí, entre la 'familia revolucionaria.' El cambio de Presidente es el despiste. Ellos se cambian, pero sólo de una oficina a la otra. Procurando siempre el mismo sueldo y más o menos la misma categoría. No importa si se van a Educación, a Agricultura, a Guerra o a Gobernación; lo importante es que tengan la misma representación y poco más o menos mismo sueldo . . . Sabe Dios hasta cuándo durará esto; opino, que la situación actual, va a superar en récord de duración a la época porfiriana" (201).

11. "La teoría de Marañón sobre el donjuanismo nos demuestra sus errores. Esa teoría es, en mi concepto, consuelo de los asexuados y refugio de los agotados. También puede serle útil a cualquiera de los que nada tienen que ver con la época actual, con esta época en la que resulta mezquino, completamente mezquino dejarse atrapar por una sola mujer" (118).

12. "Su primera pasión, que mucho tiempo fomentó secretamente, se le despertó, siendo aún muy joven, por su hermana menor, hasta que un día, desesperado, resolvió introducírsele en su alcoba. La chica al ver que su hermano como loco trataba de poseerla, gritó furiosamente pidiéndole protección a sus padres" (7).

13. "Fui allá, con Lombardo Toledano, su mujer y Diego Rivera. Cuando me vieron con ellos, las muchachas del mercado me preguntaron que por qué andaba con un gringo y dos puercos pelados. La mujer de Lombardo y Diego son gordos y blancos" (166).

14. It is probable that Cuesta influenced Marín's vision of Marxism. Nigel Grant Sylvester in his book on Cuesta says: "El peligro, tal como Cuesta lo ve, surge de una prevaleciente ideología marxista personificada por el Secretario de Educación, Narciso Bassols, y por uno de sus principales colaboradores, Vicente Lombardo Toledano, influyente promotor del sindicalismo, los cuales proponían reformas constitucionales que pusieran el sistema educacional bajo el influjo de la filosofía socialista" (According to Cuesta the danger arose from a prevalent Marxist ideology personified by the Secretary of Education, Narciso Bassols, and one of his principal aides, Vicente Lombardo Toledano, an influential promoter of unionism. They advocated constitutional reforms to put the education system under the influence of socialism; 1984: 37–38).

15. Writing about the United States, Jonathan Goldberg has noticed this interesting phenomenon: "It is a remarkable fact that in many of the states in which sodomy remains a crime, the language used is identical to that found in Renaissance

or colonial American statutes—25 Henry c. 6 cited verbatim, for example, in Massachusetts, Michigan, Mississippi, Oklahoma, Rhode Island, and South Carolina" (1992: 11).

16. "Físicamente está más feo que nunca; avejentado y flaquísimo. Uno de sus amigos me contó que todas las noches se desvela; se las pasa en *cabarets*, en compañía de su amigo al que le dicen 'Varita de nardo' " (203).

17. "En donde a las mujeres se les despiertan pasiones fulminantes por otras mujeres" (126).

18. "A pesar de que tenía una seguridad absoluta de mí misma y que ni por un momento pensé que sucediera, por no ser afecta a aparecer como que me escandalizó, me andaba yendo mal. Tú bien viste con cuánta indiferencia aparente me dejé acariciar, sólo por no descubrir mis pensamientos; pero tuve momentos terribles; te confieso que empezaba a dolerme la cabeza. No cabe dudad que una mujer así de viciosa y bella, es peligrosa. Pero qué asco prestarse a un machacamiento mágico, como le nombraría eso el Secretario de Educación" (160–161).

19. "La incluyo en su totalidad porque es importante no sólo por su contenido, sino como ejemplo clarísimo de la objetividad e inexorable argumentación de Cuesta (aún tratándose de un asunto íntimo y bajo condiciones en las que el poeta se sentía ridiculizado)" (21).

20. "Yo le expuse a usted que el carácter que habían tomado unas hemorroides que me afligen desde hace diez y seis años me habían dado el temor de que se tratara de una modificación *anatómica,* que tuviera caracteres de androginismo, como se acostumbra a llamar a estas modificaciones, o de estado intersexual, como también se acostumbra llamarle . . . No soy yo quien imagina que hay estados intersexuales, que se manifiestan *anatómicamente*. Ni soy yo quien expresa que la forma de esta manifestación anatómica puede ser, en unos casos, una desviación o degeneración de la próstata" (22–23).

21. Frida Kahlo also described Rivera's breasts: "About his chest, I would say that if he had disembarked on the island governed by Sappho, he would not have been executed by her warriors. The sensitivity of his breasts would have made him acceptable. His peculiar and strange virility also would make him desirable in the territories ruled by empresses eager for masculine love" (1995b: 143).

22. "¡Qué bestia eres pensando decir esto! Cuando menos te encarcelarán. ¡Ahora sí creo que estás loca! ¡No cabe duda que estás loca!" (251).

23. "Los libros 'en clave,' novelados sobre personajes contemporáneos, tienen el defecto, el peligro de que si como ocurre con los que Lupe recoge en el suyo, carecen de una personalidad vigorosa, imparten a la obra que animan una vigencia limitada . . . Luego quedan en jeroglíficos, y su valor documental se extingue en el interés que siguen teniendo exclusivamente para el autor que, de su vida, les incorporó su obra. Yo sí pude, claro, reconocerme en *Un día patrio;* pero más a causa de que Lupe puso en él mi nombre con todas sus letras, que porque mi retrato sea en ese libro más, digamos, que mi foto de una credencial a estas fechas inválida" (228–229).

24. "La sorprendí mirándome. Avergonzado y nervioso" (150).

25. "Necesitaba ver sangre o saber que sucedían cosas espeluznantes" (176).

26. "En lugar de disgustarse, besaría mis manos y mi cara para consolarme. Levantando la manga de mi saco, descubriría mi brazo y lo besaría infinitas veces.

Desabotonaría mi camisa y apoyaría su cabeza sobre mi pecho sucio y sudoroso. También mi cuello, mis oídos y mis cabellos serían tocados por sus labios y qué felicidad iría a invadirme al confirmar que me quería" (178).

Chapter 6. *Gossip, Power, and the Culture of Celebrity*

1. But Alexandre Dumas the elder did the opposite; he did very ideological and conservative readings of the seventeenth century to reinterpret it within the new cultural parameters of his century. Dumas appealed to the nostalgia of the Old Regime among the new bourgeois, who wanted to naturalize their new wealth in aristocratic terms.

2. Emilio Azcárraga founded XEW in 1930, following the family formula perfected in the United States: songs, sketches, contests, and novels adapted to the radio. Because the medium had not yet developed its own artists, they came from theater and vaudeville and in the Mexican case also from *carpas*, the so-called *carperos* (Merlín 1995: 21–22).

3. "En el melodrama, el suspenso equivale a una promesa: Jovencita, serás idéntica a tu madre, aprenderás la realidad en los embarazos y en las privaciones de lo que te rodea y en el deseo de que los sueños prefabricados te compensen por lo no vivido. ¡Ah!, y si quieres identidad, acude al nacionalismo, en el caso de que por nación se entienda un cúmulo de canciones, de chismes de columnistas, de programas y series, de tramas donde la pobreza accede al amor del rico y no por eso pierde su bondad o su pobreza."

4. "La forma del lenguaje del llamado homosexual, linda con los artificios de la germanía, del argot, del caló, y de aquello que organiza su defensa frente al poder dominante" (14).

5. Ralph Blumenthal in an interview with Neal Gabler notes: "Mr. Gabler traces the rise of entertainment culture to the nation's beginnings and an affinity for lowbrow amusements. 'Trash was deliberate,' he said. 'Americans were literate. They chose trash because it was a glorification of the democratic impulse' " (1998: 3).

6. "Mi condición para escribir en su nueva revista fue que la sección semanal de mi comentario acerca de sucesos que me tocaran del modo más directo y más personal: un verdadero 'Diario' que consignara mis impresiones del pequeño mundo en que me movía—como quien toma apuntes o dispara su cámara para fijar momentos, sitios y rostros en el camino de los días. Los editores aceptaron, y empezó a publicarse, todas las semanas, 'El Diario de Salvador Novo' " (7).

7. According to Daniel J. Boorstin, "In the traditional vocabulary of newspapermen, there is a well-recognized distinction between 'hard' and 'soft' news. Hard news is supposed to be the solid report of significant matters; politics, economics, international relations, social welfare, science. Soft news reports popular interests, curiosities, and diversions: it includes sensational local reportings, scandalmongering, gossip columns, comic strips, the sexual lives of movie stars, and the latest murder" (1961: 23).

8. Jesús D. González says in an interview with Bertha Zacatecas that in the 1930s radio stations in Mexico did not have news departments (Zacatecas 1996: 112).

9. "Este género de memorias pertenece inconscientemente a la ficción" (17).

10. "Con el auxilio de mi excelente memoria, y la crudeza de la descarnada objetividad que empleo aun sobre mí mismo, o sobre todo contra mí mismo" (503).

11. "Then the LORD rained on Sodom and Gomorrah sulfur and fire from the LORD out of heaven; and he overthrew those cities, and all the Plain, and all the inhabitants of the cities, and what grew on the ground. But Lot's wife, behind him, looked back, and she became a pillar of salt" (Genesis 19.24–26).

12. There is an excellent literary portrait of General Maximino Avila Camacho as General Ascencio in Angeles Mastretta's *Arráncame la vida* (Oropesa 1996b).

13. "Aquella sociedad conoció las jerarquías que establece el individualismo" (271).

14. "La ideología de una grave crisis de inconsistencia de status" (294).

15. "Este individualismo (que está muy lejos de haber roto todas sus vinculaciones con el orden del mundo jerarquizado, aunque fuera considerado como un primer golpe temible y amenazador contra aquél) empieza por afirmar el valor del individuo, de todos los individuos" (294–295).

16. "Una de mis frustradas ambiciones; quizá la más alta, recurrente y neurótica, consistió siempre en ser una persona ordinaria, humilde, anónima y común y corriente" (281).

17. "Todavía el domingo, la víspera de volar a Acapulco, visité a mi tío Manuel, también le mostré mis análisis, y me prescribió un tratamiento rápido de sulfas, Redoxon, hígado y vacunas de colibacilos, que surtí al regresar a casa, añadiéndolo a la dotación de medicinas que por mi propia cuenta, y sin comunicárselo a ninguno de estos eminentes facultativos, había yo empezado a ingerir desde hace unos días" (284).

Bibliography

Primary Sources

Balbuena, Bernardo de. 1963. *Grandeza mexicana y fragmentos de siglo de oro y el Bernardo.* Mexico City: UNAM.

Beloff, Angelina. 1986. *Memorias.* Trans. Gloria Taracena. Mexico City: SEP/UNAM.

Bertolucci, Bernardo, and Franco Arcalli. 1973. *Bernardo Bertolucci's "Last Tango in Paris."* New York: Delacorte.

Böll, Heinrich. 1975. *The Lost Honor of Katharina Blum: How Violence Develops and Where It Can Lead.* Trans. Leila Vennewitz. New York: McGraw-Hill.

Cervantes de Salazar, Francisco. 1964 [1939]. *México en 1554: Tres diálogos latinos traducidos.* Trans. Joaquín García Icazbalceta. Mexico City: UNAM.

Cuesta, Jorge. 1991. *Ensayos críticos.* Ed. María Stoopen. Mexico City: UNAM.

Esquivel, Laura. 1989. *Como agua para chocolate: Novela de entregas mensuales con recetas, amores y remedios caseros.* Mexico City: Planeta.

García Lorca, Federico. 1953 [1923]. *Títeres de cachiporra.* Buenos Aires: Ediciones de Losange. Translation: *The Slapstick Puppets.* Trans. Anne Ketcham Blodgett and Marion Lipscomb Miller. Ithaca, N.Y.: n.p., 1967.

———. 1987 [1927]. "La imagen poética de don Luis de Góngora." In *Obras completas,* vol. 3, 223–247. Madrid: Aguilar.

———. 1994 [1940]. *Poeta en Nueva York.* Ed. María Clementa Millán. Madrid: Cátedra. Translation: *Poet in New York.* Trans. Ben Belitt. New York: Grove Press, 1983.

———. 1996. *Sonetos.* Granada: Fundación García Lorca/Editorial Comares.

Góngora y Argote, Luis de. 1993. *Soledades.* Ed. John Beverley. Madrid: Cátedra. Translation: *The Solitudes of Luis de Góngora.* Trans. Gilbert F. Cunningham. Baltimore: Johns Hopkins University Press, 1968.

Kahlo, Frida. 1995a. *The Diary of Frida Kahlo: An Intimate Self-Portrait.* Ed. Claudia Madrazo. New York and Mexico City: Harry N. Abrams and La Vaca Independiente.

———. 1995b. *The Letters of Frida Kahlo: Cartas Apasionadas*. Ed. Martha Zamora. San Francisco: Chronicle.

Lazo, Agustín. 1947[?]. *La huella: Drama romántico en tres actos*. Mexico City: Sociedad General de Autores de México.

———. 1948. *El caso de don Juan Manuel*. Mexico City: Atenea.

Marín, Guadalupe. 1938. *La única*. Mexico City: Jalisco.

———. 1941. *Un día patrio*. Mexico City: Jalisco.

Mastretta, Angeles. 1985. *Arráncame la vida*. Mexico City: Ediciones Océano.

Novo, Salvador. 1933. *El joven*. Mexico City: Imprenta Mundial.

———. 1934. *Seamen Rhymes*. Drawings by Federico García Lorca. Buenos Aires: Francisco A. Colombo.

———. 1935. *Continente vacío (viaje a Sudamérica)*. Madrid: Espasa-Calpe.

———. 1955. *Poesía 1915–1955*. Mexico City: Impresiones Modernas.

———. 1961. *Poesía: XX poemas/Espejo/Nuevo amor y poesías no coleccionadas*. Mexico City: FCE.

———. 1964. *La vida en México en el período presidencial de Lázaro Cárdenas*. Ed. José Emilio Pacheco. Mexico City: Empresas Editoriales.

———. 1965. *La vida en México en el período presidencial de Manuel Avila Camacho*. Ed. José Emilio Pacheco. Mexico City: Empresas Editoriales.

———. 1967. *La vida en México en el período presidencial de Miguel Alemán*. Ed. José Emilio Pacheco. Mexico City: Empresas Editoriales.

———. 1978 [1970]. *Sátira: El libro ca . . .* Mexico City: Diana.

———. 1979. "Memoir." In *Now the Volcano: An Anthology of Latin American Gay Literature*, ed. Winston Leyland, 11–47. San Francisco: Gay Sunshine Press.

———. 1982. "Agustín Lazo." In *Agustín Lazo 1898–1971* by Museo Nacional del Arte, 8. Mexico City: MUNAL.

———. 1992 [1946]. *Nueva grandeza mexicana*. Mexico City: Hermes. Translation: *New Mexican Grandeur*. Mexico City: Petróleos Mexicanos, 1967.

———. 1998. *La estatua de sal*. Prologue by Carlos Monsiváis. Mexico City: Consejo Nacional para la Cultura y las Artes.

Pérez Galdós, Benito. 1979. *Tormento*. Madrid: Alianza.

Poniatowska, Elena. 1987 [1978]. *Querido Diego, te abraza Quiela*. Mexico City: Era.

———. 1992. *Tinísima: Novela*. Mexico City: Era. Translation: *Tinisima*. Trans. Katherine Silver. New York: Farrar, Straus, Giroux, 1996.

Valle-Inclán, Ramón del. 1988. *Sonata de primavera; sonata de estío: Memorias del Marqués de Bradomín*. 15th ed. Introduction by Pere Gimferrer. Madrid: Espasa Calpe. Translation: *Spring and Summer Sonatas: The Memoirs of the Marquis of Bradomín*. Trans. Margaret Jull Costa. Sawtry, England: Dedalus, 1997.

———. 1993a. *Luces de bohemia: Esperpento*. Ed. Alonso Zamora Vicente. Madrid: Espasa-Calpe.

———. 1993b. *Three Plays: Divine Words, Bohemian Lights, Silver Face*. Trans. María M. Delgado. London: Methuen Drama.

Villaurrutia, Xavier. 1991 [1966]. *Obras*. Ed. Miguel Capistrán, Alí Chumacero, and Luis Mario Schneider. Mexico City: Letras Mexicanas.

Werfel, Franz. 1931. *Juárez y Maximiliano*. Trans. Enrique Jiménez D. Mexico City: La Razón.

Secondary Sources

Acero, Rosa María. 1998. "Novo ante Novo: Un novísimo personaje homosexual." Diss., University of California, Santa Barbara.

Aguilar Camín, Héctor, and Lorenzo Meyer. 1993. *In the Shadow of the Mexican Revolution: Contemporary Mexican History, 1910–1989.* Trans. Luis Alberto Fierro. Austin: University of Texas Press.

Aguilera, Juan, and Manuel Aznar Soler. 1999. *Cipriano de Rivas Chérif y el teatro español de su época: 1891–1967.* Madrid: Asociación de Directores de Escena de España.

Agustín, José. 1990. *Tragicomedia mexicana: La vida en México de 1940 a 1970.* 2 vols. Mexico City: Planeta.

Alderson, Michael. 1994. "Introduction about the Author." In *The War of the Fatties and Other Stories from Aztec History* by Salvador Novo, ix–liii. Austin: University of Texas Press.

Altamiranda, Daniel. 1994. "Juana Inés de la Cruz." In *Latin American Writers on Gay and Lesbian Themes: A Bio-Critical Sourcebook,* ed. David William Foster, 192–198. Westport, Conn.: Greenwood Press.

Alvarado, Ana María. 1980. "Función del prostíbulo en *Santa* y *Juntacadáveres.*" *Hispanic Journal* 2 (1): 57–68.

Barkan, Leonard. 1991. *Transuming Passion: Ganymede and the Erotics of Humanism.* Stanford: Stanford University Press.

Beardsell, Peter. 1992. *A Theater for Cannibals: Rodolfo Usigli and the Mexican Stage.* London and Toronto: Fairleigh Dickinson University Press.

Beverley, John R. 1980. *Aspects of Góngora's "Soledades."* Purdue Romance Monographs in Romance Language. Amsterdam: John Benjamins B.V.

———. 1994. "Gracián o la sobrevaloración de la literatura (Barroco y posmodernidad)." In *Relecturas del Barroco de Indias,* ed. Mabel Moraña, 17–30. Hanover, N.H.: del Norte.

Binding, Paul. 1985. *Lorca: The Gay Imagination.* London: GMP.

Blanco, José Joaquín. 1980. "La crítica de Novo." In *La paja en el ojo ajeno: Ensayos de crítica,* 92–105. Puebla: Universidad Autónoma de Puebla.

———. 1983. *Crónica de la poesía mexicana.* 4th ed. Mexico City: Katún.

Blumenthal, Ralph. 1998. "Roll 'Em: Life as a Long Starring Role." *New York Times,* Books Online Edition, December 9.

Bobes Naves, María del Carmen. 1987. *Semiología de la obra dramática.* Madrid: Taurus.

Boorstin, Daniel J. 1961. *The Image; or, What Happened to the American Dream.* Kingsport, Tenn.: Kingsport Press.

Brenkman, John. 1993. *Straight Male Modern: A Cultural Critique of Psychoanalysis.* New York: Routledge.

Brushwood, John S. 1966. *Mexico in Its Novel: A Nation's Search for Identity.* Austin: University of Texas Press.

Butler, Judith. 1990. *Gender Trouble: Feminism and the Subversion of Identity.* New York: Routledge.

Buxó, José Pascual. 1960. *Góngora en la poesía novohispana.* Mexico City: UNAM.

Cagiao, Pilar. 1992. "Incorporación al mercado laboral e inseción social." In *Histo-*

ria general de la emigración española a Iberoamérica, vol. 1, 275–330. Madrid: Historia 16.

Calabrese, Omar. 1992. *Neo-Baroque: A Sign of the Times*. Trans. Charles Lambert. Princeton, N.J.: Princeton University Press.

Camp, Roderic A. 1982. *Mexican Political Biographies 1935–1981*. 2nd ed. Tucson: University of Arizona Press.

Cascardi, Anthony J. 1989. *"The Revolt of the Masses:* Ortega's Critique of Modernity." In *Ortega y Gasset and the Question of Modernity*, ed. Patrick H. Dust, 337–368. Minneapolis: Prisma Institute.

Castillo, Debra. 1992. "Rosario Castellanos: 'Ashes without a Face.'" In *De/Colonizing the Subject: The Politics of Gender in Women's Autobiography*, ed. Sidonie Smith and Julia Watson, 242–269. Minneapolis: University of Minnesota Press.

Cernuda, Luis. 1957. "Federico García Lorca (1898–1936)." In *Estudios sobre poesía española contemporánea*, 207–220. Madrid: Guadarrama.

Charnon-Deutsch, Lou. 1999. "María de Zayas y Sotomayor." In *Spanish Writers on Gay and Lesbian Themes: A Bio-Critical Sourcebook*, ed. David William Foster, 188–190. Westport, Conn.: Greenwood Press.

Cohen, Ed. 1991. "Who Are 'We'? Gay 'Identity' as Political (E)motion (A Theoretical Rumination)." In *Inside/Out: Lesbian Theories, Gay Theories*, ed. Diana Fuss, 71–92. London and New York: Routledge.

Coke-Enguídanos, Mervyn R. 1988. "Rubén Darío Encounters Quevedo." *Hispanófila* 93: 45–57.

Coll, Edna. 1964. *Injerto de temas en las novelistas mexicanas contemporáneas*. San Juan: Juan Ponce de León.

Coontz, Stephanie. 1992. *The Way We Never Were: American Families and the Nostalgia Trap*. New York: Basic Books.

Covarrubias, Sebastián de. 1987 [1674]. *Tesoro de la lengua castellana o española*. Ed. Martín de Riquer. Barcelona: Alta Fulla.

Crabbe, K. B. 1974–1975. "An Alternate Interpretation of the Poetry of Salvador Novo: A Jungian Archetypal Approach." *Reflexión* 3–4: 81–99.

Curtius, Ernst Robert. 1955 [1948]. *Literatura europea y Edad Media latina*. Trans. Margit Frank Alatorre and Antonio Alatorre. Mexico City: Fondo de Cultura Económica.

Dauster, Frank. 1961. "La poesía de Salvador Novo." *Cuadernos Americanos* 116: 209–233.

———. 1971. *Xavier Villaurrutia*. New York: Twayne.

Debroise, Olivier. 1983. *Figuras en el trópico y plástica mexicana 1920–40*. Barcelona: Océano.

Deleuze, Gilles, and Felix Guattari. 1977. *Anti-Oedipus: Capitalism and Psychoanalysis*. Trans. Helen R. Lane, Robert Hurley, and Mark Seem. New York: Viking.

Díaz Arciniega, Víctor. 1989. *Querella por la cultura "revolucionaria."* Mexico City: FCE.

Díaz-Ortiz, Oscar A. 1999a. "Francisco de Quevedo y Villegas." In *Spanish Writers on Gay and Lesbian Themes: A Bio-Critical Sourcebook*, ed. David William Foster, 126–133. Westport, Conn.: Greenwood Press.

———. 1999b. "Luis de Góngora y Argote." In *Spanish Writers on Gay and Lesbian*

Themes: A Bio-Critical Sourcebook, ed. David William Foster, 80–87. Westport, Conn.: Greenwood Press.

Doane, Mary Ann. 1987. *The Desire to Desire: The Woman's Film of the 1940s.* Bloomington: Indiana University Press.

Dyer, Richard. 1991. "Believing in Fairies: The Author and the Homosexual." In *Inside/Out: Lesbian Theories, Gay Theories,* ed. Diana Fuss, 185–201. New York: Routledge.

Echeverría, Bolívar, ed. 1994. *Modernidad, mestizaje cultural, ethos barroco.* Mexico City: UNAM.

Egido, Teófanes. 1973. *Sátiras políticas de la España moderna.* Madrid: Alianza.

Eisenberg, Daniel. 1999. "Miguel de Cervantes." In *Spanish Writers on Gay and Lesbian Themes: A Bio-Critical Sourcebook,* ed. David William Foster, 46–49. Westport, Conn.: Greenwood Press.

Espinosa Altamirano, Horacio. 1985. *El inconmensurable, inaudito, inverosímil e inusitado Diego Rivera.* Mexico City: EDAMEX.

Etreros, Mercedes. 1983. *La sátira política en el siglo XVII.* Madrid: Fundación Universitaria Española.

Fernández, Lluís. 1990. "Neobarroco: en la vorágine del pop." *El País Temas,* April 26: 6.

Fernández Rosado de Levin, Rosa Bernardina. 1989. "El autor y el personaje femenino en dos novelas del siglo XX: *Santa* de Federico Gamboa y *La gloria de don Ramiro* de Enrique Larreta." Diss., Colorado University.

Forcadas, Alberto. 1972. "Más sobre el gongorismo de Rubén Darío." *Papeles de Son Armadans* 66 (196): 41–55.

Forster, Merlin H. 1976. *Fire and Ice: The Poetry of Xavier Villaurrutia.* Chapel Hill: University of North Carolina Press.

Foster, David William, ed. 1994. *Latin American Writers on Gay and Lesbian Themes: A Bio-Critical Sourcebook,* ed. David William Foster. Westport, Conn.: Greenwood Press.

———, ed. 1999. *Spanish Writers on Gay and Lesbian Themes: A Bio-Critical Sourcebook.* Westport, Conn.: Greenwood Press.

Franco, Jean. 1985. *La cultura moderna en América Latina.* Trans. Sergio Pitol. Mexico City: Grijalbo.

———. 1989. "Writers in Spite of Themselves: The Mystical Nuns of Seventeenth-Century Mexico." In *Plotting Women: Gender and Representation in Mexico,* 3–22. New York: Columbia University Press.

Frantz, David O. 1989. *Festum Voluptatis: A Study of Renaissance Erotica.* Columbus: Ohio State University Press.

Gabler, Neal. 1994. *Winchell: Gossip, Power and the Culture of Celebrity.* New York: Alfred A. Knopf.

———. 1998. *Life the Movie: How Entertainment Conquered Reality.* New York: Alfred A. Knopf.

Gallop, Jane. 1988. *Thinking through the Body.* New York: Columbia University Press.

Garber, Marjorie. 1992. *Vested Interests: Cross-Dressing and Cultural Anxiety.* New York: Routledge.

————. 1995. *ViceVersa: Bisexuality and the Eroticism of Everyday Life.* New York: Simon and Schuster.

García Canclini, Néstor. 1995 [1990]. *Hybrid Cultures: Strategies for Entering and Leaving Modernity.* Trans. Christopher L. Chiappari and Silvia L. López. Minneapolis and London: University of Minnesota Press.

García de la Concha, Víctor. 1990. "Barroco: Categoría, sistema e historia literaria." In *Estado actual de los estudios en el Siglo de Oro,* ed. Manuel García Martín et al., vol. 1, 59–74. Salamanca: Universidad de Salamanca.

García Gutiérrez, Rosa. 1999. *Contemporáneos: La otra novela de la Revolución Mexicana.* Huelva: Universidad de Huelva.

Gide, André. 1920. *Los límites del arte y algunas reflexiones de moral y literatura.* Trans. Jaime Torres Bodet. Mexico City: Cultura.

Gilbert, Sandra M., and Susan Gubar. 1984 [1979]. *The Madwoman in the Attic: The Woman Writer and the Nineteenth-Century Literary Imagination.* New Haven and London: Yale University Press.

Goldberg, Jonathan. 1992. *Sodometries: Renaissance Texts, Modern Sexualities.* Stanford: Stanford University Press.

González Echevarría, Roberto. 1993. *Celestina's Brood: Continuities of the Baroque in Spanish and Latin American Literatures.* Durham and London: Duke University Press.

González Mateos, Adriana. 1988. "Novo amor: Una sátira." In *Multiplicación de los contemporáneos: Ensayos sobre la generación,* ed. Sergio Fernández, 149–165. Mexico City: UNAM.

Goodwin, Joseph P. 1989. *More Man Than You'll Ever Be: Gay Folklore and Acculturation in Middle America.* Bloomington and Indianapolis: Indiana University Press.

Gorostiza, José. 1988. "Juventud contra molinos de viento." In *Cauces de la poesía mexicana y otros textos,* ed. José Emilio Pacheco, 23–26. Mexico City: Universidad de Colima.

Goytisolo, Juan. 1977. "Quevedo: La obsesión excremental." In *Disidencias,* 117–135. Barcelona: Seix Barral.

Griffin, Dustin. 1994. *Satire: A Critical Introduction.* Lexington: University of Kentucky Press.

Harris, Daniel. 1997. *The Rise and Fall of Gay Culture.* New York: Hyperion.

Hart, Thomas R. 1977. "The Pilgrim's Role in the First *Solitude.*" *Modern Language Notes* 92: 213–226.

Hauser, Rex. 1993. "Settings and Connections: Darío's Poetic *Engarce.*" *Revista Canadiense de Estudios Hispánicos* 17 (3): 437–451.

Helm, MacKinley. 1941. *Modern Mexican Painters.* New York: Harper.

Herrera, Hayden. 1983. *Frida: A Biography of Frida Kahlo.* New York: Perennial Library.

Herrera-Sobek, María. 1990. *The Mexican Corrido: A Feminist Analysis.* Bloomington and Indianapolis: Indiana University Press.

Hutcheon, Linda. 1988. *A Poetics of Postmodernism: History, Theory, Fiction.* New York: Routledge.

Irwin, Robert. 1999. "La homosexualidad cósmica mexicana: Espejos de diferencia racial en Xavier Villaurrutia." *Revista Iberoamericana* 65 (187): 293–304.

Jameson, Fredric. 1986 [1981]. *The Political Unconscious: Narrative as a Socially Symbolic Act.* Ithaca: Cornell University Press.

———. 1992 [1991]. *Postmodernism or the Cultural Logic of Late Capitalism.* Durham: Duke University Press.

Jammes, Robert. 1967. *Etudes sur l'oeuvre poétique de Don Luis de Góngora y Argote.* Bordeaux: Institut d'Etudes Ibériques.

Jiménez, A. 1970 [1960]. *Picardía mexicana.* 43rd impression. Mexico City: Costa-Amic.

Johnson, Julie Greer. 1993. *Satire in Colonial Spanish America: Turning the New World Upside Down.* Austin: University of Texas Press.

Juaristi, Jon. 1997. *El bucle melancólico: Historias de nacionalistas vascos.* Madrid: Espasa.

Kael, Pauline. 1973. "Introduction." In *Bernardo Bertolucci's "Last Tango in Paris"* by Bernardo Bertolucci and Franco Arcalli, 9–19. New York: Delacorte.

Kandell, Jonathan. 1990. *La Capital: The Biography of Mexico City.* New York: Owl Book.

Katz, Friedrich. 1992. "The Liberal Republic and the Porfiriato, 1867–1910." In *Mexico since Independence,* ed. Leslie Bethell, 49–124. Cambridge: Cambridge University Press.

Keller, Gary D. 1977. *The Significance and Impact of Gregorio Marañón: Literary Criticism, Biographies and Historiographies.* New York: Bilingual Press/Editorial Bilingüe.

Krauze, Enrique. 1994. *Siglo de caudillos: Biografía política de México (1810–1910).* Mexico City: Tusquets.

Laín Entralgo, Pedro. 1969. *Gregorio Marañón: Vida, obra y persona.* Madrid: Espasa-Calpe.

Lauretis, Teresa de. 1984. *Alice Doesn't: Feminism, Semiotics, Cinema.* Bloomington: Indiana University Press.

———. 1994. *The Practice of Love: Lesbian Sexuality and Perverse Desire.* Bloomington and Indianapolis: Indiana University Press.

Long, Mary Kendall. 1995. "Salvador Novo: 1920–1940: Between the Avant-Garde and the Nation." Diss., Princeton University.

Ly, Nadine. 1985. "Las *Soledades:* '. . . Esta poesía inútil . . .'" *Criticón* 30: 7–42.

Mailer, Norman. 1973. "A Transit to Narcissus." In *Bernardo Bertolucci's "Last Tango in Paris"* by Bernardo Bertolucci and Franco Arcalli, 199–224. New York: Delacorte.

Manrique, Jaime. 1999. *Eminent Maricones: Arenas, Lorca, Puig, and Me.* Madison: University of Wisconsin Press.

Maravall, José Antonio. 1980. *La cultura del barroco: Análisis de una estructura histórica.* 2nd ed. Barcelona: Ariel. Translation: *Culture of the Baroque: Analysis of a Historical Structure.* Trans. Terry Cochran. Minneapolis: University of Minnesota Press, 1986.

———. 1986. *La literatura picaresca desde la historia social (siglos XVI y XVII).* Madrid: Taurus.

Marías, Julián. 1990. *Understanding Spain.* Trans. Frances M. López-Morillas. Ann Arbor and San Juan: University of Michigan Press/Editorial de la Universidad de Puerto Rico.

Marof, Tristán. 1934. *México de frente y de perfil.* Buenos Aires: Claridad.

Mejía Prieto, Jorge. 1985. *Así habla el mexicano: Diccionario básico de mexicanismos.* Mexico City: Panorama.

———. 1990 [1985]. *Albures y refranes de México.* Mexico City: Panorama.

Méndez Ródenas, Adriana. 1983. *Severo Sarduy: El neobarroco de la transgresión.* Mexico City: UNAM.

Mercado, Tununa. 1992. "Margo Glantz: Enciclopedia, amor y zapatos." *Vogue-México* (February): 124–128.

Merlín, Socorro. 1995. *Vida y milagros de las carpas: La carpa en México 1930–1950.* Mexico City: INBA.

Michelson, Peter. 1993. *Speaking the Unspeakable: A Poetics of Obscenity.* Albany: State of New York University Press.

Molloy, Sylvia. 1991. *At Face Value: Autobiographical Writing in Spanish America.* Cambridge: Cambridge University Press.

Monsiváis, Carlos. 1985. *Jorge Cuesta.* Mexico City: Terra Nova.

———. 1986. "García Lorca y México." *Cuadernos Hispanoamericanos* 433–434: 249–255.

———. 1988a. *Escenas de pudor y liviandad.* Mexico City: Grijalbo.

———. 1988b. "Salvador Novo: Los que tenemos unas manos que no nos pertenecen." In *Amor perdido,* 265–296. Mexico City: Era.

———. 1992. "Prologue." In *Nueva grandeza mexicana* by Salvador Novo, 9–17. Mexico City: Hermes.

Monterde, Francisco de. 1963. "Introducción." In *Grandeza mexicana y fragmentos de siglo de oro y el Bernardo* by Bernardo de Balbuena, v–xxxii. Mexico City: UNAM.

———. 1964. "Juárez, Maximiliano y Carlota, en la obra de los dramaturgos mexicanos." *Cuadernos Americanos* 23 (136): 231–240.

Moretta, Eugene Lawrence. 1971. *The Poetic Achievement of Xavier Villaurrutia.* Cuernavaca: Centro Intercultural de Documentación.

Museo Nacional del Arte. 1982. *Agustín Lazo 1898–1971.* Mexico City: MUNAL.

Navarrete, Ignacio. 1995. *Orphans of Petrarch: Poetry and Theory in the Spanish Renaissance.* Berkeley: University of California Press.

Navarro, Joaquina. 1955. *La novela realista mexicana.* Mexico City: Compañía General de Ediciones.

Nomland, John B. 1967. *Teatro mexicano contemporáneo (1920–1950).* Trans. Paloma Gorostiza de Zozaya and Luis Reyes de la Maza. Mexico City: INBA.

Nunokawa, Jeffrey. 1995. "The Disappearance of the Homosexual in *The Picture of Dorian Gray.*" In *Professions of Desire: Lesbian and Gay Studies in Literature,* ed. George E. Haggerty and Bonnie Zimmerman, 183–190. New York: MLA.

Núñez Noriega, Guillermo. 1994. *Sexo entre varones: Poder y resistencia en el campo sexual.* Hermosillo: El Colegio de Sonora.

Olea Franco, Rafael, and Anthony Stanton, eds. 1994. *Los Contemporáneos en el laberinto de la crítica.* Mexico City: El Colegio de México.

Oropesa, Salvador A. 1992. "*Como agua para chocolate* de Laura Esquivel como lectura del *Manual de urbanidad y buenas costumbres* de Manuel Antonio Carreño." *Monographic Review/Revista Monográfica* 8: 252–260.

————. 1994. "Salvador Novo." In *Latin American Writers on Gay and Lesbian Themes: A Bio-Critical Sourcebook*, ed. David William Foster, 290–293. Westport, Conn.: Greenwood Press.

————. 1995a. "La mala leche barroca en la poesía satírica de Salvador Novo." *Monographic Review/Revista Monográfica* 10: 70–78.

————. 1995b. "La representación del yo y del tú en la poesía satírica de Salvador Novo: La influencia del albur." *Chasqui* 24 (1): 38–52.

————. 1996a. "Hacia una identidad nacional: La relación México-España en *Santa* de Federico Gamboa." *Romance Languages Annual* 8: 627–632.

————. 1996b. "Popular Culture and Gender/Genre Construction in *Mexican Bolero* by Angeles Mastretta." In *Bodies and Biases: Sexualities in Hispanic Cultures and Literature*, ed. Roberto Reis and David W. Foster, 137–164. Minneapolis and London: University of Minnesota Press.

————. 1999. "Emilio Prados." In *Spanish Writers on Gay and Lesbian Themes: A Bio-Critical Sourcebook*, ed. David William Foster, 125–126. Westport, Conn.: Greenwood Press.

Pacheco, José Emilio. 1964. "Nota preliminar." In *La vida en México en el período presidencial de Lázaro Cárdenas* by Salvador Novo, 11–14. Mexico City: Empresas Editoriales.

Panabière, Louis. 1983. *Itinerario de una disidencia: Jorge Cuesta (1903–1942)*. Trans. Adolfo Castañón. Mexico City: FCE.

Paz, Octavio. 1974. *Los hijos del limo: Del romanticismo a la vanguardia*. Barcelona: Seix Barral. Translation: *Children of the Mire: Modern Poetry from Romanticism to the Avant-Garde*. Trans. Rachel Phillips. Cambridge, Mass.: Harvard University Press, 1974.

————. 1982. "El reino de la Nueva España." In *Sor Juana Inés de la Cruz o las trampas de la fe*, 21–86. Barcelona: Seix Barral. Translation: *Sor Juana or the Traps of Faith*. Trans. Margaret Sayers Peden. Cambridge, Mass.: Harvard University Press, 1988.

————. 1987. *Generaciones y semblanzas: Escritores y letras de México*. Ed. Octavio Paz and Luis Mario Schneider. Mexico City: FCE.

————. 1991 [1977]. "Xavier se escribe con equis." In *Antología* by Xavier Villaurrutia, 9–61. Mexico City: Fondo de Cultura Económica.

————. 1994. "Poeta secreto y hombre público: Jaime Torres Bodet." In *Los Contemporáneos en el laberinto de la crítica*, ed. Rafael Olea Franco and Anthony Stanton, 3–12. Mexico City: El Colegio de México.

Pérez de Mendiola, Marina. 1996. "*El diario de José Toledo:* A Queer Space in the World of Mexican Letters." In *Bodies and Biases: Sexualities in Hispanic Cultures and Literatures*, ed. David William Foster and Roberto Reis, 184–202. Minneapolis: University of Minnesota Press.

Picasso, Pablo. 1985 [1948]. *Góngora*. Intro. John Russell. New York: George Braziller.

Pollard, Patrick. 1991. *André Gide: Homosexual Moralist*. New Haven and London: Yale University Press.

Ramón, David. 1997. *Dolores del Río*. Vol. 2. México City: Clío.

Read, Malcolm K. 1984. "Language and Body in Francisco de Quevedo." *Modern Language Notes* 99 (2): 235–255.

Rehbein, Edna A. 1992. "Agustín Laro." In *Dictionary of Mexican Literature,* ed. Eladio Cortés, 359–360. Westport, Conn.: Greenwood Press.

Rivera Marín, Guadalupe. 1997. *Diego el Rojo.* Mexico City: Patria.

Rodríguez, Juan Carlos. 1974. *Teoría e historia de la producción ideológica, 1: Las primeras literaturas burguesas (siglo XVI).* Madrid: Akal.

Rodríguez Chicharro, César. 1964. "Disemia y paronomasia en la poesía de Xavier Villaurrutia." *La Palabra y el Hombre* (April–June): 249–260.

———. 1966. "Correlación y paralelismo en la poesía de Xavier Villaurrutia." *La Palabra y el Hombre* (January–March): 81–90.

Ross, Andrew. 1989. *No Respect: Intellectuals and Popular Culture.* New York: Routledge.

Ross, Kathleen. 1993. *The Baroque Narrative of Carlos de Sigüenza y Góngora: A New World Paradise.* Cambridge: Cambridge University Press.

Rossi, Paolo. 1995. "The Scientists." In *Baroque Personae,* ed. Rosario Villari, trans. Lydia G. Cochrane, 263–289. Chicago and London: University of Chicago Press.

Roster, Peter J., Jr. 1978. *La ironía como método de análisis literario: La poesía de Salvador Novo.* Madrid: Gredos.

R[oura], A[lma] L[ilia], and J[ulia] S[oto]. 1982. "Reseña biográfica." In *Agustín Lazo 1898–1971* by Museo Nacional del Arte, 13–14. Mexico City: MUNAL.

Sabat de Rivers, Georgina. 1996. "Las obras menores de Balbuena: Erudición, alabanza de la poesía y crítica literaria." *Revista de Crítica Literaria Latinoamericana* 22 (43–44): 89–101.

Safire, William. 1990. "Virile Women Target Tobacco Men." *New York Times Magazine,* March 11: 18.

Sahuquillo Vázquez, Angel. 1986. *Federico García Lorca y la cultura de la homosexualidad: Lorca, Dalí, Cernuda, Gil-Albert, Prados y la voz silenciada del amor homosexual.* Stockholm: Stockholms Universitet.

Sarduy, Severo. 1972. "El barroco y el neobarroco." In *América Latina en su tradición,* ed. César Fernández Romero, 167–184. Mexico City: Siglo XXI.

Sedgwick, Eve Kosofsky. 1985. *Between Men: English Literature and Male Homosocial Desire.* New York: University of Columbia Press.

———. 1990. *Epistemology of the Closet.* Berkeley and Los Angeles: University of California Press.

Sefchovich, Sara. 1987. *México, país de ideas, país de novelas: Una sociología de la literatura mexicana.* Mexico City: Grijalbo.

Sen, Kanishka. 1997. "Queering the Mexican Stage: Theatrical Strategies in Xavier Villaurrutia and Salvador Novo." Thesis, Arizona State University.

Sheridan, Guillermo. 1984. "México, los 'Contemporáneos' y el nacionalismo." *Vuelta* 87: 29–37.

———. 1985. *Los Contemporáneos ayer.* Mexico City: FCE.

Silver, Philip W. 1997. *Ruin and Restitution: Reinterpreting Romanticism in Spain.* Nashville, Tenn.: Vanderbilt University Press.

Smith, Paul Julian. 1986. "Barthes, Góngora, and Non-Sense." *PMLA* 101 (1): 82–94.

Sontag, Susan. 1966. *Against Interpretation and Other Essays.* New York: Farrar, Straus and Giroux.

Sylvester, Nigel Grant. 1984. *Vida y obra de Jorge Cuesta (1903–1942)*. Puebla: Premiá.

Thomas, Hugh. 1995 [1993]. *Conquest: Montezuma, Cortés, and the Fall of Old Mexico*. New York: Touchstone.

Tomás y Valiente, Francisco. 1990. "El crimen y pecado contra natura." In *Sexo barroco y otras transgresiones premodernas*, ed. Francisco Tomás y Valiente et al., 35– 55. Madrid: Alianza.

Torriente, Loló de la. 1959. *Memoria y razón de Diego Rivera*. Vol. 2. Mexico City: Renacimiento.

Valender, James. 1996. "Cartas de Salvador Novo a Federico García Lorca." *Cuadernos Hispanoamericanos* 548: 7–20.

Velázquez Chávez, Agustín. 1969 [1937]. *Contemporary Mexican Artists*. Freeport, N.Y.: Books for Libraries.

Vilanova, Antonio. 1952. "El peregrino de amor en las *Soledades* de Góngora." In *Estudios dedicados a Menéndez Pidal*, vol. 3, 421–460. Madrid: CSIC.

———. 1972. "Nuevas notas sobre el tema del peregrino de amor." In *Studia Hispánica in Honorem R. Lapesa*, vol. 1, 563–570. Madrid: Gredos.

Villari, Rosario, ed. 1995a. *Baroque Personae*. Trans. Lydia G. Cochrane. Chicago and London: University of Chicago Press.

———. 1995b. "The Rebel." In *Baroque Personae* by Rosario Villari, trans. Lydia G. Cochrane, 100–125. Chicago and London: University of Chicago Press.

Walsh, John K. 1995. "A Logic in Lorca's *Ode to Walt Whitman*." In *¿Entiendes?: Queer Readings, Hispanic Writings*, ed. Emilie L. Bergmann and Paul Julian Smith, 257– 278. Durham and London: Duke University Press.

Williams, Raymond. 1985 [1977]. *Marxism and Literature*. Oxford: Oxford University Press.

Wolfe, Bertram D. 1963. *The Fabulous Life of Diego Rivera*. New York: Stein and Day.

Zacatecas, Bertha. 1996. *Vidas en el aire: Pioneros de la radio en México*. Mexico City: Diana.

Index